GENDER AND THE NAME OF GOD

Also by Ruth C. Duck

Bread for the Journey (editor)
Everflowing Streams: Songs for Worship
    (editor with Michael G. Bausch)
Flames of the Spirit (editor)
Touch Holiness (editor with Maren C. Tirabassi)

GENDER AND THE NAME OF GOD

The Trinitarian Baptismal Formula

Ruth C. Duck

The Pilgrim Press
New York

Scripture quotations are from the New Revised Standard Version Bible, copyright 1989, Division of Christian Education of the National Council of the Churches of Christ in the United States of America, and are used by permission.

The following persons and organizations have graciously given permission to quote from sources as noted: Hoyt Hickman, James F. Key, Eugene E. Laubach: Correspondence; Carole Bohn and J. Frank Henderson: Unpublished works; Elisabeth Schüssler Fiorenza and the Faith and Order Commission of the World Council of Churches: Extensive quotations of published works.

The call to prayer on page 92 is from *More Than Words: Prayer and Ritual for Inclusive Communities* by Janet Schaffran and Pat Kozak, copyright 1988, by the editors. Reprinted by permission of the Crossroad Publishing Company.

The hymn text at the beginning of Chapter 2 is by the author and is copyrighted 1989. The hymn text at the beginning of Chapter 5 is by the author and is copyrighted 1988. The hymn text at the beginning of Chapter 7 is attributed to Patrick of Ireland, fifth century, and was translated in 1889 by Cecil F. Alexander.

Library of Congress Cataloging-in-Publication Data
Duck, Ruth C.
    Gender and the name of God : the Trinitarian baptismal formula /
Ruth C. Duck.
        p. cm.
    Includes bibliographical references and index.
    ISBN 0-8298-0894-9 (alk. paper) : $16.95
    1. God—Name. 2. God—Fatherhood. 3. Patriarchy—Religious
aspects—Christianity. 4. Liturgical language. 5. Baptism
(Liturgy) 6. Trinity. I. Title.
BT180.N2D82 1991
231'.044'014—dc20   91-16764
                                                            CIP

This book is printed on acid-free paper.

Printed in the United States of America.

10   9   8   7   6   5   4   3   2   1

The Pilgrim Press, 475 Riverside Drive, New York, NY 10115

DEDICATION

To friends,
    whose stories gave me a reason to complete this work.
To John,
    who says the rain baptizes everyone.
To children of today and tomorrow:
    May they inherit a world becoming free of violence and
    domination.

CONTENTS

ACKNOWLEDGMENTS

This book is based on my dissertation for the Doctor of Theology degree in Theology and Worship at Boston University School of Theology. I have rewritten and reorganized it and incorporated new research.

Horace Allen and Elizabeth Bettenhausen were important sources for this book, both through their excellent teaching at Boston University and their astute questions in response to my class work and dissertation research. They prodded me to reflect further on trinitarian theology. As a result, for two weeks in 1986 I took the course "The Mystery of God" taught by Catherine Mowry LaCugna at the University of Notre Dame. LaCugna's own constructive theology and the readings she assigned (as well as a course on the History of Christian Doctrine taught by Carter Lindberg at Boston University) shaped my interest in and understanding of the Trinity. LaCugna's articles have provided a continuing source of information and reflection, even though my own position is somewhat different from hers.

I am grateful to many people who have responded to my requests for information; they have elaborated their own ideas or suggested books and articles for my reading. These persons include Janet Cawley, Linda J. Clark, Mitzi Eilts, Walter Farquharson, Rebecca A. Ferguson, Cheryl Townsend Gilkes, Dennis Groh, Jeffrey Gros, J. Frank Henderson, Hoyt Hickman, David R. Holeton, Thomas Hopko, Robert Jewett, James F. Kay, Krzysztof Kuczma, Eugene E. Laubach, Hallett Llewellyn, Christopher Morse, Carolyn Nikkal, Harold H. Oliver, Jeanne Audrey Powers, Marjorie Procter-Smith, Faith Robinson, Daniel Schowalter, Laurence H. Stookey, Geoffrey Wainwright, and Margaret Wiborg. (Ferguson, Gros, Oliver, Powers, Procter-Smith, as well as the Feminist Liturgy Group of the North American Academy of Liturgy, Keith Watkins, and Brian Wren, have also read and commented upon all or part of the dissertation in draft or final form.) These persons have provided me with valuable information and ideas to which I could not have had access without their help.

Many of them are actively involved in scholarly, denominational, and ecumenical discussion of the concerns that are central to this dissertation. A group of women doctoral students at Boston University School of Theology also provided their insights in response to a paper on the baptismal formula. Members of the group at the time when this discussion took place were Jeanne Gallo, Allison Moore, Marjorie Scott, Barbara Darling Smith, Valerie Jones Stiteler, and Dodie Stowe.

Still others have been important to the process of turning the dissertation into a book. Stephanie Egnotovich and Larry Kalp at Pilgrim Press worked with me in the first stages. Gail Ramshaw, as reader for Pilgrim Press, provided a most helpful working plan for turning the dissertation into a book. I am grateful that Pilgrim Press saw fit to invite me to develop my dissertation into a book. Barbara Withers has worked closely with me in editing the final manuscript.

The Board of Higher Education of the United Methodist Church, in a matching grant with Garrett-Evangelical Theological Seminary, provided a grant to help me complete the project. Thus I was able to engage Dori Baker, a recent M.Div. graduate of Garrett-Evangelical, as a research assistant. Her contributions are particularly evident in Chapter 2, in which the social context of patriarchal language about God is explored. She gathered more recent data on child abuse and rewrote several sections of the chapter; she also provided suggestions for rewriting the whole volume. Through the grant, I was also able to gain the secretarial and editorial assistance of Linda Koops, who typed part of the final manuscript and who provides excellent support services to me and several other faculty members at Garrett-Evangelical Theological Seminary. The following Ph.D. students at Garrett-ETS/Northwestern helped in the last stages of completing the manuscript: Ellie Stebner (bibliographical work and manuscript editing); and Khiok-Khng Yeo (Greek and Hebrew transliterations). My thanks to President Neal Fisher and Dean Richard Tholin for their confidence in me in providing this research grant.

GENDER AND THE NAME OF GOD

INTRODUCTION

> This is the water of baptism.
> Out of this water we rise with new life,
> forgiven of sin
> and one with Christ,
> members of Christ's body.

So begins the order for baptism of the United Church of Christ (United Church of Christ Office for Church Life and Leadership 1986, 136). Baptism is a momentous occasion. Through the grace of God working in baptism, we receive new life and forgiveness and become one with Christ and the church. To share in Christ's baptism is to stake one's life with Christ on self-affirming and self-giving love lived out in community in solidarity with all humanity, especially suffering and oppressed peoples. To share in Christ's baptism is to enter a new life, to receive a new calling, and to become part of a community encouraged by the presence of the Spirit to seek peace and justice in the world.

Baptism is an action interpreted by words. Empowered by the promise of Jesus Christ's presence (Matt. 28:20), the church administers water as a sign and sacrament of divine love and vocation reaching out to children, women, and men. The words spoken at baptism focus the meaning of the event. An occasion of such great importance calls for words that are carefully chosen and that speak the heart's truth. At the dawning of one's life as a Christian, the words spoken give direction to all that is to come. Then, overheard each time new people pass through the water, these words provide a constant reminder of Christian identity and calling.

The words of baptism witness to the church's welcome of God's new order. The old order of this world, by contrast, is characterized by patriarchal patterns of relationship and power. Elisabeth Schüssler Fiorenza has described patriarchy as a male pyramid "of graded subordinations and exploitations" based not only on sex, but also on the class, race, country, or religion of the

3

men to whom women "belong" (Schüssler Fiorenza 1984, xiv). This definition highlights on the one hand the differing access to power and resources shared by people of different races, classes, or other groups, and on the other, the subordination of women to the men in their groups. The patriarchal arrangement of power is destructive to human beings and societies, and is not consistent with structures of Christian community instituted by Jesus Christ. Not only does patriarchy prevent the full development of all peoples, but even more tragically, it entails the exploitation, deprivation, physical abuse, and violent death of many in order to keep the system in place to benefit a powerful few. Like war (in the poster of the 1960s), patriarchy "is not healthy for children and other living things."

The very structure of language in patriarchal cultures reflects the patriarchal pyramid of power, making invisible or devaluing women, people of color, people of differing abilities, and any who are not dominant in society. Frequent use of masculine language for God in Christian worship, when feminine images are never used, is of concern to feminists because it both expresses and undergirds the sociopolitical system of patriarchy. Further, to use masculine language less frequently but to require it in the most important acts of Christian worship (such as baptism) also undergirds patriarchy.

The trinitarian baptismal formula, "I baptize you in the name of the Father and of the Son and of the Holy Spirit," is used by most churches worldwide today when the water of baptism is administered.[1] It epitomizes the contradiction between the church's offer of new life through Jesus Christ and its use of language reflecting patriarchal social systems. Baptism means conversion from the ways of this world to new life in community; it means participation in the death and resurrection of Jesus Christ in solidarity with the oppressed. These and other meanings of baptism are contradicted when the pivotal words of the formula reflect old ways of patriarchy. The words spoken when

---

1. For example, the trinitarian baptismal formula appears in all but one of the twenty-four modern baptismal liturgies included in *Baptism and Eucharist: Ecumenical Convergence in Celebration* (World Council of Churches 1983). In the one exception, the Church of the Czech Brethren, there is no mention of the formula; it may be assumed to be part of the term "Act of Baptism." Confession of faith in "God, Father, Son and Holy Spirit" takes place early in the service (World Council of Churches 1983, 81–82).

water is administered express the heart of the Christian faith in capsulized form. Although "Father" has a place in Christian worship among other metaphors for God, I have come to believe that this metaphor should not be so predominant in Christian worship. Using the Father/Son metaphor in the formula is not adequate to the task of summarizing Christian faith. Speaking of God in masculine but not feminine terms, it reinforces patriarchal patterns of valuing the male and devaluing the female. Moreover, "Father" has unfortunate associations for many in North American society, in which patriarchal values condone the abuse of children by their fathers. Further, "Father" has been used so incessantly as a metaphor for God that for many people it has lost its metaphoric power to evoke wonder and reflection; seeming to be a literal statement about God, it may also become an idol. New ways must be found to affirm baptismal faith in the triune God; the traditional trinitarian baptismal formula is simply inadequate for affirming faith in the God of Jesus Christ who meets us in baptism.

One major source of resistance to changing the formula is the concern for mutual recognition of baptism, which has become important to those who have worked for Christian unity in the twentieth century. Churches must recognize one another's baptisms before they can approach structural church union; in the meantime, mutually recognizing baptisms enables churches to acknowledge one another as authentic expressions of the church of Jesus Christ. Because baptism incorporates persons into the universal Christian church, to fail to recognize another denomination's baptism is to deny the Christian identity of that church and its members.

Mutual recognition of baptism becomes a concern on the local level when people change their denominational affiliation. People who join a church that does not recognize their former denomination's baptism are often rebaptized, despite most churches' agreement that baptism should not be repeated. Laurence H. Stookey tells of a woman named Lucy who was baptized on five occasions to satisfy the demands of churches that she joined through the influence of various family members (Stookey 1982, 11-12). In the early 1950s, after marrying my mother, my father wanted to join the Baptist church, but the local Baptist church would not accept his Methodist baptism by immersion and confession of faith. My father refused to be rebaptized, so my family joined the Methodist church. Such stories illustrate the dilemmas posed on the local level when churches do not accept one another's baptisms — a problem that may become more frequent until the ecumenical church addresses problems raised by the exclusively masculine language of the traditional baptismal formula.

The Consultation on Church Union consensus document of 1984 (*The COCU Consensus*) also illustrates the current dilemmas concerning church unity, mutual recognition of baptism, and masculine bias in language. It argues that lack of church unity "imperils the credibility of the gospel" and leads to "injustices which hinder peace among the nations" (COCU 1984, 7). The consensus statement recognizes that the "sexism which permeates the language and practice of worship" is a threat to Christian unity (9). It also holds mutual recognition of baptism to be basic to unity, stating that baptism is administered "in the name of the Father, the Son, and the Holy Spirit" (25, 37). It does not, however, address the tension posed by the exclusive language of the formula on the one hand and its role in mutual recognition on the other.

Responses to the 1982 *Baptism, Eucharist, and Ministry* (BEM)[2] document show both the importance and the difficulty of reaching agreement on the baptismal formula. (Refer to the Appendix for a more detailed review of responses to BEM related to the baptismal formula.) Although some churches said they would recognize only baptisms administered "in the name of the Father and of the Son and of the Holy Spirit," three churches questioned the masculine language of that formula. Some groups rejected "baptism in the name of Jesus," whereas others use that form. Further, the difference between the Western form beginning "I baptize you" and the Eastern form "*Name*, servant of God, is baptized" is important to some, because the Eastern form emphasizes a theology of baptism in which God and not the presider or baptizand is the main actor. Further discussion of the words used

---

2. I sometimes refer to the World Council of Churches' *Baptism, Eucharist, and Ministry* document as "BEM." Notes will hereafter refer to the document as "Faith and Order 1982"; unless otherwise noted, I refer to paragraph numbers in the section on baptism. References to other documents of the World Council of Churches Faith and Order Commission will also be abbreviated to "Faith and Order."

at baptism is needed on the one hand to enable mutual recognition of baptism, and on the other to avoid supporting patriarchal dominance in the church.

I do not advocate waiting for ecumenical consensus before seeking alternatives to the traditional baptismal formula. Partly due to ecumenical concern, some churches that generally advocate inclusive language retain the trinitarian baptismal formula. For example, the United Church of Christ and the United Methodist Church have retained the formula in traditional form in their most recent worship books. Unfortunately, this implies that what we say when we baptize is insignificant and — unlike the ordination of women — can easily be sacrificed for the sake of Christian unity. I want in this book to challenge the assumption that the words of the formula are unimportant. To the contrary, they are significant; changing the formula cannot be delayed until the worldwide ecumenical community agrees upon an alternative. I also want to challenge the assumption that no alternative to the present baptismal formula can express trinitarian Christian faith with integrity. Several alternatives are strong enough in their present or potential form to demonstrate that the church can — if it will — find a way beyond exclusively masculine language, even in the baptismal formula. The search for Christian unity and the search for inclusiveness, far from being at odds with each other, are compatible. Christian unity should be based on the search to build community "in which the full possibilities of each person and all peoples can be realized in harmony and mutuality" (Cardman 1984, 84). "Christian unity" that accepts patriarchal ideology is fraudulent; for in patriarchal systems, unity is based on domination, subordination, and violation, and not on the mutual relations of love proper to Christian unity. "Christian unity" that leaves no room for difference, that mainly represents the interests of dominant groups, is fraudulent.

Because the need for change is immediate, I proceed in this book to provide an alternative baptismal formula that restores the practice of confessing baptismal faith through a dialogue of questions and answers. For centuries, the pivotal words of faith at Christian baptism were not a declarative formula the presider spoke, but a dialogue between the presider and those being baptized or bringing children for baptism. In my own alternative to the formula, I restore this dialogue in its ancient threefold form:

Do you believe in God, the Source, the fountain of life?
Do you believe in Christ, the offspring of God embodied in Jesus
  of Nazareth and in the church?
Do you believe in the liberating Spirit of God, the wellspring of
  new life?

Those being baptized or bringing infants for baptism would answer together with the whole community, "I believe," and then each time water would be administered. This dialogical method of affirming faith is both linguistically inclusive and non-hierarchical — for the affirmation of faith is made not only by the presider, but also by those coming or bringing others for baptism and the whole community of faith. I have intentionally chosen language that is rich in metaphorical associations, with the theme of water appearing in each question. These metaphors are grounded in scripture and Christian tradition, yet they are fresh and evocative.

This proposal demonstrates the possibility of developing lively metaphorical language for trinitarian affirmation in baptism. I regard it to be a model that can generate further reflection, rather than an answer that closes out all other possible alternatives.

THE LINES OF THE ARGUMENT

Broad interdisciplinary research supports my proposed alternative. Here are the lines of my argument.

I begin in Chapter 1 by considering liturgical language, with emphasis on its metaphorical nature. I affirm understandings of metaphor that highlight the tension of "like" and "unlike" (McFague 1982 and 1987; Ricoeur 1976) and the importance of connotations in making metaphorical meaning (Clark 1980; Black 1962). I also emphasize the revelatory potential of liturgical language. I consider "Father" as a metaphor for God in light of these understandings. In Chapter 2, I explore the cultural context for predominantly masculine and paternal imagery for God. I show how this imagery, used to the exclusion of feminine imagery, supports the patriarchal abuse of power, and particularly the abuse of children by their fathers. In Chapter 3, I trace the developments by which masculine and paternal imagery became central in Christian worship. I find that the dominant use of such imagery does not depend so much on the prayer and teaching of Jesus as on other developments, particularly the way the trinitarian controversies influenced worship.

Because masculine language came to predominate through historical process, it can also be changed. In Chapter 4, I explore methods of reconstructing language so that it will reflect God's new order and not patriarchal social patterns. We can develop new patterns of language for Christian worship using hermeneutics developed for scripture study (Schüssler Fiorenza 1983 and 1984; Tracy and Grant 1984; and Nida 1964). We can detect patriarchal bias through a hermeneutics of suspicion. Then, we can shape new language as we retrieve diverse images from past tradition, as we translate traditional images into new terms, and as we draw on the contemporary faith experience of women and men.

Following this interdisciplinary consideration of liturgical language, in Chapter 5, I consider the meaning of baptism. In Chapter 6, I trace the historical developments that led to prevalent use of the trinitarian baptismal formula. Then, in Chapter 7, I consider the meaning and liturgical function of the baptismal formula, developing criteria for a revised baptismal formula. Next, in Chapter 8, I reflect critically on alternatives to the formulas that have already been offered. Finally, in Chapter 9, I develop and support my own alternative to the traditional formula and briefly explore strategies for implementing revision of the formula in the churches.

Research and reflection have led me to two conclusions: first, that revision of the baptismal formula is urgently needed; and second, that a question-and-answer method is better than a declarative formula as a way to affirm baptismal faith in the Trinity. I hope, in offering this exploration, to stimulate thought and discussion about the words spoken at the momentous occasion of baptism so that churches will find ways to change their practice. "God the Father" has reigned at the pinnacle of patriarchal power. For the sake of effective Christian witness, for the sake of loving Christian community, for the sake of children yet to be born, we must find ways to speak of God that dethrone this false idol and that witness to the God made known to us in Jesus Christ.

CHAPTER 1

THE LANGUAGE OF WORSHIP

How we speak to and about God matters. That is why we must move beyond patriarchal ways of speaking about God, and that is why we must move with care as we add and subtract, invent and reclaim language for Christian worship.

Words matter because, for Christians, they play an important part in our relationship with God. Mystics may wordlessly contemplate God. Perhaps most Christians have mystic moments when the presence of God is so real that words would fail to praise or to name. But more often, we pray and praise using words; and, we dare to claim, God uses the medium of human words — in scripture text and even in our fragile contemporary words — to speak to us.

The words of worship matter. Christian community also knows mystic, silent moments when God seems near and when many spirits become one spirit in God's presence. They stand, and bow, and sign themselves, and hold hands, and dance. But words are vehicles that can draw us near to God and one another as we praise, pray, and witness to God's love made known in Jesus the Christ. Even though sacraments use physical symbols, they are not silent events; through prayers and blessings, we focus the meaning of liturgical action. Through words, too, we encourage one another to live in new ways in the world.

Words matter, for they build and break relationships. This is also true in the community of faith. Through the words of worship, our relationship with God and one another is nurtured or undermined. As Mark Searle writes, "The role of liturgical language is not simply to convey supernatural 'facts,' but to engage us in relationship" (Searle 1981, 100). God, who has sought loving relationship with humanity from the beginning of time, drew near to us especially in Jesus Christ. Even now, God seeks us; and, we dare to say, the Holy Spirit moves through our words, apt or inept, to bring us into a loving relationship with God, one another, and the whole creation.

Liturgical language should be of essential concern to the church. Robert A. Bennett has written that words can be the occasion for forming the new being:

> In the sacred moment and sacred place, these shapers of one's reality [words] converge and are experienced not merely as neutral tools for expressing one's faith in God, but as the occasion for forming a new being. Language within worship has the power to renew and enliven or to oppress and destroy. (Bennett 1987, 549)

Liturgical language can create or destroy in the lives of individuals and communities. It can reveal or obscure, build up or break down. So with respect and loving care, those who have a role in shaping the language of worship must reflect on its meaning.

LITURGICAL LANGUAGE IS METAPHORICAL

To begin, it is important to recognize that the language of worship is metaphorical, for "God" is not just any subject of relationship. Tillich expressed it this way: "The being of God is being-itself. The being of God cannot be understood as the existence of a being alongside others or above others" (Tillich 1951, 235). He argued that terms beyond "being-itself" or "ground of being," even terms such as "infinite" or "supreme being," are symbolic, not conceptual, language:

> God as being-itself is the ground of the ontological structure of being without being subject to this structure.... Therefore, if anything beyond this bare assertion is said about God, it no longer is a direct and proper statement, no longer a concept. It is indirect, and it points to something beyond itself. In a word, it is symbolic. (Tillich 1951, 239)

Even the terms "being-itself" or "ground of being" may not be concepts in the ordinary sense. But here Tillich defines the problem of talking to or about God: as soon as we begin to address or describe God in terms based on human experiences and relationships, we are speaking metaphorically. What can be predicated if God is the subject? Harold H. Oliver has written that the "symbolic depth" of God as subject "reduces all 'predicates' to partial signifiers" (Oliver 1987, 43). Thus, according to Oliver, statements about God are not "cognitive claims" in the same sense that some other statements are. David Tracy has explored this problem in relation to the words "God is love":

> The metaphorical statement "God is love" . . . insists that *God* is whatever this reality, *agape*, may be. Several clues emerge here. First the very use of the word "God" in this statement (like the kingdom *of God* in the parables) serves as a radicalizing qualifier upon the entire statement. In sum, the use of the expression "God" signals the presence of religious-as-limit use of language. (Tracy 1979, 109; the emphasis is his.)

The use of the term "God" signals metaphorical use of language. Such terms as "rock," "father," "mother," or "love" can refer literally to human experience, but when they refer to God they become metaphors, not literal, cognitive statements. God is neither rock nor human being, and God shows love in ways that transcend human love. It follows that the language of worship is highly metaphorical, because it speaks much of God and the divine-human relationship.

A new understanding of metaphor has been becoming important to biblical and theological studies, and increasingly to the study of Christian worship.[1] Until recently, a metaphor was considered to be a figure of speech substituted for a missing or absent literal word (Ricoeur 1976, 48). In this understanding, a metaphor sometimes filled in language gaps when no word yet existed to talk about something. Thus, the appendages of an airplane were called "wings" because they resembled birds' wings, but in time "wing" became a literal term. Or a metaphor could be a rhetorical device designed to please hearers or readers, while not adding anything to the meaning of a statement. A metaphor is thus understood to be a simile with the comparative term ("like" or "as") omitted; it is a naming based on the similarity between the two terms. It says nothing that could not be said some other way.

---

1. Norman Perrin, Amos Wilder, and Dominic Crossan are among the scholars who have applied contemporary understandings of metaphor to biblical studies. Sallie McFague has developed what she calls a "metaphorical theology." For treatment of metaphor in liturgical studies, refer to Mark Searle 1981; Gail Ramshaw 1986a; and A. C. Thiselton 1975. Titles and publication data for most of these authors are provided in the reference list.

By contrast, in the understanding developed by persons such as Ricoeur, McFague, and Tracy, which I support, a metaphor produces meaning not only by the similarity but also by the dissimilarity of the two terms.[2] "Metaphor exists within the tension of identity and difference," writes Handelman (1982, 23). In this new understanding, metaphors may sometimes function as language inventions, as ornaments, or as similes with the comparative terms omitted. Characteristically, however, metaphors involve the interaction of two systems of meaning that contain elements that are both alike and not alike (Black 1962, 44–47). This interaction occurs at the level of sentences and not merely of individual words; it is not that one word is substituted for another, but that two systems of meaning are put in relation to one another to make a statement. Bringing together that which does not ordinarily go together creates a tension that reveals meaning:

> If metaphor does not consist in clothing an idea in an image, if it consists instead in reducing the shock engendered by two incompatible ideas, then it is in the reduction of this gap or difference that resemblance plays a role. What is at stake in a metaphorical utterance, in other words, is the appearance of kinship where ordinary vision does not perceive any relationship.... A new, hitherto unnoticed, relation of meaning [springs] up between the terms that previous systems of classification had ignored or not allowed. (Ricoeur 1976, 51)

Metaphors bring forward unnoticed dimensions of reality by forging connections where they would not ordinarily be expected. They can stretch the limits of human thought and perception so that we grasp new meanings.

The meanings emerging from metaphors cannot, however, be put precisely into other words. The more metaphors are based on the tension between "like" and "unlike," the less they are translatable into other terms. They can be paraphrased, but paraphrase cannot exhaust their meaning (Ricoeur 1976, 53). By creating an apparent contradiction, they lure persons toward a new perception of some reality. This is how they communicate meaning.

---

2. See works by Handelman, Ricoeur, Black, and Wheelwright in the reference list. Ricoeur (1976, 49) credits I. A. Richards with the pioneering work in developing a new understanding of metaphor.

Max Black has pointed out that metaphors create meaning through "systems of associated commonplaces." He says that the metaphor "a man is a wolf" evokes meaning not so much through the dictionary definition of a wolf, as through what people associate with a wolf in a culture. An expert on wolves might know the commonplaces to be incorrect, but still would grasp the metaphor, knowing what is commonly thought about wolves:

> From the expert's standpoint, the system of commonplaces may include half-truths or downright mistakes (as when a whale is classified as a fish); but the important thing for the metaphor's effectiveness is not that the commonplaces should be true, but that they should be readily and freely evoked. (Black 1962, 40)

Metaphors depend on associations people have as whole people, with thoughts, feelings, bodies, and histories.

Linda Clark has applied Max Black's thought to the church's use of "Father" as a metaphor for God. She writes:

> One cannot disassociate the word "father" from its usage in the ordinary speech of everyday life. We could not communicate anything by this phrase if the words did not conform in some way to their accepted connotations. Max Black points out that the accepted commonplaces are altered through their use in the metaphor, but not beyond recognition. (Clark 1980, 25)

When the metaphor "Father" refers to God in Christian worship, the meaning evoked is necessarily influenced by the meaning of "father" in everyday life, and not only by understandings in scripture and church tradition. Metaphors make meaning through association with lived experience; and, even if a systematic theologian declared how worshipers *should* understand the metaphor, that would not affect their actual experience of the metaphor.

Because metaphors create meaning by association, one cannot control or predict exactly how they will be heard. Beverly Rice, a Christian educator, tells of a group of church school teachers who developed a curriculum designed to help children expand their images of God (class discussion, Garrett-Evangelical Theological Seminary, July 1990). They began by discussing "Shepherd." How surprised the teachers were to discover that the children's only associations around the word "shepherd" were of German shepherds! To appropriate the church's metaphor "Shepherd" for God, the children had drawn upon their own experience. This story highlights the need for loving care in choosing metaphors for worship and Christian education. Just at the age when younger children are forming their understandings of God, they think quite concretely; they will not call on abstractions to make sense of religious language. Either they will draw on associations from living experience, or they will not make sense of such talk at all. If only for the children, we must take care with the metaphors we use.

Using terms together in a metaphor creates further associations, affecting the way both terms are experienced. Max Black argues that to say "a man is a wolf" not only affects one's perception of men, but also one's perception of wolves: "If to call a man a wolf is to put him in a special light, we must not forget that the metaphor makes the wolf seem more human than he otherwise would" (Black 1962, 40, 44). The wolf metaphor brings out characteristics of "a man" such as fierceness, hunger, and constant engagement in struggle. In turn, juxtaposing a "wolf" and a "man" in a metaphor influences our perceptions of a wolf, screening out characteristics that could not be applied to men and making it seem that wolves experience human intentionality. This aspect of metaphorical language means that if we call God "Father," something godlike rubs off on human fathers by association.

The distinction between "live" and "dead" metaphors is also important to the study of liturgical language. In a live metaphor, the tension between the juxtaposed terms is still perceived and therefore can lure toward new discovery of meaning. A dead, or literalized, metaphor has little power to evoke new perception because it has become so commonplace. McFague says that the greatest danger of metaphor is "assimilation — the shocking, powerful metaphor becomes trite and accepted" (McFague 1982, 41). At first, a metaphor may seem so shocking as to evoke disbelief; then, when it is a living metaphor, through tension it evokes insight; then, it becomes dead or literalized. Ricoeur says, "There are no live metaphors in a dictionary" (1976, 52). If this is true, then "Father" is not a live metaphor, because my 1988 *Random House College Dictionary* (Revised edition) gives "the first person of the Trinity" as one definition of "Father." In live metaphor, the tension between the "is" and "is not" is still present.

Metaphors that have been used in worship over time may no longer provoke insight. For example, as McFague has observed, "Jesus said, 'This is my body,' and instead of surprise, joy, or disbelief, we do not even hear the metaphor" (McFague 1982, 41). We must use metaphor to speak about God. Yet when Christian worship repeats the same metaphors over centuries, the tension between "is" and "is not" is lost. As the tension disappears, so does power to evoke fresh awareness of God, particularly when liturgies use only a few metaphors for God.

Metaphors sometimes lose their evocative power because the associated commonplaces on which they draw change or disappear. For example, the associations evoked by royal metaphors for God have changed over the years. Daniel Stevick has shown that royal metaphors were more prominent in the *Book of Common Prayer* than they were in scripture, and that the imagery is used differently, drawing on sixteenth-century experiences (Stevick 1970, 43–48). According to Stevick, English-speaking people in the twentieth century have a still different experience; they no longer live in social structures in which an "accepted, permanent, unbridgeable gap in status" and power exists between king and subject (68). God's transcendence, to which Stevick believed king-and-subject metaphors point, could now be better represented in terms of "radical newness in history," rather than "a realm above history" (68).

Sometimes, when the tensive quality of a metaphor referring to God is lost, people assume a particular way of speaking about God to be literally true. They forget that God is both like and unlike whatever human terms are used to speak about God. As McFague has argued, there is a "necessity for many complementary models to intimate the richness and complexity of the divine-human relationship. If this criterion is not accepted, idolatry results" (McFague 1982, 145). When one way of talking about God becomes dominant to the exclusion of others, as McFague argues the metaphor "Father" has become (145), an idol has been established.

Finding living metaphorical language for worship is a crucial task for the church as it seeks to be a means by which God may address the world in love and grace. In practice, this often means juxtaposing new or neglected metaphors with enduring metaphors. These enduring metaphors (often called "root metaphors") generate new metaphors, and they themselves shift in importance and meaning over the years, as we have noted with the metaphor "king." Various authors have named "God is love," "the reign of God," "the saving acts of God," and "the death and resurrection of Christ" as root metaphors of the Christian faith.[3] Root metaphors endure over time in the context of a rich diversity of metaphors, as Christians witness to the God of Jesus Christ.

In other uses of language, writers avoid mixing metaphors; but, says Ramshaw, "In liturgical speech metaphors mix freely" (1986a, 9). Liturgical language requires a network of metaphors because of the inadequacy of any one metaphor, by itself, to speak about God. Juxtaposed metaphors clarify and delimit one another. (Refer to Thiselton 1975, 6, for a helpful discussion of this aspect of metaphor.) For example, in Psalm 18, the LORD is called "my rock" (verses 2, 31, 46), but it is also said, "He reached down from on high, he took me; he drew me out of mighty waters" (verse 16). God's "reaching" and "drawing" indicates that God is not an inanimate object; that is not the way God is a "rock." On the other hand, the "rock" metaphor gives a clue that God is not literally an embodied human being, as the "reaching" and "drawing" metaphors might indicate. The two metaphors work together to reveal something that might in propositional terms be called "God's faithfulness" in relation to the person praying.

A diversity of metaphors brings out the meaning of well-worn metaphors, which may be repeated almost as if by rote. For example, "God is love" has become such a commonplace saying that it no longer even seems to be a metaphor. In his hymn "God of Many Names," Brian Wren has given new life to the metaphor "God is love" by juxtaposing it with more surprising metaphors, for example, "Womb and birth of time" and "Carpenter of new creation" (United Methodist Church 1989, hymn 106).

---

3. Ricoeur (1976) offers a particularly helpful discussion of root metaphors. McFague calls "the kingdom of God" the root metaphor of Christianity (McFague 1982, 109). David Tracy argues that "God is love" is the root New Testament metaphor (Tracy 1979, 100). For Thiselton, the phrase "saving acts of God" is central in Christian liturgy (Thiselton 1975, 15); Searle, on the other hand, calls the death and resurrection of Jesus the root metaphor of Christian worship (Searle 1981, 111–112).

FATHER AS A METAPHOR FOR GOD

This understanding of metaphor leads to several observations about the use of "Father" as a metaphor for God. First, if even terms such as "love" are metaphorical, in the sense that they speak of God by borrowing from human experience, surely "Father," as a way of talking about God, is a metaphor, and not, as is sometimes claimed, an ontological statement about God's being (*contra* Bloesch 1985, 36). The question revolves around how language functions. Like most metaphors, naming God "Father" creates meaning through the tension of the likeness and unlikeness of the two terms of the metaphor. God is both like and unlike human fathers. But, through incessant use, the metaphorical quality of the name "Father" has been lost. When the tension is lost, and God is seen as only like, and not unlike fathers, the metaphor loses its power to evoke new perception through tension and wonder. Claims that the term "Father" applied to God is analogy, not metaphor, again reveal that the metaphor has lost its power. Analogies make meanings by way of partial likeness and not through the tension of likeness and unlikeness. Even the most loving fathers are limited human beings who are unlike God, though the finest father-child relationships mirror something of the divine-human relationship.

Understanding that metaphors create meaning through a system of associated commonplaces also makes nonsense of the idea that "Father," when used of God, has nothing to do with the everyday usage of the word. Bloesch claims that "the trinitarian names for God are ontological symbols based on divine revelation, rather than personal metaphors having their origin in cultural experience" (Bloesch 1985, 36). What sense does it make to point to "divine revelation" communicated through words deeply embedded in human experience and then to ask believers to suspend their experience related to these words? Children make sense of religious language by drawing on their life associations, and even adults bring associations from human experience to a metaphor such as "father." "Father," as a way of speaking to or about God, is a metaphor, and it makes meaning through association with the human experience of fatherhood.

LITURGICAL LANGUAGE MAY BE REVELATORY

Liturgical language may be revelatory; that is, through it we may enter into deeper understanding of and communion with God. To say that liturgical language is metaphorical is not to challenge its claim to truth, but to consider how it does reveal truth.

The language of Christian worship opens the doors to communion with and understanding of God through ordinary human language. As Gail Ramshaw says, "Christian speech is not a Sanskrit, a wholly other language required and reserved for sacred purposes" (Ramshaw 1986a, 3). The words of worship are words of human speech, in the vernacular, drawing from daily life. The metaphor "God is love" draws on associations with friends, lovers, and family to intimate something about the nature of God. "Justification by faith," a key metaphor of the Protestant Reformation, derives from Paul's use of courtroom metaphors to describe God's "acquittal" of humanity in Jesus Christ. Other key Christian metaphors — for example, "the kingdom of God" — grow out of human experience and language. Even the title "Christ" or "Anointed One," acted out in ritual by the unnamed woman of Mark 14:3-9, grows out of rituals of anointing a king or other leader. The language of Christian worship grows out of embodied human experience.

The language of Christian worship draws on entirely human language, yet through this language Christians witness and respond to divine revelation with praise and thanksgiving. Drawing on Paul's metaphor (2 Cor. 4:7), Letty Russell says in *The Household of Freedom:* "When we think and talk about God we always use metaphors, because God's self-revelation is known to us through our 'earthen vessels' of experience" (Russell 1987, 36). Theologians differ in how they describe the relation of metaphorical language to the reality of God. Here Russell posits a "self-revelation of God" of which human metaphors are the vehicle. By contrast, some other theologians are more reserved in claiming that human metaphors may have any direct relation to the reality of God. For example, in *Metaphorical Theology* (if not as much in the more recent *Models of God*) McFague appears to be more skeptical than Russell about the relation of human metaphors to divine reality. For example, McFague writes:

> The tradition says that we are created in the image of God, but the obverse is also the case, for we imagine God in *our* image. And the human images we choose for the divine influence the way we feel about ourselves, for these images are "divinized" and hence raised in status. (McFague 1982, 10)

Healthy skepticism about the limits of our knowledge of God is warranted; but, as Karl Barth points out (*CD* II/1, 224), extreme skepticism amounts to denial that it is God's good pleasure to be revealed to humanity in Jesus Christ.[4] Thus Russell's careful distinction that "God's self-revelation is known to us through our 'earthen vessels' of experience" is helpful (Russell 1987, 36). Christian metaphors about God are more than projections of the human image on the divine; they witness with thanksgiving and humility to the way God has been made known to us.

Barth has carefully explored the nature of human knowledge of God (Barth *CD* II/1, 179–254). To begin, the limits of human knowledge of God must be admitted. We humans cannot on our own attain to the knowledge of God by our views (Barth's word for "images," *CD* II/1, 181) or concepts. Even in being revealed, God remains hidden, for human beings cannot fully comprehend God. However, in the Word through the Spirit, God is pleased to become known in relationship with human beings. Thus the "hidden" God is not inconsistent with God revealed in Word and Spirit (Barth *CD* II/1, 210). Human views and concepts are imperfect vehicles through which Christians witness to God's self-revelation, through the grace of God. Through grace, God may use human ideas and images as a means of revelation in the proclamation and worship of the church. The first and primary human response to God's self-revelation is praise and thanksgiving for God's free gift. This leads to a journey of learning about God in a relationship of trust and obedience, leading to approximate views and concepts that are never complete and

---

4. All references to Karl Barth in this book are from the *Church Dogmatics* (*CD*). The notes give the volume (in Roman numerals), the part (in Arabic numbers), and the page references in the *Church Dogmatics* as translated by G. W. Bromiley; refer to the Reference List for publication data.

always open to discussion. By grace, we can speak about God; by grace, we accept the limits of our speaking about God.

Barth's exploration of the adequacy of human images and concepts of God suggests the context in which discussion of the metaphorical nature of language about God ought to be understood. To say that liturgical language, and specifically language about God, is metaphorical, is not to say it has no reference in divine reality. Christians claim to speak metaphorically about God in response to God's self-revelation in Jesus Christ. Thus the metaphors of Christian faith are more than a projection of human experience upon a divine screen. At the same time, they are "earthen vessels," not identical with the Living Water of which they may be carriers. No one metaphor, no one image, no one concept, can be the final word about God. Yet God has been faithfully revealed in Jesus Christ and continues to be revealed through the work of the Holy Spirit in the church, in and through human words.

Given the limits and potentials of language in witnessing to God, metaphorical language is uniquely suited for worship. Metaphor "exists within the *tension* of identity and difference" (Handelman 1982, 23; emphasis added), as does the human language we use to witness to God's self-revelation. Analogical language makes meaning by connecting two realities that are more or less alike. Because God is both like and unlike whatever terms we use, to regard as analogical any images for God based in human experience is to claim too much. If, on the other hand, we considered only God's dissimilarity to any human language or images, we could worship only in silence or by saying what God is not. Metaphorical language, however, keeps alive the tension between likeness and unlikeness, and between the possibility and limits of all human language about God. The tension of metaphor can express meanings that cannot otherwise be expressed. If our images of God are necessarily metaphors, this is not only limit but also possibility, for metaphors reveal meaning in a way that concepts do not. To say language about God is metaphorical is not to deny its truth claims, but to affirm a particular way of communicating truth.

Scripture plays a key role in mediating God's self-revelation, and thus in generating metaphors for Christian worship. Scripture witnesses to God's self-revelation in Jesus Christ, as well as to

God's faithfulness to Israel, the covenant people. These writings are not, strictly speaking, revelation but witness to revelation, which, through the Spirit, may occasion new revelation (Barth *CD* I/1, 99–111). Still, the Bible is prototypical for Christians, for it contains the earliest witnesses to God's coming in Jesus Christ, and it documents the formation and continuation of God's covenant with Israel and the church.

Christian worship has always plumbed scripture for its language, but it has done so with increasing selectivity, as will be seen in Chapter 4. The terms "Father," "King," "Lord," and "Son," along with "Spirit," "Christ," and "God" are the main scriptural names for God now used in English language liturgies. (Wren documents this in regard to hymns; Wren 1989, 115–122). Writers of liturgies have neglected other scriptural names for God. This, in turn, influences what people perceive is found in scripture. Then, with this limited perception of how God is named in scripture, some people make a further move: they claim that these few names must forever dominate Christian worship. Note the circularity of this argument. Some others recognize that other metaphors exist, but claim that "Father," "Lord," "King," "Son," "Christ," "Spirit," and "God" have unique revelatory status because they occur more frequently in scripture than do other metaphors. Surely statistical analysis is an inadequate way to recognize divine revelation, even in North America! Moreover, neither of these first two arguments deals with whether YHWH, the untranslatable name for God, used with great frequency in Hebrew scripture, is best transferred into the liturgy through the name "Lord."[5]

Another line of argument claims that because "Father" is a name for God used frequently in the New Testament, it is uniquely revelatory; but this implicitly rejects the witness of the Hebrew scriptures, something most Christians have been unwilling to do. Even the claim that because Jesus called God "Father," that name must forever dominate Christian liturgy, does not hold up under scrutiny, as we shall see in Chapter 4. Most flimsy of all is the claim

---

5. In back of this paragraph are arguments by Donald Bloesch in *The Battle for the Trinity* (1985), who argues that "Lord," "Father," "King," "Son," "Spirit," "Christ," and "God" must remain the predominant divine names. Plaskow's thought helped me recognize how liturgical use affects our perception of what is in scripture (1990, 128–134).

that "Father," being an "analogy," brings "real knowledge" of God, whereas "rock" or "mother," being a metaphor, brings only "intuitive awareness" (Bloesch 1985, 23). This claim to revelation is based either on a false understanding of language or a denial that God is in any way unlike a human father; further, it does not do justice to the revelatory potential of metaphors, apparently identifying "real knowledge" with (supposed) conceptual knowledge.

I believe, by contrast, that scripture is a prototype for metaphors that reveal God's nature, inviting rather than excluding new metaphors for Christian witness. We may take our lead from the very diversity of scriptural metaphors for God. Forbidding graven images, scriptures use a plurality of names to speak about God. Those who pick out just a few names for God from scripture and call them uniquely revelatory reject scripture's own method and substitute idols of their own.

The center of the Christian revelation is not scripture, but Jesus Christ. Scripture is prototype for our liturgical metaphors because it contains the witness to God's self-revelation in Jesus Christ, which, mediated through the witness of church and Spirit, brings about a response in faith. Those who do respond in faith, then, may freely give witness to their faith through praise, prayer, and proclamation. The metaphors they use may come from scripture or from daily life. Always scripture will be a touchstone in this ongoing circle of witness and faith response. It provides a starting point, not a limit, for our language about God.

The church calls on a great variety of names to witness to God's self-revelation. God has been and continues to be revealed among humanity, and human beings use available language to respond and to describe that revelation. We always stretch language beyond its limits to say anything about God. Yet Christians use the materials at hand — a multitude of metaphors drawn from scripture and human experience — to construct some way of praising God. By grace, revelation may occur through this human construction.

LITURGICAL LANGUAGE IS COMMUNAL

Worship is the act of a community with God through the Spirit; ideally, it engages the hearts and minds of all who are present. Thus, in worship we must speak in ways that enable the heartfelt participation of all who have gathered together to worship God and engage in the life of Christian community. Because worship both forms and expresses faith, those who shape liturgical language must balance sensitivity to people's present understandings of God with the desire to nurture growth in life and faith. Common worship is nourished by the private prayer of the community while it is apart, as well as by traditions of the whole church throughout time and space. In turn, the shared experience of public worship shapes private prayer. Public worship calls for language that can be "the meeting ground for the faith of many" (Ramshaw 1983, 426). Common language is intelligible, authentic, scriptural, and appropriate to its context.

Intelligibility

If the language of worship is to express and shape the faith of the Christian community, it must be intelligible to all or most worshipers. Therefore, for example, the Protestant reformers and the architects of the Vatican II reforms called for worship in the vernacular. The vocabulary and grammar of worship must be such that worshipers can understand it.

The metaphorical nature of liturgical language presents particular challenges to intelligibility. Thus, as Thiselton argues, the need for metaphoric tension must be balanced with the need for intelligibility:

> If language is so highly metaphorical as to be naturally unintelligible to the average worshiper, it defeats its own ends. For it cannot be conveying meaning *powerfully*, if not conveying meaning *at all*. (Thiselton 1975, 26)

To seek intelligibility in worship does not mean reducing images to cognitive discourse; metaphorical language is not translatable into concepts. Instead, it means asking whether a metaphor evokes live associations for worshipers. For example, when singing the hymn "Come, Thou Fount of Every Blessing," do worshipers know the meaning of "Here I raise mine Ebenezer"? The language of worship ought to be intelligible to most worshipers without reducing metaphoric language to conceptual language and without depending on just a few metaphors.

It is a mistake to try to make worship intelligible mainly by removing metaphorical language. Thiselton argues that Today's English Version of the Bible makes the mistake of sacrificing metaphorical language for the sake of clarity:

> An example of this problem may be considered by comparing the way in which Today's English Version of the Bible consistently softens the force of Biblical metaphors because it aims above all else at clarity of meaning. Thus "put on Christ" (Gal. 3:27) becomes "take upon themselves the qualities of Christ." Readers are no longer left to ask the question for themselves: how does one "put on" not new clothes, but a person? The ambiguity has been removed, but so has the self-involvement and appeal for a reaction. (Thiselton 1975, 26)

We need not sacrifice metaphoric tension for the sake of intelligibility. Evocative metaphors use words known to the hearers, yet they are open-ended enough to lure hearers into responding in their own ways. Thus the words of worship come alive in ever new ways.

Authenticity

Besides being intelligible to members of the community, the language of worship must authentically express the faith of the community. One must ask, Can worshipers honestly pray a prayer, whether aloud from a printed text or silently along with a liturgical presider? A discussion in *The Christian Century* about contemporary prayers of confession illustrated this problem. In an article, Browne Barr took issue with a prayer in which congregants were expected to confess buying designer sheets. He himself did not know what designer sheets were, and he objected to the trend toward very specific prayers of confession that may not apply to everyone. He asked for a return to prayers of confession with "general, sweeping poetic phrases" so that worshipers may confess "the sins we have dredged up, not ones laid on us" (Barr 1987, 844). However, a respondent to the article, although not defending the prayer about designer sheets, argued that prayers that are too general may fail to speak for anyone: "All too often everybody's confession is nobody's confession" (Wade 1987, 1100). He argued that more specific prayers are more likely to name people's sin, even though "not every phrase will apply to every worshiper every Sunday" (1100). Although the two writers took different approaches to the problem, both acknowledged the need for the language of worship to be authentic to the experience of the community. Providing common language that most worshipers can recognize as their own includes accurately naming the experience of a community. Thus sensitive listening to and participation in the joys and struggles of the worshiping community and the world is an important discipline for those who shape the words of worship, as writers of prayers, hymns, and other liturgical texts. In this way, the language of worship will be more intelligible and authentic to Christian communities.

Scripture As a Source for Common Language

Although the way in which different Christian communities interpret scripture varies, they all share this document as an important part of their lives. To one degree or another, Christians are familiar with the stories and images of scripture. With the introduction of lectionaries since the early 1970s, scripture is becoming more central in the worship of many churches. For all these reasons, scripture is an important source for common language in worship.

Given the patriarchal context in which scripture originated, scriptural metaphors must be carefully chosen for use in Christian worship. The church must reclaim a broader range of scriptural metaphors. The ecumenical lectionary, if supplemented by other scriptures to avoid masculine bias, can help churches to base their worship around a broader range of scripture passages and discover more diverse metaphors for God in their common worship.[6]

Common Language Is Contextualized

Seeking intelligibility, authenticity, and scripture resonance are ways of helping people pray in common. These goals refer to the *content* of common language for worship. I would also like to comment on the *process* of seeking common liturgical language.

---

6. Refer to Duck and Tirabassi 1990, 129-135, for suggestions for supplementing the lectionary from a feminist perspective.

People often assume that the best path toward language adequate for common prayer is to convene a denominational committee. The church empowers these experts and representatives to develop language for worship that will be considered orthodox in theology and adequate for every church in the denomination. Alternatively, people entrust the local church pastor or editor of published worship resources with the task of shaping liturgical language. Especially when these committees and individuals listen to God, scripture, church, and world, empowering a few to shape liturgical language may be a good way to call upon gifts and divide tasks in the church. Many good efforts have come out of such committees, pastors, and writers, but the church has generally neglected the possibilities of developing resources by communities (not only pastors) on the local level.

One insight that people working on feminist liturgies bring to the life of the church is their emphasis on local context. Indeed, as Marjorie Procter-Smith has noted, such groups are often reluctant to publish worship materials they develop, in the conviction that worship can best be developed on the local level (Procter-Smith 1990, 21–22). Even when they do publish their liturgies, it is usually with the disclaimer that these are only models to inspire other groups' work, rather than orders to be followed word for word, action for action. In this approach, common language for worship comes from worshiping communities themselves.

"Common liturgical language," in its truest sense, is contextualized; it grows out of actual worshiping communities. Judith Plaskow, writing from a Jewish feminist perspective, muses that the discovery of postpatriarchal language appropriate for worship may await the creation of new egalitarian faith communities (Plaskow 1990, 159). Certainly, any who assert that worship is the people's work must admit that metaphors drawn from the faith and lives of persons in local communities must complement words for worship developed denominationally.

Developing common language based on the worship and faith of local communities need not be done in isolation. Denominational worship commissions can help congregations learn from one another by publishing collections of resources developed on the local level or by gathering worship leaders for mutual sharing. At such events, they can also help congregations develop theological and liturgical sensitivity in planning worship. And, when an official hymnal or worship book is needed, they can draw on the experiences of local communities, even as they seek to present new models for local use.

Developing the language of worship in local contexts calls us to embrace diversity rather than to demand uniformity. Common language is not the same thing as uniform language. Uniform language may be idolatrous, or represent the faith of only a small, homogeneous, dominant group within a community. Common language, on the other hand, encompasses the rich diversity of worshiping communities, with metaphors as diverse as the people who worship together (refer to Gray 1990, 56–57, and Plaskow 1990, 154–169). Recognizing diversity brings ferment to worship communities. When people in a congregation with varied experiences shape their worship cooperatively, a degree of discomfort or conflict often occurs. This very conflict or discomfort is often the sign of a community that is growing in faith and mutual understanding.

I recognize that this is a revolutionary approach to common language, especially beyond my own congregationalist context in the United Church of Christ. I acknowledge, too, that entrusting the choice of liturgical language to higher church authorities or pastors may sometimes safeguard the continuity of worship with church tradition. But women and many other groups participated in very limited ways in shaping that tradition. It is time now to open up the process of shaping liturgical language to women, lay people, and people of many cultures, along with men, clergy, and Westerners. As all levels of the church join in this open process, the heartfelt participation of worshiping communities will grow. Worship will be more authentic and intelligible to more people, even as it draws upon a wider range of metaphors from scripture and human experience.

LITURGICAL LANGUAGE CHANGES

As communities, their historical contexts, and their word associations change, the language that will be appropriate for worship also changes. Theological reflection may lead toward shifts in religious language; indeed, Nelle Morton argues that people of every generation must consciously reflect on the adequacy of the

metaphors they use, if these metaphors are not to become idolatrous (Morton 1985, 180–183). Changes in the life of the church
and the world will also occasion changes in patterns of metaphors.
Change occurs in several ways. Predominant metaphors shift to
roles of less importance or are used differently. Some metaphors
become more prominent, and new metaphors emerge.

Some points in the history of the church provoke much questioning, reflection, and creativity. Certainly the present is such
a time. Speaking of hymn writing, Thomas Troeger has argued
that working creatively with the tensions between the language
of the past and the human experience of the present allows the
church to witness vitally to its faith as years go by: "The tension between a poet's experience and the faith which the poet has
received from the church is often a source for creative energies
and for the discovery of language that revitalizes faith" (Troeger
1987, 10). This tension can in fact "mobilize the imaginations
of poets so that the tension becomes a source of revelation into
the workings of God" (10). Troeger demonstrates how Psalm 19
transformed ancient traditions received from Israel and the ancient Near East, and then how poets such as Addison and Watts
paraphrased the psalm in light of the changing cosmologies of
their times. This creative working with the tension between received religious language and contemporary cultural experience
is, in fact, an ongoing process. Though it is only human to fear
change, I agree with Troeger that this time of great change, generated in part by feminist critique of traditional Christian theology
and worship, is a time of great opportunity and creativity.

The evolution of the language of Christian worship is a historical process involving persons and communities in all their
complexity. The language of worship is human language that
can be changed based on consideration of its evocative power,
its theological adequacy, its aptness in expressing the faith of
community, and its ethical ramifications. Because the language
of worship forms and expresses the faith of community, and because it is directed at praise and thanksgiving to God, the church
must continue seeking the most adequate language possible, even
as it admits the limits of all its attempts to do so. If liturgical revision is the work of a relative few, it is work on behalf of the
whole church, which seeks a common language of praise and
thanksgiving, proclamation and love.

CHAPTER 2

BEYOND THE FATHER'S FEARFUL MASK

O Holy Wisdom, show your face
beyond the father's fearful mask.
We seek your healing and your grace;
for battered lives your peace we ask.

O Well of Silence, send your voice,
unheard in names of wanton power.
O Word of Love, may we rejoice
to hear you speaking in this hour.

O Fragrant Scent of Liberty,
with your aroma wrap us round.
O Blessed Heart of Harmony,
unite us in a rainbow sound.

Reveal your image in us each
long bound by patriarch's decree.
Resound as silence comes to speech
and Truth returns to set us free.*

This hymn text expresses my conviction that the traditional language of Christian worship imparts patriarchal values. "Patriarch's decree" has bound the image of God in many of us, male and female, limiting us to the gender roles of patriarchy. Also, patriarchal language, including the constant use of "father" in naming God, creates a mask that conceals, rather than reveals, the loving God of Jesus Christ. I pray that the Holy One will guide us in discovering new words for worship that can heal and free.

---

*Words by Ruth C. Duck, copyright 1989.

In this chapter, we will see how predominantly masculine language for God is part of the overall gender bias of the English language. Not only does gender bias in language reflect patriarchal values; it helps to keep the whole social construct of patriarchy in place.

"Father" language about God, when used predominantly, without feminine images, is part of the overall pattern of gender bias in language. Moreover, it draws on associations from the patriarchal family, legitimating the domination of mothers by fathers and children by parents. In North America, this legitimated domination often leads to domestic violence. Although many Christians have positive associations about their fathers, for significant numbers of people the predominant father image, associated with the patriarchal family, becomes a mask that hides rather than reveals God's love. At the same time, it becomes a part of the social reality that makes patriarchal domination and abuse possible.

I am convinced that the churches must address the problem of predominantly masculine and paternal imagery for God — for the sake of faithful Christian witness and for the sake of precious human lives. In this chapter I give the reasons for my conviction by showing how gender bias in language supports patriarchy, and by explaining why "Father" as a predominant metaphor for God is problematic in patriarchal society.

GENDER BIAS IN LANGUAGE

Although masculine imagery and pronouns for God have prevailed in Christian worship, thoughtful Christians have often noted that God transcends categories of sex. For example, Gregory of Nazianzus, in his Fifth Theological Oration, warns against considering God to be male in sex because "he" is called "God and Father" (Collins 1985, 300). However, although God is not male in *sex*, in worship Christians again and again attribute masculine *gender* to the divine.

Sex and gender are two different categories of human development. The word *sex* refers to mating behavior and to biological differences such as sexual organs, which distinguish males and females (Oakley 1972, 16, 18; Lott 1987, 6; Schneiders 1986, 8-11). The word *gender*, on the other hand, is a cultural and psychological term identifying behaviors women and men learn, which do not depend on biological differences (Oakley 1972, 158; Lott 1987, 6). This includes roles assigned to and personality characteristics expected of males and females. Cultures assume that gender traits naturally and automatically grow out of biological sex differences. However, cross-cultural research reveals that social expectations determine gender roles. What one culture considers to be a masculine characteristic, another considers to be feminine and vice versa. Bernice Lott notes that "every social behavior performed by men is also done by some women within the same culture or another"; and, except for "a universal responsibility for the care of infants, ... women's behavior across cultures varies dramatically" (Lott 1987, 1). Culture, not biology, defines masculinity and femininity.

Because the word *sex* and the terms *male* and *female* have to do with biological characteristics, it is rightly said that God has no sex and that God is neither male nor female. At the same time, a society's gender expectations come into play whenever God is described using masculine or feminine pronouns and metaphors. Metaphors for God such as "Father," "King," and "Lord" are thus "masculine" and not "male," for they refer to gender, to socially learned behavior, and not to biological sex. When masculine metaphors are used in speaking to and about God, they do not refer to sex (as if God had sex organs or male chromosomes), but to gender (by associating "God" with some role, trait, or behavior usually expected of human males). God is not a male, but given the predominance of masculine imagery for God, people often assume that God is masculine. The metaphoric status of masculine language for God is forgotten, leading to such nonsensical statements as "God is a Spirit. He is neither male nor female." The statement "neither male nor female" acknowledges that God is not male in sex; but the pronoun "he" attributes masculine gender to God.

The use of predominantly masculine language for God in English language liturgies reflects gender constructs operating in the English language. A culture's language reflects its gender assumptions. Linguistics scholar Julia P. Stanley argues that in the English language, "the semantic space is dominated by males" (Stanley 1977, 74), and that the "sex-role dichotomy perpetuated by our society [is] embedded within our language" (44).[1] Gender bias is embedded within the language through several strategies, including predominantly masculine language for God.

Male dominance is embedded in the English language through so-called generic language. The use of terms such as "he," "man," and "mankind" to refer to persons of unidentified sex or to groups including both sexes reveals that males are the social standard (Stanley 1977, 50). "Generic" use of these terms is ambiguous because in some contexts they refer specifically to persons of male sex, whereas in other contexts they refer to either males or females or to both. An 1850 British law illustrates the problem. It decreed that words "importing the masculine gender" should be taken to include females, unless otherwise provided. John Stuart argued unsuccessfully for repeal of the law lest women be included in such provisions as "every male person paying rent, and occupying a house of a certain value, should be entitled to a vote" (Baron 1986, 140). "Man" or "male person" could be interpreted to include a woman if she broke the law, but to exclude her if she wanted to vote. The ambiguous reference of generic language thus allows those empowered to interpret language to exclude or include women as they please.

God is not male in sex; so the prevalent use of masculine pronouns for God in English language liturgies is, in part, an extension of the idea of male generic language. Grammars written in the eighteenth and nineteenth centuries defended the growing use of the masculine nouns and pronouns to speak of both males and females by invoking the "doctrine of worthiness," that is, male superiority (Baron 1986, 97–98). One grammarian wrote that God is "in all languages *Masculine*, inasmuch as the masculine Sex is the superior and more excellent; and as He is the Creator of all, the Father of Gods and Men" (Baron 1986, 99, quoting James Harris, *Hermes*, 1751 [1765], 50). Another, James Beattie, claimed that "we" speak of the divine as masculine, but "idolatrous na-

---

1. A growing number of scholars of the English language support her claim. Those who agree that gender bias is embedded in the English language include Alleen Pace Nilsen, Haig Bosmajian, and H. Lee Gershuny, who co-edited *Sexism and Language* (1977) with Stanley. Others who have studied the way in which gender assumptions are reflected in the English language include Dale Spender (1980), Casey Miller and Kate Swift (1976 and 1980), and Dennis Baron (1986).

tions" will even use feminine names for the Supreme Being (1788, quoted by Baron 1986, 99).

Today the term "customary gender" has replaced the term "most worthy gender" to justify the use of masculine terms to include both male and female persons or to refer to God (Baron 1986, 99). However, Baron charges that this less revealing name still assumes male superiority: "The modern paraphrases of the doctrine of worthiness are but thin masks for the underlying assumption of male superiority in life as well as language" (100). "Generic" masculine language reinforces male dominance in society. The predominant use of masculine language for God both reflects and exemplifies the masculine bias of the English language.

Another form of the "most worthy" principle operates through word order; masculine forms precede feminine ones; for example, "brothers and sisters" or "God our Father and Mother." Grammars of previous centuries explicitly based this practice on belief in the superior worthiness of the masculine (Baron 1986, 3). The principle also operates when people insist that masculine imagery must be used at the most important times in the church's life, such as baptism and ordination (refer to White 1983, 107).

Studies have shown that generic masculine words evoke pictures of male human beings more than nongendered words do (Miller and Swift 1976, 21, 24). Thus, when masculine pronouns are used to refer to God, people are more likely to picture a male person. Moreover, when masculine pronouns predominate and feminine pronouns are missing, even nongendered terms tend to evoke masculine images. If God is usually called "Father" or "he," even the second-person address "you" will evoke masculine images.

Indeed, some grammarians hold that in English, words about people assume masculine reference unless they refer explicitly to females or both males and females. Writes Baron: "Even today, many linguists assume that the masculine is the normal, or unmarked, gender and that all English nouns are masculine unless specially marked" (Baron 1986, 97). Gender marking reflects stereotypes. The suffix "-man," in occupations like "longshoreman" or "mailman" assumes that men will load the boats and carry the mail. When "poet" becomes "poetess" and "pastor" becomes "lady pastor," the marker ("-ess" or "lady") reveals that society expects poets and pastors to be men (refer to Miller and Swift 1976, 159; 1980, 111–112). Society expects nurses to be women, as the term "male nurse" reveals. Terms such as "career woman" and "family man" reinforce the idea that men belong in offices and women in the home. On the other hand, Stanley believes that to avoid gender marking may render women invisible (Stanley 1977, 74).

Because gender-marked terms often reflect stereotypes about male and female roles, using such terms to refer to God presents particular challenges. "King" and "queen," "father" and "mother," "lord" and "lady" are not equivalent in their connotations. Using "king," "father," and "lord" and none of their feminine counterparts is tempting, if one wishes to portray God as powerful. To use these metaphors, however, not only implies that God is masculine; it also supports the gender role stereotypes that attribute power to males. Even using an unmarked term such as "shepherd," which is related to a marked term such as "shepherdess," may seem to imply that God is masculine. On the other hand, the way feminine words for God are used may perpetuate gender role expectations. Only when masculine and feminine images are used in nonstereotypical ways will they help to overcome masculine bias in language.

The prevalent use of gender markers to indicate role stereotypes leads to questions about imagery for God in Christian worship. Are masculine images for God used because God's praiseworthy acts correspond to roles usually filled by men in society? Should we assume that nouns with no gender marking refer to males? Is "God" then a masculine term? In my opinion, to admit that all nouns are masculine unless proven otherwise is to surrender too much semantic space to the masculine. One may then ask whether such terms as "Creatrix" or "Goddess" concede that "the Creator" or "God" is masculine. Miller and Swift point to the tension involved:

> *Goddess* and *Creatrix* have recently seen increased usage among people who want to call attention to the once widespread worship of a supreme deity conceived of as female. For others, however, the use of such terms implies that *God* and *Creator* refer to a male deity, a concept most thoughtful religious people reject as idolatrous. (Miller and Swift 1980, 112)

"Goddess" may seem to be a diminutive name for the divine; it may give credence to the idea that "God" is masculine. But explicit feminine terms for God, including "Goddess," are needed to remove the "Father" mask so that we can understand God with more clarity and less idolatry. Nelle Morton persuasively argues that the use of the "Goddess" may be the best way "to shatter the old male God image . . . in a sexist culture and sexist religion" (Morton 1985, 145).

The tendency in theology and language to associate women with evil exacerbates the problem created by overuse of masculine imagery for God (refer to Ruether 1983, 93–115). Linguist Dale Spender argues that naming God in masculine terms and associating woman with evil in Christian tradition reinforce the superiority of men and the inferiority of women in Western society. Women are associated with evil not only in the Genesis account of the Fall, but also in the English language. Among words in English that have gender markers, those with masculine markers greatly outnumber those with feminine markers. Yet among gender-marked words with negative associations, feminine words outnumber masculine words (Nilsen et al. 1977, 34–35). In addition, many words with feminine markers have sexual overtones. In one study, Julia Stanley found 220 words for a sexually promiscuous female, but only 20 for a sexually promiscuous male (cited in Spender 1980, 15). The masculine — but not the feminine — is generally associated with God in the English language. The feminine — more than the masculine — is associated with evil in the English language. Thus a man, by association, is godlike; a woman is not. The contrast of associations reflects and reinforces male dominance in society.

The embedding of gender expectations in language through the false generic, word order, and gender marking reflects and reinforces the male domination of society. So does the association of God with the masculine and evil with the feminine. Other aspects of language reinforce domination and subordination based on race, class, differing abilities, and so on, so that, for example, God is identified with whiteness (Jones 1987, viii). As Wren has written, it is important to evaluate how faithful certain ways of talking about God may be, but it is also important to ask, "Who benefits from speaking of God in this way, from this or that pattern of language and metaphor?" (Wren 1989, 82). Linguistic bias helps to keep oppressive social systems in place. In fact, according to historian Gerda Lerner, the movement toward exclusively masculine symbols for the divine helped to establish patriarchal control of society (Lerner 1986, 6, 219).

To identify God with males and masculinity, and at the same time to identify the feminine and females with evil, is to engage in idolatry. Mary Daly has written: "If God is male, then the male is God" (Daly 1973, 19).[2] Using masculine or feminine pronouns is not in itself idolatrous, for God is "not less than personal" (Tillich 1951, 245), and the English language uses masculine and feminine pronouns to refer to persons. But when masculine and never feminine terms refer to God, one partial image of God is equated with the whole. This is idolatry.

Referring to God only in terms of dominant social groups — such as males in patriarchal society — risks identifying God with oppression. To the contrary, African American, feminist, and liberation theologians have asserted that God identifies with and advocates for the oppressed in their struggle for justice.[3] Major Jones persuasively argues that all people (including Caucasian males) should be free to imagine God in terms of their color and gender, remembering the limits of all images of God, yet honoring the image of God within themselves. However, by imagining God as only and essentially white, white people have been able to "remain comfortably unconcerned about the oppression that Black people and their God suffer" (Jones 1987, viii). He argues that African Americans must become free of alien Caucasian images of God to affirm their "personal, full humanity," and that women must be free to refer to God as "she" for the same reasons (ix). To insist that everyone speak of God using language associated with a dominant social group condones oppression.

A less powerful group can claim its own worth by using language for God associated with its own experience and not with the experience of a group that has power over it. Moving away

---

2. The theology of Mary Daly has continued to evolve since 1973, but I continue to find her insights of 1973 helpful. In her 1987 *Wickedary*, she defined "godfather" in part as "the fictional divine father of worldly godfathers; heavenly puppet of popocrats, which they have fashioned in their image and likeness and which functions as their figure/head" (Daly 1987, 203). Clearly, she has moved far "beyond God the father" (Daly 1973, title)!

3. For example, see Cone 1975, 63–77; Ruether 1985, 41–74; Tamez 1987, 144; and Gustavo Gutiérrez 1973, 189–212.

from exclusively white or masculine ways of imaging God can be a part of the liberative process.

Delores S. Williams, an African American theologian and poet, says that an important but often-overlooked aspect of *The Color Purple* (Walker 1982) is the relation between Celie's changing notion of God and her ability to refuse victimization: "Walker makes it absolutely clear that Celie moves beyond the passive acceptance of her victimization as her understanding of God, sexuality, and church changes" (Williams 1986, 231). By accepting Shug's perspective, including her notion of a God who is not an "old white man" but who is connected with "every living thing," Celie is changed:

> With these new perspectives, Celie is no longer a passive victim anticipating release from oppression through death. Celie renounces her old understanding of God and says, "[T]he God I been praying and writing to is a man. And act just like all the other mens I know. Trifling, forgitful and lowdown.... If he ever listened to poor colored women the world would be a different place." (Williams 1986, 231)

Moving toward a new way of speaking to and about God beyond white masculine images, Celie is able to confront and leave her brutally abusive husband. Williams observes that in *The Color Purple*, concepts about God either "support the oppression of black women or complement their struggle for liberation" (231). Celie's new understanding of God comes not from a mystical experience but from a human relationship in which she is guided in the process of liberation from oppression. Williams affirms that "many of us black women have seen ourselves and our experience of God in *Purple*."[4] As Williams's remarks about *The Color Purple* suggest, moving beyond the white masculine bias of language can be one aspect of moving toward liberation.

Including feminine pronouns and metaphors also enhances the revelatory potential of religious language by opening a wider pool of metaphors to complement traditional metaphors. When God is called "Father," and never "Mother," we are more likely

---

4. Williams 1986, 232; refer to Thistlethwaite 1989, 57–58, 90, and 115 for a critique of white feminist interpretations of *The Color Purple*.

to forget that God is not Father in any literal sense. Literalizing metaphors is dangerous. McFague writes:

> One of the classic difficulties with metaphors that become models, such as that of God the father, is that they are often reified, petrified, and expanded so as not only to exclude other models but also to pretend to the status of definitions. (McFague 1987, 39)

Moving past masculine bias in liturgical language enhances its authentic revelatory power, which rests in metaphor and not in definitions that make exclusive models of any human way of talking about God.

In summary, then, by adopting the various strategies of masculine bias in the English language in its worship, the church exalts the male as the normative human being and supports oppression. A few masculine metaphors are reified into definitions, which we idolatrously associate with God.

On the other hand, when we move past masculine bias in the language of liturgy, we support the liberation of all people from patriarchal oppression. We discover a richer pool of imagery for God, thereby reducing the danger of idolatry and enhancing the revelatory potential of liturgical language. For the sake of faithful Christian witness, we must move past gender bias in language.

GENDER BIAS IN LANGUAGE AS A MEANS OF SOCIALIZATION

Moving past gender bias is particularly urgent when we consider its effect on girls and boys as they are growing up. Gender bias in language is an effective tool of socialization. It helps children to internalize and live out their culture's gender expectations.

The socializing power of words was demonstrated by a study of children exposed to a curriculum in which consonants were personified as male persons and vowels were personified as female persons. The gender stereotypes in this curriculum were extreme, showing girls as sick, dainty, afraid, and complaining, and boys as strong, healthy, dominant, and hostile toward girls. A study comparing children who used this curriculum to those who did not showed a statistically significant relation between children's exposure to the curriculum and their identification of certain domains as male or female (Nilsen et al. 1977, 168).

The generic use of terms like "man" and "he" is no longer a part of colloquial English; it is learned at school and not at home by both girls and boys (refer to Nilsen et al. 1977, 178; and Baron 1986, 140–141). Nilsen speculates that because boys are referred to with masculine pronouns, they may learn this language "rule" more easily than girls. She argues that neither males nor females ever fully learn to include female persons in masculine generic words (Nilsen et al. 1977, 178). Thus, "generic" language helps to socialize children to accept gender role expectations by including thought patterns in which the male is the normative human being.

In her book *Sex-Role Stereotypes: Traditions and Alternatives*, psychologist Susan A. Basow explores the process by which sex-role socialization takes place. Among social forces beyond the family that contribute to sex-role socialization, she lists language first, holding that "social and linguistic change are interactive, each promoting change in one another" (Basow 1980, 138). She cites a study of ten cultures that found a positive correlation between "structural sex bias in a culture … and the proportion of male to female gender nouns in use" (138). Language is not the only factor in sex-role socialization; Basow finds that language, role models, play activities, media, schools, and religious settings all convey a consistent message in which "the two sexes are depicted as differing widely in behavior and status" (162). These stereotypes affect a young person's developing self-concept, behavior, and mental and physical health.

Both Basow (1980, 159) and Spender (1980, 165) argue that the use of predominantly masculine language for God is one way people are socialized to accept male dominance of society. Caroline Walker Bynum, an editor of *Gender and Religion*, agrees:

> What people understand themselves to be qua male and female is learned and shaped within culture, and religious symbols are one of the ways in which such meanings are taught and appropriated. (Bynum 1986, 7)

Studies in *Gender and Religion* indicate that cultures that use feminine symbolism for the divine are not always correspondingly free from male dominance of women. Feminine symbolism can serve various ends. Feminine images may either reinforce, challenge, or ignore cultural stereotypes about women and men. And language that challenges or ignores gender stereotypes is not enough by itself to change systems of male dominance (Bynum 1986, 16). Religious symbolism is only one way in which people learn cultural expectations about gender. Religious language interacts with political structures and gender expectations to create cycles of socialization. Male-biased language interacts with other patterns of male dominance, which together teach a child to live in patriarchal society and encourage an adult not to question patriarchal norms.

The masculine bias of the English language, including predominantly masculine references to God in Christian worship, helps to socialize persons into patriarchal ways of believing and acting. By contrast, the language of worship forms and expresses the Christian faith and practice of communities and individuals. The church has often failed to recognize that the goal of socializing persons into patriarchal society conflicts with the goal of forming persons in the Christian faith.

When Christians intentionally or unintentionally pay homage to the powers of this world, they subvert the primary goal of worship — to thank and praise God. To exalt masculine gender expectations and to support male privilege through association with the God of Jesus Christ is to subvert true praise and thanksgiving. The purpose of worship, which liturgical language ought to serve, is not socialization into gender roles but praise of God.

The goal of worship is also to witness to the gospel of God's love made known in Jesus Christ and to call persons and communities into faithful discipleship. On the other hand, the goal of gender socialization is to maintain the present social system; thus it subverts Christian freedom to respond to the call of God who "has brought down the powerful from their thrones and lifted up the lowly" (Luke 1:52). Liturgical language should witness to the gospel and call persons to faithful discipleship, rather than to support the powers and structures of this world.

Language about God that does not serve to socialize persons into patriarchal culture may include both feminine and masculine metaphors. However, neither masculine nor feminine pronouns would predominate in frequency, in importance, or in excellency. Further, such metaphors would not be used in a way that conformed to gender role stereotypes. Michael A. Williams says that the author of *The Hypostasis of the Archons*, a Gnostic text, speaks of Wisdom in feminine terms, without stressing gender: "The author does not seem so interested in Wisdom as female, but rather in Wisdom as divine fashioner, revealer, begetter of Life" (M. Williams 1986, 213). Williams interprets this lack of interest in gender as a lack of positive valuation of the female (219). I would argue instead that using both masculine and feminine images of the divine without stressing gender avoids socializing worshipers into patriarchy and frees the church to praise and proclaim the God of Jesus Christ. Using language free of gender stereotypes helps to form communities in which women and men can freely respond to God's call.

Liturgies of baptism, a key time for Christian formation, should reflect Christian rather than patriarchal values. The traditional baptismal formula, with its predominantly masculine language, reflects patriarchal values. Reforming the baptismal liturgy is an essential movement from patriarchal socialization toward formation of Christian identity.

THE SOCIAL CONTEXT OF FATHER AS A NAME FOR GOD

The "Father" metaphor, so prevalent in Christian worship, is problematic simply as one part of the gender bias of Christian liturgical language. In North America, it is also problematic because of associations many bring to "Father" as a metaphor for God. And, as discussed in Chapter 1, metaphors draw on "associated commonplaces" in the creation of meaning. Discussion of "Father" or "Mother" as metaphors for God must take into account actual experiences of parent-child relationships in a culture. In considering these cultural associations, I will focus on father-child relationships, because "father" is much more prevalent than "mother" as a metaphor for God in Christian worship. I will, however, attend to associations that may come into play when we use maternal imagery for God.

Many people in worshiping congregations in the United States have generally positive associations about their fathers. For many others, however, the everyday experience of "father" is of one who harms, mistreats, and abuses, rather than one who loves and provides. Patriarchy has permitted, and sometimes encouraged, abuse of the less powerful people in the system, including women and children (Bohn 1985, citing work in progress by Judith Herman). In recent years, child abuse victims, incest survivors, therapists, pastors, and researchers have broken the long-standing silence about child abuse. Unfortunately, these voices make us aware of widespread problems in father-child relationships in United States society.

The exact extent of child abuse is difficult to document. Even definitions vary. Child abuse can be said to fall into four categories: physical abuse, physical neglect, sexual abuse, and emotional maltreatment (National Center on Child Abuse Prevention Research 1990, 8). Although these categories help to define child abuse, definitions for each category vary widely. The narrowest definitions of physical abuse include only violence resulting in injury, whereas the broadest include mild physical punishment. Definitions of sexual abuse can include only genital penetration, or they may include any inappropriate touching or seductive talk. Available statistics measure varied things (Widom 1988, 260).

Moreover, available statistics on child abuse reflect only reported cases, which, researchers insist, vastly underrepresent the problem. Child abuse within the family is reported even less frequently than that perpetrated by strangers. MacKinnon cites a study showing that only 2 percent of child sexual abuse by family members is reported, compared with 6 percent of abuse by persons outside the family (MacKinnon 1987, 290). Both underreporting and such differences in reporting various categories make it difficult to assess the extent of child abuse in the United States, in and beyond the family.

Even the number of reported cases is staggering. The National Committee for the Prevention of Child Abuse collected 1989 data from social service agencies in 48 states and the District of Columbia. In 1989 they counted 2.4 million cases of child abuse — up 10 percent from the year before (Daro, Casey, and Abrahams 1990, 6).[5] These included about 27 percent who

---

5. Catherine Spatz Widom, in a study on the difficulties of obtaining reliable statistics on child abuse, wrote: "Using official agency records for information on the incidence of child abuse produces low estimates that only hint at true incidence" (1986, 265). She also believes that middle- and upper-class families are less likely to be counted in agency statistics.

were injured by physical abuse, 55 percent who were neglected, 8 percent who were emotionally maltreated, and 16 percent who were sexually abused (National Center on Child Abuse Prevention Research 1990, 8). According to this study, at least 1,237 children died as a result of child abuse in 1989 (13). Some socioeconomic classes may be more prone to a specific category of child abuse than others. Physical neglect is more often reported in low-income single-parent families, where support and resources for parenting may be limited or nonexistent. Sexual abuse appears to be reported more often in higher income families (Daro 1988, 37). However, each type of abuse occurs across broad socioeconomic lines, regardless of race, class, income, education, or ethnic heritage.

Emerging data suggest that as many as one in three girls and one in eleven boys have been sexually abused as children (Pellauer, Chester, and Boyajian 1987, 8; Tennis 1985, 46; Pellauer suspects that sexual abuse of boys may be underreported). In one study, 16 percent of women reported being sexually abused within the family by age eighteen, but only 2 percent of these cases were reported (Chester 1987, 14). In a 1979 study of college students by David Finkelhor, 19 percent of the women and 9 percent of the men reported being sexually abused as children, often by family members (Lott 1987, 152). A study by Diana Russell found that 38 percent of women and 10 percent of men had been sexually abused as children (MacKinnon 1987, 41). A 1985 *Los Angeles Times* survey "found that 22 percent of Americans — 27 percent of the women and 16 percent of the men — had been victims of child sexual abuse" (cited in Golden 1988, 43). Although the percentages may differ, these studies all confirm that sexual abuse of children is widespread. Also, victims of childhood abuse commonly repress all memory of the abuse once it ceases, recalling it only in middle adulthood (Nikkal 1988, 6). Even the shocking statistics that are now available probably underrepresent the problem.[6]

---

6. Refer to Lott 1987, 152–153, for a more complete review of the literature. Diana Russell (1986, 297–298, 308) also reports a review that she and David Finkelhor conducted of literature on child sexual abuse. They found that the great majority of victims whose cases were reported were female and the great majority of perpetrators were male, the largest single group being fathers and father figures. Refer also to Wren 1989, 41–43.

Fathers are the largest single group who abuse children sexually (Pellauer, Chester, and Boyajian 1987, 5–9). For example, in the *Boston Globe Magazine*, Daniel Golden reported that according to the records of the Massachusetts Department of Social Services, fathers represented 27.5 percent of those referred for prosecution for charges of child sexual abuse. Other categories included "strangers (16.8 percent), boyfriends of the mother (11.6), stepfathers (11.4), male caretakers (10.1), uncles (9.9), brothers (6.1), and mothers (4.3)" (Golden 1988, 43). For purposes of our discussion, note that many of the nonfathers (stepfathers, caretakers) are in a parental role and may be called "father" by children; men in a parental role thus include 49 percent of this sample, or 60.6 percent if boyfriends of the mother are included. Remember also that these statistics represent cases that were prosecuted, and that sexual abuse within the family is less likely to be reported (MacKinnon 1987, 290). Thus, though fathers are the largest group in Golden's study, they are most likely *under*represented at 27.5 percent. Such statistics should give us pause when we consider using "father" week after week in Christian liturgy.

Although some mothers abuse their children physically, sexually, or through neglect, and some boys are victims of abuse, the majority of child abusers are men, and the majority of victims are females (Mollenkott 1982, 17; Halsey 1984, 6). The dominance of men over women and adults over children that allows this structure of abuse to continue is one expression of the patriarchal pyramid. Parental responsibility to nurture and set limits for children includes a certain kind of control, but it does not entitle parents to use children for their own needs or treat them like property. Child abuse is an expression of the patriarchal system, with its hierarchies of domination and submission. Bohn has argued that domestic violence, including child abuse, should not be considered to be a private, personal matter; rather, it manifests and supports the patriarchal system:

A firm connection between the personal and the political must be made. Acts of individual violence must be seen for what they are: the sinful violation of a relationship and products of a sociopolitical system that encourages and enables them.... It is not enough to treat the victim and reform the abuser.... Private pain has to become a social, systemic issue, and be healed at its very roots. To make such a connection requires the recognition that patriarchy itself is built on a sinful, limiting concept of persons. (Bohn 1985, 7–8)

Child abuse should not be seen as the deviation of individuals from societal norms, but as the tragic outcome of those norms.

The tradition of *patria potestas*, inherited from ancient Roman society, encourages abuse of children by their fathers. The social system of *patria potestas* gave the *patria* (male heads of households) absolute control (*potestas*) over "wives and concubines, children, servants, slaves, animals and real property" (Schneiders 1986, 11). Every institution of Western society has been modeled on this system:

> When this structure was extended to other situations they were seen as quasi-families in which there is one adult and all others are minors. The feudal lord, the abbot in his monastery, the divine right monarch, the priest in his parish, the white European in the colonies, the husband in relation to his wife, the slave-holder with his "darkies," the Pope, were all father-figures caring for the "children" over which God had placed them. (Schneiders 1986, 14)

The patriarchal order, articulated as *patria potestas* in Rome and continued in other Western societies, makes some social groups dominant over others: men over women, adults over children, free men and women over slaves, clergy over laity, and humanity over nature. God, when portrayed as "omnipotent Father/King," rules at the top of the pyramid.

When fathers abuse daughters, this expresses patriarchal dominance, not just individual deviance. Patriarchal values tolerate or encourage abuse of the less powerful by the more powerful. Abuse of daughters by their fathers teaches daughters their place in the patriarchal system. And, as Bohn has argued, the overwhelming use of masculine language for God contributes to male dominance, which in turn leads to domestic violence (Bohn 1985, 7).

Child abuse is of concern to the church because of the present trauma and future distress its victims will suffer. Numerous recently published studies have established that those who have been abused as children are much more likely than others to experience various emotional and relational problems as adults.

(For a review of the literature, refer to Russell 1986, 138–139. Refer also to Roland, Zelhart, and Dubes 1989; Feinauer 1989; and Coons et al. 1989). The adult aftermath of child sexual abuse can include difficulty in establishing human relationships, serious depression, and low self-esteem (Herman 1981, 99; Lott 1987, 162–163). A very high percentage of women who are prostitutes are survivors of child sexual abuse.[7] Eighty percent of women with multiple personality disorders were sexually abused as children, according to one study; 45 percent of them were physically abused as well (Coons et al. 1989, 328). Many teenage runaways are seeking to escape sexual abuse (Russell 1986, 204; Lott 1987, 162). Men who have been sexually abused as children or who observed sexual abuse in their families often grow up to be abusers themselves (Mitchard 1980). Women who have been sexually abused as children learn to accept victimization. According to Russell's study, incest survivors were more than twice as likely as others to report rape or physical violence by their husbands or rape by an authority figure (for example, doctor, teacher, employer, minister, therapist); they were more likely to suffer other sorts of abuse as well (Russell 1986, 161). This is only a small sampling of the ill effects demonstrably suffered by survivors of child sexual abuse; the effects on society are not difficult to guess. Difficulties result from other forms of child abuse as well; for example, according to Dr. Robert ten Bensel:

> Thirty-one percent of juvenile delinquents have been severely beaten by their parents, while another 64 percent have needed medical attention for burns, broken bones, and various mutilations caused by their parents. (Mollenkott 1982, 16)

Physical abuse of children has serious effects on the lives of individuals and on society.

Just as children are more likely to be abused by family members than others, so abuse by family members can be particularly damaging to the present and future well-being of those who suffer it. When abuser and abused live in the same household, and especially when the abuser is a biological parent, frequent and prolonged abuse is possible (Halsey 1984, 2; Faller 1989, 223–224).

---

7. Nikkal 1988, 16–17, citing Florence Rush in *The Best Kept Secret: Sexual Abuse of Children* (Englewood Cliffs, N.J.: Prentice-Hall, 1980, no page cited).

In turn, greater duration and frequency of abuse often leads to greater long-term damage (Russell 1986, 141–154). Violation of a trusted relationship by child sexual abuse can result in more psychological harm than abuse by a stranger (Feinauer 1989, 54). A study by Roland, Zelhart, and Dubes (1989) found that women who had been abused by fathers or stepfathers had more psychological test scores which indicated pathology than women who were sexually abused by others. Potential and actual danger within the parent-child relationship must be considered when we reflect upon using "father" or "mother" as a metaphor for God.

Child abuse, in the dimensions present in the United States, is neither acceptable nor inevitable. It threatens individuals and society, and calls for the immediate attention of the churches — from changed attitudes to improved pastoral care to preventive education and intervention to political action.[8] One part of this healing ministry is questioning the patriarchal attitudes that keep "father" predominant as a name for God in Christian worship despite its problematic connotations in United States society.

IMPLICATIONS FOR THE CHURCH

The data now emerging indicate that a significant number of worshipers in almost any church on a given Sunday morning have experienced abuse at the hands of their fathers and, in a few cases, their mothers. For example, 1 in 19 persons responding to a broad-based 1982 survey of United Methodists reported being physically abused when children; 1 in 14 reported being sexually abused (Halsey 1984, 4). Halsey comments: "Significant under-reporting, common in all surveys of family violence, may be assumed in this one as well" (4). These statistics show that many church members, like all others in U.S. society, are affected by child abuse, as victims or perpetrators. My experience as a pastor in the United Church of Christ and other conversations with church women corroborate this. In most worshiping congregations, some members have been sexually abused as children or adolescents by their fathers, and a few perhaps by their moth-

---

8. *Christianity, Patriarchy and Abuse*, ed. Joanne Carlson Brown and Carole R. Bohn (New York: Pilgrim Press, 1989) is an important contribution to the task of theological reflection and education about abuse issues in the Christian context.

ers. Others have been severely beaten by one or the other parent. Still others have been physically neglected by their parents. All these will have painful or ambiguous associations around parental metaphors for God. Sexual or physical abuse of children and adolescents, far from being exceptional, is part of many families in our country. This fact must be taken into account when we consider "father" or "mother" as metaphors for God. Those who are fortunate enough to have experienced loving, nonabusive parents should not dismiss the problem as insignificant, but have compassion for those with more difficult memories.

As victims break the silence about child abuse, they also stir questions about the frequent use of father language for God in Christian worship at pivotal moments like baptism. The book *Sexual Assault and Abuse*, edited by Mary D. Pellauer, Barbara Chester, and Jane Boyajian (1987), attempts to alert the church to the pervasiveness of child abuse. In it, Martha Janssen, who was sexually abused by her father for several years beginning at age three, tells her story. She writes of her adolescent years:

> I was in intense conflict with myself. That conflict was magnified in the church because of a most common image — that of God, the Father. How could God be like a father? As far as I could tell, fathers did bad things. I grew up being unusually self-sufficient, for I dared not trust an earthly father, let alone one I could not see. (Pellauer, Chester, and Boyajian 1987, 61)

Another woman who was physically and sexually abused by her father from age five to sixteen told her story in the feminist spirituality journal *Womanspirit*. Like many incest survivors, she had come to hate herself, but she wrote that using feminine imagery for the divine was a part of her journey toward self-nurture:

> I am learning to trust in the love of the Goddess. I have known Her for fourteen years; but I never let Her surround me with her love and nurturing. . . . I never asked her for help with my problems. I used to pray to Her to help others, but I would tell Her that I didn't matter. I am relieved that She didn't listen to me. Instead, She has patiently given me experiences with people so that I could learn the truth about myself. . . . I have learned that I am not alone; that I am not guilty, terrible . . . that I can enjoy life. (McClimans 1982, 27)

Sharon and Thomas Neufer Emswiler report that when they began to discuss the idea of God as Father in their worshiping community (in the context of campus ministry), "we found that many people had strong negative reactions to the traditional concept of God as Father. Because of bad experiences with their own fathers, they could not accept a God cast in the same role" (Neufer Emswiler and Neufer Emswiler 1980, 28). Susan Thistlethwaite observes that white female seminarians often report difficulties with "Father" images of God in the same breath in which they tell of being sexually molested by their fathers (1989, 112).

In an issue of the *Daughters of Sarah* journal devoted to the theme of incest, a woman who was a victim of sexual abuse by her brother reported problems with the conception of God as male ("Tamar" 1987, 12). Another, in a ritual of prayer and healing from abuse by her father, draws on a maternal image for God to assure her that God will be present and nurturing: "Does a woman forget her baby, or fail to cherish the daughter of her womb? Yet even if these forget, I will never forget you. It will be all right. I will be there" ("Marty Green" 1987, 21).

Abuse survivors have not often told their stories in print or published their difficulties with the image of God the Father. However, as many Christian women begin to speak of their experiences of abuse in groups they regard as safe, they often express problems they have with paternal and masculine imagery for God. The cases just cited are far from exceptional. The stories I have told here show that some survivors of child abuse have difficulties with parental imagery for God. I suspect that the religious experience of many more is affected by the constant use of "Father" language for God, even if they have not become consciously aware of the problem.

Besides the many who have been abused by parents, others are likely to have difficulty with parental imagery for God for different reasons. A male friend confided to me that "father" was to him an empty name for God, because his relationship with his father had been so distant. Other people grow up in homes where fathers or mothers are literally absent through divorce or death. Still others have witnessed one or both parents abusing one another.

Rita Nakashima Brock has written that North American society is "brokenhearted," and that a major symptom of this brokenhearted condition is abuse and lack of love within families where children are nurtured (Brock 1988, xi–24). In one way or another, many or most of us come from brokenhearted families. Parental images for the divine may express a wistful longing for what we wish had happened in our families.

Those who come from brokenhearted families sometimes cling to the father image for God. Diane Tennis has argued that paternal imagery for God can be healing for many who have experienced fathers or men in general to be unreliable. These persons have found in God "someone trustworthy [who] is always there"; for them God is a "reliable Father." Thus they rage and mourn when feminists ask that God no longer be called Father (Tennis 1985, 20–21). She urges: "Do not abandon God the Father, because God as Father is a reliable male symbol in the lives of women and men.... For human fathers are experienced as unreliable" (9). Children experience fathers as unreliable when they are preoccupied with work, when they abandon their families, when they are emotionally absent, and when they are abusive. By contrast, the God of Israel never abandoned the covenant people, but was present and available with a love that nurtured and challenged the people. With Jesus, according to Tennis, "there is a shift toward even more emphasis on the nearness and tenderness of God as parent and less emphasis on the patriarchal motif of hierarchical domination" (84). Although patriarchal understandings of God have been intertwined with the imagery of God the Father in scripture and church tradition, fatherhood and patriarchy are not identical. Thus Tennis argues that father imagery for God ought not be abandoned, but dissociated from patriarchal understandings and complemented with feminine imagery.

There are dangers in Tennis's arguments, however. As Brock has argued, father images grounded in longing for an "unreal past" may inhibit honest naming of our experience and growth toward intimacy, respect, and love in connectedness with God and other people (Brock 1988, 54). "Father" is a one-sided image of God that emphasizes childlike dependence rather than growth toward interdependence and maturity. Another problem with Tennis's argument, according to Thistlethwaite, is that Tennis singles out African American fathers as particularly unreliable and that she ignores the Holocaust when claiming that God is reliable to Israel (Thistlethwaite 1989, 110–111). Although "father" may be a comforting image to some whose fathers were unreliable, I question whether the image leads to genuine healing, especially when dominant in Christian worship. Metaphors that gain their power through the fantasy of an unreal past are less likely to bring healing than metaphors that are based in actual loving human experience.

In North American society, paternal or maternal imagery for God may tap into a variety of unfortunate family experiences. Using predominantly masculine language in worship perpetuates patriarchal values that in turn tolerate or even encourage child abuse.

Strong cultural reasons explain why masculine imagery for God predominates in Christian worship. Such imagery is part of the masculine bias of the English language; it supports socialization into patriarchal culture. "Father" imagery for God is associated with the tradition of *patria potestas*, and absolute control often leads to abuse. It is not surprising that in a patriarchal culture, most images of God would be masculine, often paternal; but that does not mean we should continue to use only such language in our worship.

Both terms of a metaphor are affected in relationship with one another, as Max Black has argued (Black 1962, Chapter 3). Clark applied Black's concept to father imagery for God: "God is fatherlike and fathers are godlike" (Clark 1980, 25). This transfer of meaning from "God" to "father" and back has disturbing implications both for father-child relationships and for worship among Christians.

If fathers identify themselves with some paternal imagery of God in scripture (for example, Ps. 103:13f.), they may be encouraged to show compassion and wise judgment. But if fathers associate images of God the Father with the patriarchal right of fathers to control everyone in their households, children are endangered. Metaphors such as "Father Almighty" risk such associations. Calling God "the Father Almighty," who demands the death of his child as a sacrifice for human sin, may unintentionally and unconsciously encourage fathers to use their power over children in harmful ways, and may encourage children to accept this lot. Patricia Wilson-Kastner writes:

> The victims of violence, overwhelmingly women and children, have been consistently exhorted in the Christian tradition to be meek, submissive, and obedient.
>
> ... Christian theologians also reinforced ideals of male domination through the assumption that males were superior and would do what is best. Because possible victims — women and children, and even less powerful men — were not given permission to develop their own counterbalancing strengths, assailants never learned other useful ways to exercise power than to use force and ultimately violence. The popular religious image of a father-god who killed his own son to satisfy his own anger, and who was able to reward or punish his whole creation to do his will, served to reinforce the image of power as coercive and even intrusive. (Wilson-Kastner 1987, 99)

Using parental imagery for God has ethical implications; it may reinforce violent and coercive use of power by parents. Addressing predominant parental and masculine imagery is one part of seeking to prevent serious damage to individuals and society. The privileged place of paternal imagery must be called into question in a social context where father-to-child abuse is common. Even when we do use father imagery to speak of God, we should attend to the context, lifting up compassionate, not omnipotent, images of fatherhood. Continuously associating God with human fathers may negatively affect father-child relationships.

Continuously associating God with our human fathers — frail and, in some cases, violent human beings that they sometimes are — may, in turn, negatively affect people's relationship with God. Patriarchal understandings of fatherhood may lead to false understandings of God. The fact that many people experience God, so often called "Father," as angry, judging, rejecting, or absent, may reflect their experience of fathers more than any judgmental attitudes in the church. By grace, God's love can overcome cultural barriers that obscure that love, but why should we erect barriers in the first place?

The unfortunate association of God with an abusive father leads some people to reject a faith that worships God predominantly by the name of "Father." Diana Russell's carefully controlled study of incest victims discovered that among those who were raised in a religious tradition, 53 percent of victims, compared with 31 percent of those who had not been incest victims, had left the religion of their upbringing (Russell 1986, 119). Others who associate God with an abusive father continue to participate in Christian worship without experiencing the liberating power of the gospel. In *The Color Purple*, Celie was sexually abused and twice impregnated by her father. Is it any wonder that she had to move "beyond God the Father" (Daly 1973, title) to experience God as an empowering presence in her life?

Emerging statistics show that abuse of children by their fathers is widespread. Worship leaders cannot afford to pretend that none of their members are affected; in all probability, sizable proportions of members are present victims, survivors, or perpetrators. Worship leaders cannot delay addressing the issue until someone complains, as if they need be concerned about parental imagery for God only to show pastoral compassion for a few unhappy, "maladjusted" people. The question is pastoral, but it is also ethical. Movement from the literalized, idolatrous, predominant image of God as Father to a greater diversity of metaphors may help to prevent child abuse. Language use also affects human understandings of God. Developing more adequate liturgical language also will nurture people's faith in the God of Jesus Christ, when God is no longer associated mainly with our human fathers with all their strengths and limitations.

MOTHER AS A METAPHOR FOR GOD

In light of the above concerns, then, shall we substitute "Mother" wherever God has been called "Father"? That answer is clearly too simple. Feminists within and without the Christian church have often turned to maternal imagery as an alternative to predominantly paternal imagery. Maternal imagery is prominent in the Women-Church rituals published by Winter (1987) and Ruether (1985). Though this metaphor may have much symbolic power, it also has limitations. Mary Pellauer, who has sought to be sensitive to victims of child abuse in the way she leads worship, has discovered that "Mother" as well as "Father" can be disconcerting to some people as an image for God:

> When a victim of childhood abuse says that her experience
> makes it impossible for her to tolerate God the Father, I am
> asked to unravel and reweave many central portions of the faith
> we have received. No sooner have I rewoven this God-language
> than another victim of a similar abuse says that she hates her
> mother and wants nothing to do with God the Mother. (Pellauer,
> Chester, and Boyajian 1987, x)

We cannot automatically substitute "Mother" for "Father." A household in which the father is abusing one or more children is a brokenhearted household. Associations around mothers in such households may also be ambiguous, though recent studies dispute the stereotype that mothers of incest victims knowingly condone the situation (Summit 1987, 184). A small percentage of mothers physically or emotionally abuse their children, though few mothers sexually abuse their children (Mollenkott 1982, 17). Obviously, children of such households will often have problems with "Mother" as a name for God.

Moreover, the question of God as Mother may be even more complex than that of God the Father. Currently, when God is portrayed as Mother, she is often nurturing and compassionate but not powerful, which corresponds directly to the patriarchal stereotype of motherhood. In *The Boston Globe* on Mother's Day, May 8, 1988, the Abbot in "Sherman on the Mount" says, "Moms sure are patient, loving, and kind." Sherman responds, "They're worth their weight in apple pies." God the Mother often sounds rather like this cartoon version of stereotypical motherhood. Stereotypical "mother" images in worship do not challenge patriarchal understandings; they reinforce them. When we call God "Mother" in worship, we must seek broader understandings of motherhood. At the same time, we must avoid the implication that motherhood is the prime feminine attribute.

Clarissa Atkinson has traced how the image of Monica, mother of Augustine, has served as a model of Christian motherhood. The model mother devotes herself to her son, praying for his salvation, teaching him faith and virtue. In the last century, the model of Monica has also served to encourage women to limit their sphere to the home. In various ways, the image of Monica has functioned to exalt women who selflessly devote themselves to sons and husbands. Atkinson argues that such a stereotype of motherhood has expressed a male fantasy (Atkinson 1987, 165).

The same stereotype, projected onto God, only continues to reinforce male dominance. In "Contemporary Goddess Thealogy: A Sympathetic Critique," Emily Culpepper has said that the "image of the Great Mother inadequately challenges the model of female self-sacrifice" (Culpepper 1987, 64). Though the image of the Goddess as nurturing Mother may encourage many women, as a predominant image it also promotes the stereotype that "women are essentially mothers and/or that women are inherently more loving and nurturing than men" (60). Although "mother" can be a useful metaphor among others, it is not adequate as the only feminine metaphor for God in worship.

Feminine metaphors for God must range beyond maternal imagery to avoid perpetuating patriarchal gender stereotypes; and when "Mother" is used of God, it should be done in a way that avoids patriarchal stereotypes of motherhood. Predominant use of "Mother" imagery may be problematic for those who have had abusive or otherwise difficult relationships with their mothers. Parental imagery — whether maternal or paternal — is not adequate as the only or predominant way of talking about God in Christian worship.

Tennis is perhaps correct in asserting that the relationship between parents and children is too central to be abolished completely from metaphoric use in Christian theology and worship (Tennis 1985, 34). However, recognizing that parent-child relationships are often painful or ambiguous, North American churches should question the degree to which God is called "Father" in their worship. This recognition should prevent the church from substituting or adding the image of God as Mother wherever God has been called "Father" in the past. When we do use parental imagery in Christian worship, we should exercise care concerning the manner and context of its use. Paternal imagery has dominated Christian worship, excluding other metaphors and risking monotony and idolatry. The church must discover a broader range of living metaphor — going beyond "father" or "mother" — to witness and respond more adequately to the God of Jesus Christ.

Analysis of language used to speak to or about God in Christian worship must, of course, consider not only the cultural context, but also the history of such language use in Christian tradition. To that story we now turn.

CHAPTER 3

YOU FORGOT THE GOD WHO GAVE YOU BIRTH

Chiding the Israelites who turned away from God in the wilderness, who complained and worshiped their golden calves, Moses says, "You were unmindful of the Rock that bore you; you forgot the God who gave you birth" (Deut. 32:18; unaltered NRSV translation; refer to Trible 1978, 62–64, for more on the translation of this verse). Giving birth is an apt metaphor for the way God conceived and brought forth a new nation. Sometimes, however, translators injected sexist bias and translated the second half of the verse, which in Hebrew clearly refers to pregnancy, "you forgot the God who sired you." Throughout its whole history, the church has been in a process of forgetting all feminine ways of talking about God and enshrining the golden calves of patriarchal images of God.

JESUS' LANGUAGE ABOUT GOD

Some argue that "Father" must continue as a predominant name for God in Christian worship because Jesus called God "Father" and taught his disciples to do the same. Careful thought and biblical study show this claim to be on shaky ground.

Joachim Jeremias's study of the terms for Father in Aramaic (*'abbā*) and Greek (*patēr*) in the Gospels and epistles has greatly influenced the modern study of scripture, theology, and worship. Not only does Jeremias argue that Jesus' preferred term for God was *'abbā*; he asserts that "Jesus bases his authority on the fact that God has revealed himself to him like a father to a son. It represents the central statement of Jesus' mission" (Jeremias 1978, 53). Indeed, it could be said that for Jeremias the image of God as Father is the root metaphor of Jesus' teaching and of Christianity as it developed.

The Aramaic *'abbā* is related to the Hebrew word *'ab* (meaning "father"). According to Jeremias, small children called their fathers "*'abbā*," much as English speaking children call their fathers "Daddy." He emphasized the intimacy of this address to God: "It was something new, something unique and unheard of that Jesus dared to take this step and to speak with God as a child speaks with his father, simply, intimately, securely" (Jeremias 1965, 21). Jeremias's later research revealed that adults used *'abbā* to refer to fathers, teachers, and other respected men, but he continued to emphasize the origin of the term in the talk of children. People citing Jeremias have not always taken this adult use of *'abbā* into account. Jeremias himself wrote:

> One often reads (and I myself believed it at one time) that when Jesus talked to his heavenly Father he took up the chatter of a small child. To assume this would be a piece of inadmissible naiveté. We have seen that even grown-up sons addressed their father as *'abbā*. So when Jesus addresses God as *'abbā* the word is by no means simply an expression of Jesus' familiarity in his converse with God. At the same time, it shows the complete surrender of the Son in obedience to the Father (Mark 14:36; Matt. 11:25 f.). (Jeremias 1978, 62)

According to Jeremias, *'abbā* connotes not only intimacy, but also "obedience" and "surrender" by children to the father. To say the least, the term connotes respect as much as childish babbling. Rimbach is right to question the emphasis many have put on *'abbā* as "baby talk" (Rimbach 1986, 232; cf. Ramshaw 1986a, 105).

The actual Aramaic word *'abbā* is found three times in the Greek in the Christian Testament. In Mark's Gospel, Jesus prayed to God as *'abbā, o patēr* in the Garden of Gethsemane (Mark 14:36); and twice Paul speaks of prayer to God as *'abbā* (Gal. 4:6 and Rom. 8:15). Jeremias argues that often in the Gospels the Aramaic *'abbā* lies behind the Greek *patēr*, as when Matthew and Luke, in the parallels to Mark's account of Jesus in the Garden, use the Greek term *patēr* and not *'abbā* (Jeremias 1978, 55–57).

Jeremias noted that "there was a growing tendency to introduce the title 'Father' for God into the sayings of Jesus" (Jeremias 1978, 30). Jesus refers to God as father four times in Mark, fifteen times in Luke, forty-two times in Matthew, and one hundred and nine times in John (29). According to Jeremias, there are about sixteen different passages that reflect Jesus' own words calling God "Father." Seven are in Mark, Luke, or Matthew (if parallels of the same sayings are not counted), and nine in the Gospel of John. Of these, one, the Gethsemane passage, is found in Mark (Mark 14:36, paralleled in Matt. 26:39 and Luke 22:42). Three are in the material common to Matthew and Luke (once in the Prayer of Jesus,[1] Matt. 6:9, parallel Luke 11:2, and twice in the prayer of jubilation, Matt. 11:25, 26, parallel Luke 10:21ab). Two instances are in material found only in Luke (Luke 23:34, 46, sayings from the cross), and one is in material peculiar to Matthew (Matt. 26:42).

Jeremias believes the use of 'abbā or other words for "father" in naming God was rare in first-century Judaism; it connotes an intimacy with God that Jeremias believes first-century Jews would have found shocking. This is one reason he regards use of such words to be authentic to Jesus; dissimilarity with the traditions of contemporary Judaism is one criterion he uses to judge the authenticity of words attributed to Jesus. Further, Jesus prays to God as 'abbā or patēr in all layers of the Gospel tradition ("Q," Mark, material peculiar to Luke, material peculiar to Matthew, material common to Matthew and Luke, and material peculiar to John). Thus Jeremias believes one can attribute the address of God as father to Jesus himself.

According to Jeremias, in all but one of these authentic sayings, Jesus is praying or teaching about prayer (for example, Luke 11:5–13); and in all the authentic passages in which Jesus is praying, except when he calls God "Eloi, Eloi" on the cross (Mark 15:34, parallel Matt. 27:46), he calls God "Father."

According to Jeremias, Jesus uses "your father" and "my father" distinctively in the passages that are authentic to Jesus. At times he speaks of God as "my father," suggesting that he has a unique relationship with God. When he calls God "your father," he is addressing only his disciples, and not the people in general. In Jeremias's understanding, only through his intimacy with God as a son to a father can Jesus know and reveal God. When he

---

1. I am using "the Prayer of Jesus" as a substitute for the term "the Lord's Prayer" (only when "Prayer" is capitalized).

teaches the disciples to pray "Our Father," he is allowing them
to share in intimate relationship with God through him. In Galatians 4:6 and Romans 8:15, Paul says that the spirit of Christ
within Christians enables them to cry " *'Abbā!* Father!" as children of God. Jesus Christ reveals God to humanity by virtue of
mutual relationship with God:

> In that same hour [Jesus] rejoiced in the Holy Spirit and said, "I
> thank you, Father, Lord of heaven and earth, because you have
> hidden these things from the wise and the intelligent and have
> revealed them to infants; yes, Father, for such was your gracious
> will. All things have been handed over to me by my Father; and
> no one knows who the Son is except the Father, or who the
> Father is except the Son and anyone to whom the Son chooses
> to reveal him." (Luke 10:21–22, parallel Matt. 11:25–27)

Some have used this passage to make exclusive claims for the
Christian religion, but Jeremias follows C. H. Dodd in interpreting the passage as a parablelike image in which Jesus' relationship
with God was compared to the way a son learns a trade from
his father (Jeremias 1978, 51). In ancient Palestine, a son would
learn his father's trade secrets and thus would be the only one capable of sharing them with others. By this interpretation, the
father-son image elucidates how others enter into knowledge
of and relationship with God through their relationship with
Jesus.

Many scholars have followed Jeremias's understanding of
Jesus' use of *'abbā/patēr*. Biblical scholar Norman Perrin uses
Jeremias's study of *'abbā* to illustrate the criterion of dissimilarity (1967, 39–41). Theologians such as Edward Schillebeeckx
(1979, 256–271) have developed christological understandings
based on Jeremias's ideas. Schillebeeckx speaks of the unique
quality of Jesus' religious life in terms of "his (historically exceptional) *Abba* address to God" (267). According to Geoffrey
Wainwright, Jesus' naming God *'abbā* is part of "the paradigm which Jesus presents for worship" (Wainwright 1980, 21),
though "Jeremias cannot quite prove that its use as an address to God was unique to Jesus in Judaism" (22). Jeremias's
findings about Jesus' use of "Father" appear to be known and
accepted by scholars and local church pastors almost without
question.

Some persons exploring the patriarchal influence in Christianity have found Jeremias's work helpful. Robert Hamerton-Kelly (1979; 1981) argues that the intimate father addressed as *'abbā* is not a patriarch; to give allegiance to this God is to reject patriarchy. Gail Ramshaw regards "the Abba, the Servant, the Paraclete" to be a more inclusive alternative to the trinitarian formula than "the Father, the Son, the Holy Spirit" (Ramshaw 1986b, 491–498). Diane Tennis holds that to use *'abbā* language is to give more "emphasis to the nearness and tenderness of God as parent and less emphasis on the patriarchal motif of hierarchical domination" (Tennis 1985, 84). I question these interpretations. Those who are concerned about patriarchal domination would do better to reexamine the issues Jeremias raises than to accept his findings without further critical examination. I now turn to consideration of some criticisms that have been made of Jeremias's work on Jesus' use of *'abbā/patēr*.

Review of Some Critics of Jeremias's Studies of 'Abbā

Many of Jeremias's findings have been widely accepted; for example, few insist that Jesus never called God *'abbā*. However, his findings and the interpretations of others based on them have been challenged on several points, with important implications for the contemporary discussion about the naming of God.

In an article called "God as Father in the Proclamation and in the Prayer of Jesus," Dieter Zeller takes issue with Jeremias on several points. He challenges the idea that Jesus' naming of God is dissimilar to Jewish tradition, because God is sometimes referred to as Father in the Hebrew scriptures and other pre-Christian Jewish literature. Nor would a term used respectfully by adults to their fathers or teachers have been shocking to Jews; Zeller de-emphasizes the supposed derivation of *'abbā* from baby talk. Zeller approves Oesterreicher's translation of Mark 14:26: "Abba, You all-powerful One," which, he thinks, contradicts the idea of a "baby-like familiarity in the word 'Abba'" (Zeller 1981, 124). Because *'abbā* ("daddy") had nearly replaced *'ăbî* (the more formal word for "my father") in first-century Aramaic, Jesus used *'abbā*, meaning "Father," not "Daddy." Through this line of thought, Zeller refutes the idea that naming God "Father" would have been unusual in first-century Judaism. Thus he undermines attempts based on the principle of dissimilarity to support the authenticity of Jesus' sayings calling God "Father."

More than Jeremias, Zeller understands first-century Hebrew liturgical texts referring to God as "Our Father" (*'abînu*) to be relevant to Jesus' use of father as a name for God. He rejects Jeremias's idea that Sirach 51:10 originally said "You are the God of my father," and not "You are my Father" (Zeller 1981, 124; Jeremias 1965, 16–17). Thus Jesus, in naming God "father," or even "my father," was continuing Jewish tradition rather than claiming for himself a unique relationship with God (Zeller 1981, 125).

Zeller believes that Jesus mainly referred to God as Father in the Wisdom teachings, and not in prayer, as Jeremias had claimed. For example, he believes that Jesus spoke the words assuring the disciples that the Father who cares for the flowers will also care for them (Luke 12:22–31; Zeller 1981, 119–122). He believes that when New Testament passages call God *'abbā* or *patēr* in prayer, this reflects the prayer of Palestinian Christian communities, and probably not Jesus' prayer (123). The passages in which Jesus calls God *'abbā* or *patēr* in the Garden do not provide much information, to Zeller's thinking, because they are not overheard, but told by the "all-knowing narrator" (123). Zeller selects a different set of texts in which Jesus calls God "Father" as authentic words of Jesus. He interprets them in the context of Jesus' preaching of the *basileia*, and concludes:

> The Father, whom Jesus brings close to his listeners, remains the faithful God of Israel, who is linked with his people through their particular history. Yet, Jesus reinterprets God's nearness through the signs of the imminent Kingship (*Basileia*) of this same God. (Zeller 1981, 125)

According to Zeller, Jesus did not use "Father" in a shocking way, but remained in continuity with Jewish tradition.

Asher Finkel, who has examined the forms of the "Prayer of Jesus," regards the use of *'abbā* in the prayer to be authentic to Jesus. He believes that Jesus' address of God as Father is "reverential and relational" (Finkel 1981, 155), and that it finds its counterpart in first-century Jewish liturgical address of God as "our Father" in penitential prayer. He accepts evidence for first-century Aramaic prayer to God as *'abbā*, which Jeremias rejects

(Jeremias 1978, 61; Finkel 1981, 155–156). He considers Jesus' address of God as Father to be a reverent circumlocution of God's name, humble rather than shocking in its claims. It appeals to God's fatherly forgiveness:

> Thus, both forms of JP [the Prayer of Jesus] make the appeal to *'Abba*. The community or the apostles intercede for Fatherly forgiveness of sins and for Fatherly protection in time of trial. Jesus has taught his followers to use the address *'Abba* as a sincere expression of humility before God and as complete reliance on his love. (Finkel 1981, 157)

Thus, although Finkel accepts Jeremias's claim that Jesus addressed God as *'abbā*, he denies that this address was unique and interprets its meaning differently than does Jeremias. Whereas Jeremias emphasizes the uniqueness of Jesus' relation to the father as son, Finkel leans more heavily on the portrayal of God as a compassionate and forgiving father in Hebrew scripture and liturgy.

Another scholar who questioned the uniqueness of Jesus' address of God as Father was Birger Gerhardsson:

> It seems to me that Jeremias is too bold when he asserts that in the Jewish milieu of Jesus' time it was unthinkable to address God as "Abba" (Father). Our source material related to the way contemporary Jewish groups addressed God in prayer is too limited to enable us to say with certainty what was *not* done. (Gerhardsson 1979, 55)

Like Jeremias, Gerhardsson believes that Jesus prayed to God as *'abbā*, and that this contributed to the development of Son of God christology. In light of the limited source material, he does not believe one can claim conclusively that address of God as Father or even *'abbā* would have been shocking to first-century Jews.

Madeleine Boucher has been developing a critique of Jeremias's conclusions. In an article, "Scriptural Readings: God-Language and Nonsexist Translation," she challenges the idea that Jesus frequently called God "Father." Like Zeller, she questions the historicity of Mark's account of Jesus' address of God as *'abbā* in the Garden of Gethsemane: "Scholarly opinion as to whether the Gethsemane scene is historical or legendary is divided; in any case, no one was present to hear or report the words of Jesus" (Boucher 1983, 158). Although Jeremias believes the parallels in Matthew and Luke support Mark's account, Boucher calls attention to the fact that Matthew and Luke, unlike Mark, did not use *'abbā*, but *patēr*. She says this casts doubt on whether *'abbā* was a central name of God for Jesus (158). Jesus' frequent use of *patēr* for God in Matthew and Luke draws on late tradition and "does not accurately represent the usage of Jesus" (158). Like scholars cited previously, Boucher questions whether *'abbā* connotes familiarity more than respect, and says:

> The thesis that the metaphor "Father" was central and distinctive for Jesus, that it surpassed Jewish usage in frequency and intimacy, and that it was a new way of speaking about God goes beyond the evidence. (Boucher 1983, 158)

According to Boucher, because addressing God as "Father" is not so central or unique as has been claimed, we ought to regard this address as a metaphor, rather than as a name for God or a revelation that God is male.

Drawing on the findings of Boucher and other scholars, Mary Collins also has questioned the belief of some that the address of God as "Father" is nonmetaphorical in status and normative for Christian worship. She cites the rabbinic studies of G. F. Moore that led him to conclude that Jesus' use of *'abbā* was not "distinctive or unprecedented" in Jewish piety (Collins 1985, 296). She also cites Joseph Fitzmyer:

> Fitzmyer, among others, has taken exception on philological and textual grounds to the now widely repeated position of Jeremias that Abba is intentionally informal and intimate, in contrast to the more formal and distant Aramaic "Ab." (Collins 1985, 296)

Collins refers to additional research by Boucher, who judges that "four texts at best might be considered authentic sayings of Jesus, and of these only one is an address in prayer" (296). Boucher accepts as authentic the verses in which Jesus teaches the disciples to pray "(Our) Father (in heaven)" (Matt. 6:9; Luke 11:2), but questions whether evidence supports the claim that *'abbā* "represents the central statement of Jesus' mission" (Collins 1985, 297, quoting an unpublished paper by Boucher).

Collins suggests that Jesus' frequent naming of God as Father in the Gospels reflects the "early church's experience of

Jesus as the Son of God" (Collins 1985, 297). She reports that Raymond Brown, while noting how often Jesus calls God *patēr* in the Gospel of John, calls the "I am" sayings the key to the evangelist's understanding of Jesus' own experience. At the same time, Brown points to the diversity within the New Testament concerning "Jesus' own receiving of, bearing, and revealing the name of God" (Collins 1985, 298). Like Brown, Collins emphasizes diversity — and restraint — in the naming of God, and asks for critical reflection about both "father" and "mother" as names for God in worship. She calls for "linguistic resourcefulness" in naming contemporary Christian experience and "breaking our stereotypically androcentric language patterns" (304).

Criticism of Jeremias's treatment of Jesus' use of *'abbā/patēr* thus follows several lines. Some scholars question whether the use of *'abbā* or other paternal address of God would have been unique or shocking to first-century Jews. What the various language forms referring to "father" meant and how often they were used in first-century Judaism are subject to much debate (refer to Fitzmyer 1985). The idea that Jesus' prayer to God as Father was discontinuous rather than continuous with first-century Jewish prayer and liturgy has also been questioned.

One may also ask whether *'abbā* as a name for God is a shockingly intimate term derived mainly from baby talk. The etymology of the word is not even certain; claims that it is the first name a child calls its father depend on the parallel with *imma*, the child's address for mother (Jeremias 1965, 20–21). However, because *'abbā* was used to address both fathers and teachers with respect, it is unlikely that first-century people would have considered *'abbā* baby talk when spoken to God. Such address may have been no more shocking or innovative than paternal images already found in the Hebrew scriptures. Those who emphasize that *'abbā* is intimate baby talk (without reference to paternal authority) have not given adequate attention to Jeremias's later work.

There is considerable debate both on *how many* sayings in which Jesus calls God "father" are authentic to Jesus, and on *which* sayings are authentic. No sayings are accepted as authentic by all commentators. Boucher argues that the only instance in scripture that reflects Jesus' authentic prayer to God as *'abbā* was in the prayer he taught the disciples. This thesis, if correct, compromises the idea that Jesus addressed God only as *'abbā*. One instance does not prove exclusive use.

Scholars have also challenged Jeremias on his theological interpretation of Jesus' use of "father" for God. If Jeremias cannot prove that Jesus' address of God as "Father" was unique, this casts doubt on the idea that by using this address, Jesus was claiming a unique relationship with God. Traditions in which Jesus calls God his Father may grow out of the church's application of the title "Son of God" to Jesus, and not the reverse. Schillebeeckx, although accepting Jeremias's thesis that "the *'abbā* experience" was essential to Jesus' relationship with God, holds that the resurrection, and not the address of God as *'abbā*, caused the church to affirm Jesus as "Son of God" (Schillebeeckx 1979, 261–262). Luke 10:21–22, with its parallel in Matthew 11:25–27, may be considered a parable and not a direct naming of God. Jesus appears to have used "Father" and "Son" imagery in a way that was not as similar to later trinitarian doctrine as Jeremias supposed. Thus it is difficult to maintain that trinitarian affirmations must use "Father"/"Son" language because of Jesus' own usage.

We cannot be sure how frequently Jesus addressed God as Father. There is some evidence that Jesus also addressed God as Mother. The *Gospel of Thomas* (saying 101) attributes maternal imagery for the divine to Jesus:

> In the *Gospel of Thomas*, Jesus contrasts his earthly parents, Mary and Joseph, with his divine Father — the Father of Truth — and his divine Mother — the Holy Spirit. The author interprets a puzzling saying of Jesus' from the New Testament ("Whoever does not hate his father and his mother cannot be my disciple") by adding that my (earthly) mother [gave me death], but my true [Mother] gave me life. (Pagels 1979, 62)

Manuscripts of this apocryphal gospel, while dated around 200 C.E., contain traditions that are at least as primitive as the canonical Gospels (Perrin 1967, 36–37, 126–127). The *Gospel of the Hebrews*, which now exists only through references from early church writers, is dated as early as the first century (Barnstone 1984, 334). Origen quotes a passage from it in which Jesus uses maternal imagery for God (335). These traditions indicate that Jesus may have called God "Mother" at times. Certainly the likelihood that Jesus sometimes called God "Father" does not mean he never used other metaphors for God, including feminine ones. Nor does it follow (as some argue) that in using "Father" as a metaphor for God, Jesus was establishing a rule that God should only be referred to in terms with masculine gender. (Wren's discussion is helpful here; Wren 1989, 183–188).

Questions about the uniqueness, authenticity, exclusivity, and christological interpretation of Jesus' use of 'abbā all throw doubt on Jeremias's thesis that the address of God as 'abbā was central to Jesus' message.

'Abbā, *Father, and Christian Liturgical Language*

Challengers to Jeremias's findings do not deny that Jesus ever spoke of God using paternal terms, though no one *patēr/'abbā* saying is an undisputably authentic saying of Jesus. Nor do challengers insist that Christians ought never to pray to God as 'abbā or Father. However, these challenges mean that neither Jeremias's findings nor theological claims and liturgical practice based upon them can be regarded to be as conclusive as once was thought. Most New Testament references calling God "Father" probably reflect early Christians' experience of prayer more than the actual words of Jesus, who may also have addressed God as Mother.

It has often been assumed that the church has addressed God as Father in worship because Jesus did so. Critical biblical scholarship cannot fully support this claim. Or it is claimed that because Jesus used masculine terms for God, we may not use feminine ones. This claim may not be based in fact, because Jesus may have also called God "Mother" or other feminine names lost to tradition. Further, both arguments rest on the assumption that the church is limited in its language of prayer to imagery that Jesus used. In practice, in most times and places Christians have exercised the freedom to pray to God in many ways and with many forms of address, alongside the Prayer of Jesus in Matthew 6:9–13 and Luke 11:2–14. Unquestioned patriarchal assumptions, and not limits set by the Prayer of Jesus, have excluded feminine metaphors about God from Christian worship.

Another line of argument, followed even by some Christian feminists, is that "Father" has become problematic as an image for the divine only because of the patriarchal understandings of fatherhood that developed in the church. For example, Schüssler Fiorenza has argued that Jesus' words "call no one your father on earth, for you have one Father — the one in heaven" (Matt. 23:9) do not legitimate but actually subvert patriarchal domination (Schüssler Fiorenza 1983, 151). She does not question the name "Father" for God, but rejects patriarchal understandings of "Father" used by the church to legitimate patriarchal authority (150–151). She believes that, used in nonpatriarchal ways, "Father" is acceptable for Christian worship. Thus John Riggs reports that she could support the continued use of the traditional baptismal formula in the United Church of Christ:

> Rather than jeopardize the ecumenical validity of a UCC baptism by using some other formula, and after discussion with New Testament scholars such as Elisabeth Schüssler Fiorenza, the editorial committee [of the UCC *Book of Worship*] decided to leave the traditional masculine trinitarian formula and then balance the masculine imagery with strongly feminine imagery. (Riggs 1988, 63)

Catherine Mowry LaCugna also suggests that because the Father God of the patriarchal order is not "God the Father of Jesus Christ" (LaCugna 1988, 67), calling God Father "need not be repudiated as inherently sexist and patriarchal" (65). She argues that refusing ever to call God Father "concedes that God the Father is male as patriarchy has defined it" (66). As her carefully nuanced argument demonstrates, LaCugna does not makes this point to discourage use of feminine metaphors for God. She seeks to indicate grounds on which discussion can progress and by which feminists can live with present liturgical practice until change is possible. Both she and Schüssler Fiorenza rightly argue that it is at least as important to change relationships in community so that they will not reflect patriarchal domination and subordination as it is to implement linguistic change (Schüssler Fiorenza 1983, 150–151; LaCugna 1988, 66). All these arguments are sound, but it is important to address another issue — lest this line of thinking be used to delay the revision of liturgical language.

Schüssler Fiorenza is correct that "Father" as a name for God is problematic in the context of patriarchal patterns of living. However, not only the context but also the predominant use of masculine and "Father" language for God with no feminine metaphors is problematic. LaCugna is correct that the Father of Jesus Christ need not be identified with the Father God of patriarchy. We must, however, consider the powerful cultural associations that metaphors about God can evoke. As long as churches, families, and societies are structured in a patriarchal way, "God the Father" will evoke patriarchal connotations when used exclusively at key points in worship, such as the baptismal formula and the eucharistic prayer. The question is not whether masculine or paternal imagery should be used in worship, but whether such imagery should have privilege over feminine and non-gender-specific imagery. Occasionally calling God "Father" is not necessarily a patriarchal practice, but *usually* calling God "Father" does reflect patriarchal values.

Some take a still different approach by suggesting that 'abbā is a more inclusive or less patriarchal alternative to "Father" as an address for God (Ramshaw 1986b, 497–498; Hamerton-Kelly 1979, 81). Not mere baby talk, 'abbā connotes not only intimacy but "surrender" and "obedience" (Jeremias 1978, 62) to the authority of fathers over children. It is certainly a masculine term in Aramaic or translation. Therefore, to be free from patriarchal associations, 'abbā, like 'ab, patēr, and "Father," must be understood in a new light and placed in a new context (alongside feminine metaphors, for example). Further, the suggestion that 'abbā means "Daddy" does not necessarily mean that 'abbā evokes more nurturing aspects of God than does the name "Father." In a cultural context where abuse of children by their fathers is a significant problem, a metaphor meaning "Daddy" may be more problematic than "Father," because children often call their fathers "Daddy." Therefore, it is difficult to understand what we gain by introducing 'abbā into liturgical prayer.

It is likely that Jesus sometimes called God "Father"; and certainly even as the church moves past patriarchal patterns, the name "Father" may be heard at times in Christian worship. Yet, as Visser 't Hooft argues, "Father" may be corrected, enriched, and completed by the use of other ways of talking about God:

The fatherhood of God is however not a closed or exclusive symbolism. It is open to correction, enrichment, and completion from other forms of symbol, such as "mother," "brother," "sister," and "friend." (Visser 't Hooft 1982, 133)

The possibility of associating God the Father not with patriarchy, but with the compassionate and just God made known in Jesus Christ, will be enhanced precisely by placing this metaphor in a less privileged place among a more diverse and gender-inclusive system of metaphors.

DEVELOPMENT OF MASCULINE LANGUAGE IN THE CHURCH

The community that Jesus gathered was characterized by the discipleship of equals, as Elisabeth Schüssler Fiorenza has documented (1983). Women shared in leadership. The call to discipleship was a call away from patriarchal family structures to a new egalitarian community. Jesus called women to faithfulness and wholeness, rather than patriarchal submission (Luke 11:27f.).[2] Similarly, the early missionary movement led by Hellenist Christians "allowed for the full participation and leadership of women" (Schüssler Fiorenza 1983, 168). Women were influential leaders of house churches, as the salutations in Paul's letters reveal. The Hellenist and Pauline communities were egalitarian, for all members had access to authority and leadership, which shifted among members (286). The Gospels of Mark and John present egalitarian views of women and the Christian community (316-333; Brown 1979, 183-198).

The Patriarchalization of the Church

Beginning in the New Testament period, however, a process, which Schüssler Fiorenza has called the patriarchalization of the church, was taking place (Schüssler Fiorenza 1983, 285). This process included growing affirmation for Christians of Roman patriarchal household codes calling for submission of slaves to masters, children to fathers, and wives to husbands. The author of 1 Peter 2 does not support such codes. Yet he encourages women and slaves in the households of non-Christians "for the

---

2. Refer to Schüssler-Fiorenza 1983, 121, 140-154; Tennis 1985, 91-113; Hamerton-Kelly 1979, chap. 3, 52-73; and Visser 't Hooft 1982, 119-127.

sake of Christian mission [to] seek the social patterns of the people around them" (261). In other cases (such as Col. 3:18—4:1 and Eph. 5:21-33), however, patriarchal submission of Christians to Christians was asked. Some Gnostics and orthodox Christians upheld patriarchal values by asking women to "become like men" by living celibate lifestyles in order to share Christian equality (270-279).

In the pastoral letters, patriarchal forms of church organization were affirmed. Church members were enjoined to submit to the authority of their leaders; and positions of authority were shared only by male heads of households, rather than shifting in an egalitarian manner (Schüssler Fiorenza 1983, 286-287). The pastoral letters and the letters of Ignatius attempted to restrict women's leadership severely and to consolidate the authority of bishops in Christian communities. They prohibited women from teaching men and restricted the order of widows to older women under the control of bishops. Evidence of prophetic gifts as a basis for authority was de-emphasized. (Schüssler Fiorenza traces these developments in detail, 1983, 288-315).

Thus the patriarchalization of the church meant affirming patriarchal household codes and abandoning egalitarian leadership styles. By the fourth century, patriarchally oriented church leaders went so far as to condemn church groups such as the Montanists partly because they did not exclude women from leadership (Schüssler Fiorenza 1983, 304). One line along which "orthodox" groups were separated from "heterodox" groups was in their exclusion of women from church leadership and their identification with patriarchal society.

Elaine H. Pagels argues that feminine symbolism for God also distinguished "heterodox" Christian groups, especially Gnostics, from "orthodox" Christian groups (Pagels 1976, 294; 1979, 57-83). The Gnostic texts, admittedly diverse, portray "the divine Mother" (Pagels 1976, 295) in three primary ways. Some of these texts, such as the writings of Valentinus, portray God as including and harmonizing the feminine and masculine. A second group identifies the Holy Spirit as Mother. Pagels includes the feminine references to God in *The Gospel of Hebrews* and *The Gospel According to Thomas* in this second group. A third group draws on Wisdom traditions to speak of God as *Sophia* — the source of wisdom and the power of creation. Those who called themselves "orthodox" rejected these documents as "heterodox"; feminine imagery for God virtually disappeared in orthodox Christian tradition (Pagels 1976, 298–299).

In the second century, some women were attracted to heretical groups both because they included women as leaders and because they used feminine imagery for God. For example, according to orthodox bishop Irenaeus, women were attracted to Marcus's circle, in which

> prayers are offered to the Mother in her aspects as Silence, Grace, and Wisdom; women priests serve the eucharist together with men; and women also speak as prophets, uttering to the whole community what the "Spirit" reveals to them. (Pagels summarizing Irenaeus, in *Against Heresies* 1.13.7; 1976, 300)

Pagels argues that the exclusion of women from leadership in "orthodox" communities and the suppression of feminine symbolism for the divine were directly related, even if other characteristics also distinguished orthodox and heterodox groups. She calls for more research on the topic.

Schüssler Fiorenza argues that Pagels does not recognize the implications of the fact that in gnosticism the feminine principle in the divine is secondary to the masculine principle (Schüssler Fiorenza 1983, 274 and 284, n. 101). Instead, Schüssler Fiorenza emphasizes the *Sophia* tradition found in earliest Christianity and still apparent in the Gospels (130–141). In fact, she argues that "the earliest Christian theology is sophialogy" (134).

Although Schüssler Fiorenza and Pagels interpret early Christian and Gnostic sources differently, both interpretations show that feminine images for the divine played a larger role in the first and second century church than they have played since. The *Sophia* traditions, along with other traditions in which feminine imagery is used for the divine, may survive from very early Christian tradition and the teaching of Jesus himself. Later orthodox traditions suppressed feminine images, just as heterodox traditions included them though secondary to masculine imagery.

When they drew lines between heterodox and orthodox traditions, and later, when they agreed upon the canon, the orthodox group excluded traditions with feminine imagery for the divine. Predominantly masculine imagery for God in Christian worship is derived, in part, from the patriarchalization of the church that was beginning to be accomplished in the second century.

The Trinitarian Debates and Masculinization of Language

Probably as a result of second-century controversies, the church virtually eliminated feminine imagery for God in Christian worship. As a result of fourth-century controversies, the church increasingly addressed God as "Father, Son, and Holy Spirit."

Before the fourth-century controversies, the churches addressed God in a variety of ways. In the account of Polycarp's martyrdom, the bishop prayed as he stood tied to the stake, ending with these words:

> For this and for all benefits, I praise Thee, I bless Thee, I glorify Thee through the eternal and heavenly High Priest, Jesus Christ, Thy beloved Son, through whom be to Thee glory, now and for all the ages to come. (Jungmann 1959, 190)

Prayer to God through Christ was common in the first two centuries and became a primary pattern through the fourth. For example, some prayers of Serapion, bishop of Thmius, Egypt, around 350 C.E., include no reference to God as "Father" (or any masculine terms), but all address God through Christ (Deiss 1979, 183–208). During the third and fourth centuries, Christian leaders added "in the Holy Spirit" to the doxology. Origen, for example, characteristically used this form of address: "We praise Thee through Christ in the Holy Spirit" (Jungmann 1959, 191).

Arius contended that the Son was a creature of God the Father who was subordinate to the Father. He and his supporters claimed the custom of praying "through Christ" showed Jesus Christ to be a mediator, who though divine, was at a lower level than the Father. In response, the Council of Nicaea in 325 drew up a confession in which the "Lord Jesus Christ, the Son of God" was said to be "begotten from the Father...not made" (that is, not a creature), and "of one substance with the Father" (Lohse 1966, 52). This did not end the Arian controversy, however; it continued for several decades after the Council and after Arius's death in 336 (48). There was strong support for Arian ideas in many quarters of the church, and intense opposition in others. In Caesarea, Basil, an anti-Arian, initiated use of a new doxology, "(to the Father be honor) with the Son together with the Holy Spirit" (Jungmann 1959, 193). This formula made it clear that the Son and the Holy Spirit were to be worshiped as coequal with the Father. According to Basil, the older formula ("through the Son in the Holy Spirit") was acceptable as well, emphasizing instead the "voluntary abasement of the Son" (193).

Basil, Gregory of Nyssa, his brother, and Gregory of Nazianzus (the "Cappadocians"), influenced decisions made at the Councils of Constantinople in 381 and 382, in which the Father, the Son, and the Holy Spirit were declared to be consubstantial and of equal dignity (Lohse 1966, 65). With this, the Arian controversy of the fourth century ended, and Arian bishops were forced to retire (Jungmann 1959, 194).

As a result of this solution of the controversy, doxologies thought to express the orthodox position became formulaic in the liturgy. The Eastern church accepted three forms of the doxology: "Glory be to the Father with Christ together with the Holy Spirit"; "Our Lord Jesus Christ through whom and with whom be to Thee glory together with the Holy Spirit"; and "[glory] to the Father and to the Son and to the Holy Spirit, now and always and in all eternity" (Jungmann 1959, 195). The Western church borrowed the third form (195), while sometimes praying "through Jesus Christ our Lord" (Wainwright 1980, 64).

Through the new doxologies, prayer to God as Father and Son and Holy Spirit became more central and characteristic to Christian worship (Jungmann 1959, 194). Further, dogmatic discussions led to emphasis both on the distinctions and inner relations among the Father, Son, and Holy Spirit. Thus, the Council of Hippo (393 C.E.) declared, "Let no one in the prayers name the Father in place of the Son or the Son in place of the Father. At the altar, prayer should always be directed to the Father" (cited by Wainwright 1980, 255). In some cases, emphasis on distinction led to the use of the address "Father" where the undifferentiated name "God" might have been used previously. Efforts to gain a clearer understanding of intratrinitarian relations led to use of "Son" where "Christ" might have been used previously. Resolution of these theological struggles gave the impression that "Father" and "Son" were technically correct terms, rather than metaphors with bearing on the divine-human relationship. In addition, emphasis on the immanent Trinity following Augustine led to de-emphasis on the relational, metaphorical status of "Father" as an image for God (LaCugna 1987, 17–18).

The accommodation of the church and the Roman state in the fourth century may also have influenced the increasing liturgical use of *pater* (which means "father" in Latin as well as in Greek). "Father" was a central image in Roman religious, family, and political life (see discussion of *patria potestas* on page 47). Jupiter/Zeus, the supreme God of the Roman/Greek pantheon, was sometimes described or depicted as a sky-father (Ferguson 1970, 32–43). Roman emperors were often called *pater patriae* ("father of the fatherland"). They were identified with the father-gods, through prayer at their shrines, through myths of divine descent, or through themselves being adulated as divine. One Eastern inscription, dated sometime after 2 B.C.E. when Caesar Augustus was designated *pater patriae* by the Roman Senate, reads: "Caesar Augustus, Father of his own Fatherland, divine Rome, Zeus Paternal, and Savior of the whole human race" (Grant 1957, 174). The merging of divine and human fatherhood in the emperor, though not always this explicit, may well have been a factor in making "Father" a dominant name for God in Christian worship. Liturgical scholars generally agree that after the fourth century, triumphalist thinking drawing on metaphors of imperial rule entered into the theological and liturgical language of the church.[3] Christians called God "Father" long before that time. Such names as "Almighty Father" may have been used more frequently or with more overtones of patriarchal fatherhood and omnipotent rule due to imperial influence, however. Using "Father" as a title for God may have undermined emperor worship, while subtly identifying the church with pa-

---

3. Ralph Keifer, late professor of worship at Catholic Theological Union, demonstrated this new tendency toward triumphalism in liturgy by comparing pre-Constantinian and post-Constantinian liturgies in a class on the Eucharist in which I participated during summer 1980 at the University of Notre Dame. I am indebted to J. Frank Henderson and Daniel Schowalter for the concepts developed in this paragraph.

triarchal imperial power — all this while using a traditional, biblical name!

In his Fifth Theological Oration, Gregory of Nazianzus denied that God is male in sex (paragraph VII in *Nicene and Post Nicene Fathers*, series 2, vol. 7, 320, cited by Catherine LaCugna 1989, 242). The Cappadocians did not argue for addressing God as "the Father and the Son and the Holy Spirit" with the stated intent of establishing predominantly masculine terminology for God, but this was an effect of the resolution of the Arian controversy. By the end of the fourth century, "Father, Son, and Holy Spirit" became a primary name for God in Christian worship. Further theological and liturgical developments not only continued but in some cases extended the use of masculine imagery for God.

Modern Developments

Some cultural and theological trends in the nineteenth and twentieth centuries have led to increasing use of "Father" as a metaphor for God. Mary Collins observes that in the modern English liturgies, classic Roman patterns of invocation such as "Almighty and eternal God" have more and more been replaced by "Father," as a response to the impersonality of culture: "In our mass, depersonalized culture, Christian people have seemed to need to speak to a God capable of providing acceptance, consolation, nurture, and love" (Collins 1985, 301). S. Paul Schilling notes that some recent hymns have been particularly masculine in their terminology:

> Seen as a whole the hymns of the late nineteenth and early twentieth centuries contain even more sexist language than their predecessors. Ironically, lyrics influenced by the rise of the social gospel are probably the greatest offenders. (Schilling 1983, 216)

Such hymns often spoke about the "fatherhood of God" or the "brotherhood of man," unlike hymns by Wesley and Watts in which worshipers more frequently spoke of themselves in the first person and God in the second person. Modern folk hymns also have spoken often of God as Father and "men" as "brothers" (Schilling 1983, 218).

J. Frank Henderson, a member of the International Commission on English in the Liturgy (ICEL), has been undertaking a statistical study of the use of "Father," "*pater*," and equivalent terms in Christian worship. He has gathered material from major extant liturgical books throughout church history up until the present time. He has discovered a marked increase in the use of paternal imagery in several modern liturgical books, especially in the collects. Henderson found that the collects in editions of the 1570 Roman missal before the twentieth century address God as *pater* four times at most. The 1970 Roman missal (Latin edition) still addresses God as *pater* in only twenty-two of fifteen hundred collects. Astonishingly, when the missal was translated into English by ICEL, 555 collects addressed God as Father! (Henderson 1988, 44–45). Translations into German, French, and Spanish also increase the address of God in paternal language, though not nearly to the extent that the ICEL translation does (46). Two translations produced in England and Wales exactly conform to the address of God in the Latin (46).

Some modern versions of the *Book of Common Prayer* also increase paternal address for God in the collects (Henderson 1988, 48–52). The 1978 *Lutheran Book of Worship* modestly increases such address as compared with the 1958 Lutheran *Service Book and Hymnal*; but the Missouri Synod book, *Lutheran Worship*, significantly increases address of God as "Father" in the collects (57).

Summarizing his review of modern liturgical books (including those of some denominations not mentioned here), Henderson writes, "It is in the new liturgical books of the 1970s and 1980s that the greatest increase of 'Father' has occurred" (Henderson 1988, 76). Henderson suggests that modern dogmatic and liturgical discussions, a concern for euphony, and a lessening of the distance perceived between God and humanity may have led to this increased address of God as Father (76).

As Henderson's study shows, one trend in the past century has been toward increasing use of masculine language to speak to and about God, especially in English-speaking North America. Interestingly enough, the greatest concern for gender-inclusive language has also developed in North America. Although people in the British Isles sometimes in jest attribute the concern for inclusive language to the experimentalism of U.S. and Canadian churches, perhaps concern has developed where the need is greatest! Of course, there are vast differences, even among the churches of North America. Susan Thistlethwaite, drawing on the work of Cheryl Townsend Gilkes, has suggested that African American churches have not expressed much concern about "Father" language for God. The metaphor has not been particularly predominant in their churches because these churches particularly emphasize Jesus and the Holy Spirit. In fact, African American tradition has often addressed God as "father to the fatherless and mother to the motherless" (Thistlethwaite 1989, 116–117).

Whatever the differences among North American churches, North American Christians have initiated concern about masculine language for God emerging in the twentieth century (refer to Schilling 1983, chap. 13, 213–228; Hardesty 1987; Watkins 1981; and S. Neufer Emswiler and T. Neufer Emswiler 1974). Some denominations have moved toward eliminating the use of predominantly masculine language for God in their worship. For example, the editors of the UCC *Book of Worship* attempted to avoid "exclusively male terms for God" (United Church of Christ Office for Church Life and Leadership 1986, 8). Press releases about the book stressed that it was the first denominational worship book edited with a commitment to inclusive language about God and humanity, although as noted previously, it retains the traditional baptismal formula (142). Although the new United Methodist hymnal includes a few hymns with feminine imagery for God, and many with no gender-specific imagery, many still use masculine language. Erik Routley, editor of the hymnal *Rejoice in the Lord* of the Reformed Church in America, stated that

> we [the editorial committee] have not often embarked on the extremely hazardous and difficult task of adjusting all language so that it gives no offense to those who regard it as wrong to use the male pronoun for God the Father or God the Holy Spirit.... We leave this struggle to those who will edit the hymnbooks of succeeding decades. (Routley 1985, 9)

Indeed, although many English-speaking Christians have at least begun to address the issue of predominantly masculine language for God in the liturgy, the struggle for resolution of the issue will no doubt continue in succeeding decades. David Holeton has asked regarding baptismal practice:

> If the purpose of the baptismal creeds was polemic (i.e., keeping out heresy) rather than serving as a *regula fidei* (giving a thumbnail sketch of the essentials of Christian faith) then we need only to ask whether or not we need to continue fighting Valentinus and his heirs [who believed that the Father of Jesus Christ did not create this evil world]. (Holeton 1988, 71)

Holeton's remarks suggest several questions: To what extent must language growing out of ancient controversies continue to dominate the language of Christian worship? Should the language of worship grow more out of positive faith affirmations or negative antiheretical statements? What are the heresies that are most dangerous for the church today; could racism, sexism, or idolatry be among them? Do the language of worship and the language of theology mutually reinforce one another, or has the language of dogmatic and speculative theology come to dominate the language of worship? Does emphasis on the battles of the fourth century keep the church from actively seeking ways to express a living faith for the twentieth and twenty-first centuries? What *are* the most adequate ways of expressing our faith now?

Understanding the historical context in which the church came to use mostly masculine and paternal imagery in worship provides openings for future development. "Father" became a predominant metaphor for God through the process of human beings making decisions based on the theological and ethical crises of their day. Even so, "Father" may become a less prominent metaphor as Christians respond to theological and ethical crises of our day. We can and should reexamine the church's worship, life, and mission through fresh encounter with Christian traditions in light of contemporary experience, with the guidance of the Spirit.

THE DE-PATRIARCHALIZATION OF THE CHURCH AND THE LANGUAGE OF WORSHIP

The patriarchalization of the church was solidified in the second century and onward. In the twentieth century, a process of de-patriarchalization is beginning, though it is far from solidified. For example, today many church bodies ordain women, and many Christians now regard the household codes of Colossians 3:18—4:1 and similar passages as expressions of patriarchy, and not of Christian faith. Developing a more diverse and gender-inclusive system of metaphors for God is another part of de-patriarchalizing the church.

Nelle Morton speaks articulately of the need for the church to evaluate the imagery it uses in worship, theology, and education. She writes:

> A consciously aware, questioning, and growing community will reexamine and internalize intentionally some images and exorcise others from its corporate life so that its spirit life retains a dynamic and vibrant ferment, ever renewing itself yet maintaining continuity with its past. (Morton 1985, 33–34)

De-patriarchalizing the church will mean reexamining the images we use in corporate worship. We may reclaim some images that were rejected under the influence of patriarchal society, while we reject other images or give them less prominence in a reconfigured system of metaphors.

Changing the "Father/Son" metaphor for God is particularly challenging, because it has become identified with hard-won theological solutions. Letty Russell has stated the problem in this way:

> The doctrinal formulations are such that the Father-Son metaphor for God has become a part of the [trinitarian] doctrine itself, leading Christians, sometimes, to assume that the Godhead is male. Women and men who are feminists because they advocate full equality of all persons are looking for other descriptions of God that include both masculine and feminine metaphors, and also ones that move beyond gender. (Russell 1979, 29)

Such feminists as Mary Daly and Carter Heyward hold that traditional doctrine errs in declaring Jesus the Christ to be coequal with God or to incarnate God in any unique way (Daly 1973, 96; Heyward 1982, 31–49). Others, like Russell, have affirmed the positive value of trinitarian affirmation for feminists, as an image of a community of shared life at the heart of God's being and acting (Russell 1979, 26–32; Wilson-Kastner 1983, 121–127; Zikmund 1987). Such Christian feminists, among whom I count myself, have questioned the assumption that "Father, Son, and Spirit" is the only appropriate way to talk about the Trinity. Stookey has observed that it is difficult to find new modes of expression that will say so much in a few words as "Father, Son, and Holy Spirit" (Stookey 1983, 168); but the traditional formula has problems other than its masculine terms. Because a "Father" is prior to a "Son" in human experience, subordination of son to father may be inferred, especially in a patriarchal context in which fathers have control over their children. Creedal and liturgical efforts to eliminate this impression (for example, Basil's new doxology) can only be partially successful, because they work against cultural associations of the words.

I support the intent of traditional trinitarian language — to affirm both the unity of God and the unique participation of Jesus Christ in God's life. Yet trinitarian language must be reformulated to address its masculine bias as well as other unresolved problems. I will discuss possible directions for reformulation later. For now I would ask the church to recover a fuller sense of the divine mystery that goes beyond all names. "Father, Son, and Holy Spirit" does not say all that can be said either about the inner life of the Godhead or about God's relatedness to humanity in the economy of salvation. In worship we give thanks and praise in response to God's love and justice expressed in relationship with humanity. The metaphorical human language we must employ in praise and thanksgiving is not conceptual language that explains God's nature for once and for all. This distinction can be lost when we regard "Father, Son, and Holy Spirit" as the only adequate way to speak of the God made known in Jesus Christ. Dialogue leading to alternatives to "Father, Son, and Holy Spirit" for the language of Christian praise is well worth the time and effort it will require.

As the church of our day makes its own mark on ongoing tradition, we have the opportunity to develop language for praise and prayer that more appropriately witnesses to the just and loving God made known in Jesus Christ.

CHAPTER 4

CHRISTIAN WORSHIP BEYOND PATRIARCHY: METHODS OF RECONSTRUCTION

The author of Ephesians compared the church to a living temple built on the foundation of prophets and apostles with Jesus Christ as the cornerstone (Eph. 2:19-22). The church lives and grows in continuity with generations of prophets, apostles, and ordinary people of faith, in ongoing relationship with Jesus Christ. Its worship and its life change over time in continuing reformation. As the church's worship and life change, so do its systems of metaphors.

Can stones live and grow? Can hardened metaphorical systems find new life? Both transformations seem improbable. But the Spirit, always at work in the church, brings new life.

At this time, the system of metaphors used in Christian worship needs major reconstruction so that the church, instead of supporting patriarchy, will be faithful to the gospel. Because we build on the foundation of people who have gone before us, reconstructing the metaphorical system of Christian liturgy is like renovating an old house. First, its surface and structural faults must be identified; the builder has to decide what needs changing. Rotting wood and faded wallpaper are stripped away and replaced by new materials, but part of the existing decor and structure can be saved, perhaps in modified form. Critical reflection and imagination, stripping and saving, all play their part.

Reconstructing a system of metaphors, like renovating a house, calls for multiple strategies. In this chapter, I will outline four methods by which we can analyze and revise liturgical language. These methods of approaching liturgical texts draw upon methods of interpretation developed to enable present understanding and application of biblical texts written long ago. The starting point is a *hermeneutics of suspicion*, which enables a searching evaluation of worship traditions to locate any patriarchal bias. Then, through the method of *remembrance* or *retrieval*, we may recover neglected parts of past tradition for present use. At other times, the most appropriate course is a method of *translation*, which substitutes equivalent feminine or non-gender-specific terms for masculine terms. But the process is not complete without the method of *creative ritualization* through which women and men are free to build on past foundations using present experience and imagination.

THE HERMENEUTICS OF SUSPICION

The language of Christian scripture, tradition, theology, and worship developed within the social and political context of patriarchy, which marginalized and silenced women. Attempts to change Christian worship to include the witness of women, to withdraw support from patriarchy, and to witness appropriately to the God of Jesus Christ must begin with honest evaluation of Christian tradition. This calls for a feminist critical theory that names the patriarchal nature both of present social relationships and of Christian traditions, including worship.

Feminists have applied the term "hermeneutics of suspicion," developed in scripture scholarship, to feminist critical theory regarding Christian traditions (Schüssler Fiorenza 1984, 15–18). According to David Tracy, a hermeneutics of suspicion is critical analysis of a tradition to reveal systematic distortions that go beyond occasional errors or difficulties (Tracy and Grant 1984, 162). Such analysis is necessary, in Tracy's words, "to clarify, purify, correct, and challenge" traditions (184). As Schüssler Fiorenza writes, feminist critical theory does not imagine a pristine period of Christian origins free from patriarchal influence, for androcentric bias exists in all layers of scripture and tradition:

> Not only is scripture interpreted by a long line of men and proclaimed in patriarchal churches, it is also authored by men, written in androcentric language, reflective of male religious experience, selected and transmitted by male religious leadership. (Schüssler Fiorenza 1985, 130)

A hermeneutics of suspicion faces honestly the patriarchal bias of scripture and tradition, and names its destructive results, among them sexism, racism, and anti-Judaism (Schüssler Fiorenza 1985, 130). In some hermeneutical methods (for example, Hans-Georg Gadamer's "new hermeneutic"), the interpreter seeks awareness of one's biases in order to screen out interference and be open to the claims of the text (Tracy and Grant 1984, 153–166). Given the patriarchal context of scripture and tradition, however, feminists must be free not only to retrieve, but also to question traditions of the past.

A hermeneutics of suspicion begins with realizing with Segundo that "anything and everything involving ideas is intimately bound up with the existing social situation in at least an unconscious way" (Segundo 1976, 8). Not only the interpreter or translator, but also the text or tradition interpreted is influenced by social location and interest. For example, the choice of metaphors for naming God in scripture does not occur in a vacuum, but reflects social structures with which authors are familiar; scripture calls God "king," not "president."

A hermeneutics of suspicion, as practiced by liberation and feminist theologians, presupposes the commitment to transform unjust and destructive social systems. It is not neutral or "objective." Because thinking is enmeshed in social situations and is tilted toward group self-interest, neutrality is impossible. At best, one can identify and be self-critical about the way social location influences one's thinking. Liberationist and feminist interpreters find support for their stance of advocacy from prophetic strains in scripture that portray God as the champion of the poor, the oppressed, and the marginalized; even God is "interested," being on the side of justice. A hermeneutics of suspicion, like the "new hermeneutics," requires that one's presuppositions and social commitments be made as conscious as possible, enabling self-criticism and honest hearing. At the same time, through this hermeneutic, one may criticize past traditions and refuse to appropriate them in present thinking and practice.

A hermeneutics of suspicion examines the political and social ideology expressed or assumed in texts in light of their influence on present social reality. It asks what groups the text assumes to be dominant and what groups it has marginalized and silenced in the past and present. Such questions help to locate the social contexts and biases of texts, and thus to inform the work of emancipation from unjust social structures (Schillebeeckx 1984, 112).

Because a feminist hermeneutics accompanies emancipative praxis, it takes place in "women-church," those engaged in living out a discipleship community of equals and in moving toward freedom from patriarchal models of self and church.[1]

My exploration of the social and historical context of predominantly masculine language for God in Christian tradition in the preceding chapters demonstrates a hermeneutic of suspicion. I have insisted that the predominance of "Father," "King," and "Lord" as names for God in worship is based not on divine revelation, but on the social context of patriarchy. This male-dominated language is part of a whole system that socializes women and others to accept a subordinate place in society. I am committed to change this system, which not only limits vocational choices and rewards for women, but which also results in abuse and violence against all who are not dominant in the patriarchal pyramid. I claim the freedom not only to retrieve, but also to question, reject, or revise inherited traditions. Participation in worshiping communities with feminist commitment supports the individual scholarly work I do, enabling me to reflect critically on the effectiveness of language revisions.

Efforts to revise the language of Christian worship are a part of emancipative feminist reflection and practice. New and revised language for God develops through reflection and testing in a community's worship. Reflection on any new practice, as well as continued reflection on Christian traditions, leads to further revision. For example, the pastors of The Riverside Church in New York City developed a new baptismal formula and then revised it based on the community's response.

Reshaping Christian worship so that it does not reinforce patriarchal domination and violence but witnesses appropriately to a just and loving God begins with a hermeneutics of suspicion. This method lays the groundwork for retrieval or translation of past traditions and creation of new ones. Critical reflection reveals the need for a reconfiguration of the metaphors used in

---

1. Refer to Schüssler Fiorenza 1984, xiv, and Ruether 1986, 141, for a fuller discussion of "women-church"; they are not identical with each other or with me in their definitions.

Christian worship. One way to approach this reconstruction is through a hermeneutics of retrieval or remembrance.

THE METHOD OF REMEMBRANCE

The method of remembrance reconstructs the language of worship by identifying or recovering images from past tradition that are still appropriate for use in present Christian worship. It includes reconstructing how women participated in biblical history and church tradition (Schüssler Fiorenza 1985, 133). "Remembrance" (*anamnēsis*) is central to Christian worship traditions. Although it primarily refers to *anamnēsis* of God's self-disclosure in the life, death, and resurrection in Jesus Christ, *anamnēsis* includes witness to God's faithful love for humanity in all times and places (Procter-Smith 1987).

A feminist method of remembrance draws on sources of scripture and church tradition to recover the stories and perspectives of women and to reclaim feminine and gender-free images of God for worship to replace or balance masculine images. Through the method of remembrance, Christians can remain in continuity with tradition even while giving some parts of tradition a less central role in worship. Communities who strongly emphasize the authority of scripture and church tradition will appreciate this method, which emphasizes recognized sources of traditional orthodox Christian faith. Thus, in her book *Inclusive Language in the Church*, evangelical Nancy Hardesty finds sources for revision mainly in scripture and in mystics such as Julian of Norwich (Hardesty 1987, 91-102). I have found that her presentation persuades evangelically oriented students that biblical traditions leave far more room to change liturgical language than they had previously imagined.

Through a method of remembrance, the stories and experiences of women take their place alongside the stories and experiences of men as a part of Christian worship. Women's memory must be recovered, because remembrance is central to Christian worship. Worship that honors men's experience and mostly ignores women's experience is distorted. From memory, human beings "construct our identity, interpret the significance of experience, and live in relationship with others" (Procter-Smith 1987, 407-408). The method of remembrance entails examining traditional liturgical texts to identify "distortions, omissions, and misuses of women's memory" and to discover "surviving fragments" of the memory of women's participation in the church and its worship (423). The liturgical texts mined include official liturgies, sermon texts, hymns, and collections of prayers from the diverse traditions of Christian worship: orthodox and heterodox, Protestant, Catholic, and Orthodox, past and present. The literature of Christian devotion — with its many women authors — is another source for liturgical language that is not patriarchal yet is firmly rooted in Christian tradition.

Retrieval from Canonical Scriptures

Scripture is a primary source for a feminist hermeneutics of remembrance. Through a hermeneutics of remembrance, we can interpret scripture anew to discover women participating as worship leaders. Procter-Smith has shown that the unnamed woman who anointed Jesus' head in Mark 14:3-9 was performing a liturgical act, for anointing was a part of early Christian baptisms (Procter-Smith 1987). The story, placed at the beginning of the Passion narrative, links Christian baptism to dying with Christ (as Mark does elsewhere, cf. 10:35-40). Because "Christ" means "anointed one," Mark here implies that the very meaning of "Christ" and "Christian" is deeply connected with the Passion. Recovering this symbolism reveals the liturgical significance of the woman's act.

A hermeneutics of remembrance also brings forward the memory of women who suffered in scripture and church tradition, and the women who lamented them. One such woman was Jephthah's daughter (name unknown), sacrificed because of a vow her father made in hopes of gaining a military victory. The daughter spends two months in the mountains mourning with her female friends before her death. Later women remembered her liturgically: "There arose an Israelite custom that for four days every year the daughters of Israel would go out to lament the daughter of Jephthah the Gileadite" (Judg. 11:39b-40). In all its tragedy, this story provides a model for remembering women's lives, because, as Phyllis Trible has written, "the women with whom she chose to spend her last days have not let her pass into oblivion"

(Trible 1984, 106-107). To lament the suffering of women of the past leads to solidarity with women who suffer now.[2]

Just as it remembers women who led liturgies of anointing or lament, a feminist hermeneutics retrieves nonpatriarchal language about God for worship. Scripture speaks of God in many ways that are not androcentric; for example, a psalmist says, "For with you is the fountain of life; in your light we see light" (Ps. 36:9). Other scriptural images of God are feminine. Some emphasize mutuality rather than domination and subordination; for example, the Holy Spirit as *parakletos* befriends rather than dominates. A hermeneutics of remembrance seeks to recover images and expressions from scripture that are appropriate for contemporary liturgical practice.

Mollenkott has explored feminine images for God in scripture in her book *The Divine Feminine* (Mollenkott 1983). She recovers images of God as a woman giving birth, and as a nursing mother, midwife, mother bear, mother eagle, homemaker, female beloved, and *'ēzēr* ("partner" or "helper"). Trible has demonstrated that the Hebrew word *rehem* ("womb") is the source for the word *rahămîm*, so often used in Hebrew scriptures to speak of God's mercy (Trible 1978, 31-59); and that the divine image is both male and female (1-30). Note that many, though not all of these images depend on stereotypical feminine roles in patriarchy; they tend to portray God only as a nurturing mother. Divine wisdom (*Sophia*) as a scriptural image of God may have greater promise for Christian worship. Sophia, portrayed as feminine, does not fit the patriarchal stereotypes, but rather participates in the creation of the world and the instruction of those who are faithful (for example, Prov. 8:22-36).[3]

Persons seeking to revise the language of Christian worship have often drawn upon a feminist hermeneutic of remembrance (refer to Hardesty 1987, 18-39; Neufer Emswiler and Neufer Emswiler 1980, 102-106; Watkins 1981, 30-47). Thus, the eucharistic prayer used at a consultation of Methodist clergywomen in Ox-

---

2. Procter-Smith 1987, 415; refer to Winter 1987, 91-98 and 143-161 for rituals of lament for women who have suffered in patriarchy.

3. Refer to Russell 1985 for approaches and examples of feminist biblical scholarship, as well as a good basic bibliography on the subject. Works by Trible and Swidler in the reference list exemplify a feminist hermeneutics of remembrance.

ford, England, in 1984 begins with an image of Divine Wisdom: "By your creative word, O Eternal Wisdom, you established us and all things living in your saving presence" (Morley and Ward 1987/1988, 35). The following call to prayer portrays God as a mother bird and the woman searching for a lost coin, drawing on scriptural images:

Leader: As a mother hen gathers her young around her,
All: So too does the Spirit of God shelter us in the shadow of her wings.
Leader: As a woman celebrates when the lost coin has been found,
All: So too does our God rejoice when she finds compassion in the hearts of her children.
Leader: As Mary recognized human need at the wedding feast in Cana and made it known to her child,
All: So is our God moved by the needs of her people and makes them known to us.

(Schaffran and Kozak 1988, 120-121)

In recent years, those seeking to supplement the traditional metaphors of Christian worship have retrieved many such images from scripture.

Retrieval from Noncanonical Scriptures

Nonpatriarchal language about God may also be retrieved from traditions that lost the debates that established the limits of Christian orthodoxy. Both maternal and wisdom imagery for God survived in these traditions. The Gospel of Thomas is not in my view an adequate witness to God's self-revelation in Jesus Christ; the author even says that women must make themselves men to enter the reign of heaven. At the same time, the feminine imagery for God used in some noncanonical texts may reflect authentic memories from the earliest Christian communities — memories that were later suppressed in orthodox communities.

Retrieval from Mystical Traditions

Feminine and nongendered images are also found in the literature of Christian mystical traditions. Many of these writings were prepared for devotional instruction and not for public worship, yet they contain some alternative images appropriate for Christian worship (refer to Hardesty 1987, 95–97). In the twelfth and thirteenth centuries, maternal imagery for God was used by such persons as Bernard of Clairvaux, Gertrude of Helfta, Mechtild of Hackeborn, and Mechtild of Magdeburg (Bynum 1982, 170–262). In the late fourteenth and early fifteenth centuries, Julian of Norwich developed a trinitarian theology in which Christ as Wisdom of God was called Mother, both in the orders of creation and redemption (J. P. Clark 1982, 211–214; Julian of Norwich [1978], 18–19). Riverside Church drew on her imagery in revising their baptismal formula. Hildegard of Bingen (1098–1179 C.E.), a mystic, preacher, and hymn writer, spoke of God using feminine, masculine, and nongendered imagery, especially from the Wisdom tradition. She portrayed Wisdom as the Bride of God and "creatrix and ruler of the world she has made" (Newman 1987, 48). Her work is another historic source for alternative images of God.

Retrieval from Liturgical Sources

It is fairly rare to find well-known traditional Christian liturgical texts that are completely free from gender bias. Like Wesley's hymn "Love Divine, All Loves Excelling," these exceptional texts often address God in the second person. Few traditional texts use feminine imagery, but some use nongendered imagery; and we can balance the masculine imagery of older texts with feminine images from other sources. Or we can retrieve older material simply through new translations that remove sexist bias in translation. Both Schilling and Henderson have shown that many older hymns and prayers were less masculine in their language than those of the past century; retrieving these older texts provides another source for reconstructed liturgical language. We can retrieve some alternative images for God from traditional liturgical texts, even though the very narrowness of their imagery makes reconstruction necessary.

THE METHOD OF TRANSLATION

Through the method of translation, texts that were originally cast in predominantly masculine language are recast to balance or remove gender reference. The method of translation developed here derives from the translation of scriptures from Hebrew to Greek to other languages. As I am using it, this method can mean seeking gender inclusivity by recasting terms in the same language or providing new translations from one language to another. Translation is not too strong a term, because a new culture beyond patriarchy requires a new language.

Eugene A. Nida has developed "dynamic equivalence" as a method of scripture translation (Nida and Taber 1969; Nida 1964). Today's English Version of the Bible was translated under the guidance of Nida. This method seeks to make texts as intelligible as possible to the reader, communicating a meaning close to that of the original. The emphasis is on meaning, not on form. Dynamic equivalent translation seeks to remain close to the intent of the original text, yet it expresses itself in the natural speech of the receptor language. Grammatical forms change; active verbal forms ("God created the world") may replace passive or nominal forms ("the worlds were created" or "the foundation of the world"). A metaphor may be translated into discursive language or into another metaphor, so that "as white as snow" becomes "very, very white" or "as white as egret feathers" (Nida and Taber 1969, 4). Or metaphoric language may replace discursive language. The goal is to communicate effectively so that modern hearers will be able to understand and respond to the text in much the same way the first hearers did (24).

In contrast to "dynamic equivalence," the method of "formal correspondence" reproduces not only the message, but also its form in syntax, part of speech, word order, and so on. The Revised Standard Version of the Bible tends toward formal correspondence. It sometimes translates idioms word for word; it transliterates the word *drachma*, a coin, without giving any idea of its value. An accurate translation that many cannot understand may result from a formally correspondent translation.

Dynamic equivalent translation can help the church communicate with people who have not been raised in the Christian faith. An "unchurched" young woman from our church's program with drug-culture teenagers was quite willing to read scripture in a worship service. However, after she practiced reading the text from the Revised Standard Version, she threw it down in frustration, saying, "I can't read this s — !" She was able to read when

I offered her a paraphrase that was closer to her own language. Dynamic equivalent translation helps to reach the unchurched, even as it brings fresh meaning to people who have always been active in the church.

Dynamic equivalent translation examines the component meanings and references of a phrase and then transfers them into equivalent meanings in the new language. Thus the phrase "our beloved ruler" might become "we love the one who rules over us" with no loss of meaning:

> The object (*our*) performs the event (*beloved*, i.e., love), of which the goal is the object element in *ruler*. But this same object performs the event of ruling the first object, *our*. This may be paraphrased as "we love the one who rules over us." (Nida and Taber 1969, 41)

Paraphrase need not mean sloppy, subjective translating, but rather a rigorous approach to the transfer of meaning that involves "no additions, no deletions, [and] no skewing of relationships" (Nida and Taber 1969, 47). Providing biblical translations that not only will be accurate but also will communicate effectively requires imagination, according to Nida and Taber (100, 158). Translating predominantly masculine liturgical language into new nonpatriarchal language without compromising Christian faith also requires imagination, time, and effort.

Recasting traditional texts into a language that is not gender biased calls for a method of translation. A dynamic equivalent method makes it possible to remain close to the meaning and style of the original, while allowing freedom to make formal changes to keep the translation graceful. Routley's advice about adapting hymns applies to dynamic equivalent adaptation of all traditional worship texts, however. He asked that any new version stay close to the style and content of the original hymn writer:

> The modified version must be something the original author could have written, and which, if we were able to consult that author, could arouse in her or him no objection beyond a specific disagreement with this particular principle. (Routley 1982a, 234)

Those using this method of translation would recast liturgical texts into inclusive terms, without otherwise interjecting ideas not already present.

Translating traditional terms to remove gender bias presents great challenges. Metaphors are not fully translatable into non-metaphorical language and are not easily replaced by other metaphors. A full understanding of the associations ancient hearers would bring to a metaphor is not available to the modern interpreter. Thus dynamic equivalent translation can produce only approximate results. Further, the way systems of metaphors work together also presents challenges. To replace "Father-Son-Spirit" with "Creator-Child-Spirit" in a trinitarian affirmation upsets the system of metaphors, because it might seem the first person of the Trinity creates the second. This would deny the Nicene Creed's affirmation that the "Son" is "begotten, not made, of one being with the Father." The challenge is to consider how metaphors work together in a particular context so that we maintain theological integrity even while avoiding predominantly masculine language.

Another difficulty with translation as a method of revising the language of worship is that, given the polarization of gender roles in patriarchal society, feminine and masculine gender terms are rarely equivalent in a direct way. Linda Clark has raised the question in relation to trinitarian language:

> If we are created in the image of God and we are both male and female, if God has no gender... why not simply alternate God the Father and God the Mother week by week in the Trinitarian formula? That question raises enormous problems, both theological and historical. But it immediately points up the difference in the meaning of the words (and functions) of fathering and mothering and the different relationship between a father and a son and a mother and a son. (L. J. Clark 1978, 20)

Patriarchal society assigns gender roles differently to fathers, who have authority over mothers and children, and mothers, who perform most of the day-to-day nurturing tasks. Thus, though both "mother" and "father" refer to biological parenting, they have different connotations in a patriarchal culture; "mother" or even "parent" is not a directly equivalent translation for "father." This difficulty of translating predominantly masculine language into inclusive language shows how changes in language interact with changes in culture. When fathers share responsibilities and prerogatives of parenting with mothers, "mother" will become more adequate as a dynamic equivalent term for "father."

Providing adequate dynamic equivalent translations of traditional texts is extremely challenging, yet it is a worthwhile challenge if we are to move past predominantly masculine imagery for God. A church with no place in worship for the hymns, creeds, and writings of the past would in large part have lost its connection with the church of the past and thus with its own sense of communal identity. Yet the masculine bias of a large portion of inherited liturgical texts means that they must be translated if they are to be reclaimed. Also, church leaders must introduce new material gradually for congregations to participate actively in worship. Many a congregation would rather change a few words in a beloved hymn than replace it with a new hymn; and those who would change worship traditions must respect what their congregations love. Translation is only one method of addressing the need for non-patriarchal language, but as part of an overall strategy, it is important.

Providing inclusive language renderings of scripture for reading during public worship is important; for as Burton Throckmorton has said, it allows worshipers to hear the Word of God: "The church must provide its members with a version of its scriptures that opens the way for congregations of women and men at worship to hear and appropriate the Word of God" (Throckmorton 1984, 743). Robert A. Bennett adds that recasting language helps people to encounter the word as "creative and redemptive":

> The legitimacy of the task of recasting language for use within worship today is based upon its practical, pragmatic, and functional role of assisting the hearer of the divine word to encounter it as creative and redemptive. (Bennett 1987, 550)

Both Throckmorton and Bennett were part of the National Council of Churches committee that prepared *An Inclusive-Language Lectionary*. This lectionary intentionally used the formal correspondence method in providing alternatives from exclusively masculine imagery. In adapting the Revised Standard Version, the committee replaced "the Father" or "God the Father" with "God the Father [*and Mother*]" (National Council of Churches 1986, 13). They made substitutions at the level of words, not sentences, in their process of modifying language "to reflect in English an inclusiveness of all persons" (6).

By contrast, Gail Ramshaw and Gordon Lathrop used a dynamic equivalent method in producing their inclusive language adaptation of the Revised Standard Version of the Bible, *Lectionary for the Christian People* (refer to Ramshaw 1984, 29–36; Ramshaw and Lathrop 1987). They recast sentences and altered syntax when necessary, paying attention to the sound of words for public reading (Ramshaw and Lathrop 1987, xi, xii). Unfortunately, they did not change or supplement metaphors such as "Lord" and "Father," eliminating only exclusive references to humanity and masculine pronouns for God.

The version of lectionary readings edited by Lathrop and Ramshaw shows the advantages of using a dynamic equivalent method of adapting scripture texts. Ramshaw had criticized the formal equivalence method of *An Inclusive-Language Lectionary,* saying, "It is a rewrite of the RSV with individual word substitutions, and thus it suffers, greatly in some places, from jerkiness, lack of poetry, ungainliness" (Ramshaw 1984, 36). In my judgment, *Lectionary for the Christian People* suffers less from "jerkiness, lack of poetry, ungainliness" than *An Inclusive-Language Lectionary.* This, in part, grows out of the combination of Ramshaw's substantial poetic gifts with Lathrop's skill as a scripture scholar. On the other hand, the standards for gender inclusivity followed by Lathrop and Ramshaw are less adequate than those of the National Council of Churches committee. Were the translation goals of *An Inclusive-Language Lectionary* carried out with the method of *Lectionary for the Christian People,* scripture readings more adequate than either could result.

Hymns, prayers, or other worship materials that paraphrase scripture passages can be revised through dynamic equivalent translation. Routley preferred "scriptural resonance," in which hymn texts correlate scripture and contemporary experience, to strict metrical translation of scripture in congregational singing (Routley 1982b, 120–125). Sometimes it is better to paraphrase scripture rather than to quote it in worship materials; for example, a quotation often reads awkwardly in a prayer. But when the words of worship quote scripture, a dynamic equivalent paraphrase may be appropriate.

Translation — dynamic equivalent or formal — makes it possible to sing hymns that have in the past used masculine language for God to the exclusion of feminine language. Churches have often found it acceptable to alter the hymn texts of historic authors for theological reasons (Schilling 1983, 49–51). For example, John Wesley changed the first line of Isaac Watts' hymn "Our God, our help in ages past" to "O God, our help in ages past" because he felt it improper for Christians to sing "our God" as if they "owned" God. Now the same hymn has been adapted for inclusivity. For example "Time, like an ever-rolling stream bears all its sons away" has been changed to "…bears mortals all away" (Ecumenical Women's Center 1974, hymn 4). Hymns are a part of the living faith of the church, especially the free churches. Through the method of translation, we can sing our faith without supporting patriarchy.

Some hymns or liturgies need extensive change; at other times, a change in pronouns suffices. The English Language Liturgical Consultation (1987) replaced the third person masculine pronouns with second person pronouns in one version of the Magnificat (Luke 1:46–55), addressing God as "you" (English Language Liturgical Consultation 1988, 50). Miriam Therese Winter's metrical version of the Magnificat generally avoids pronouns, but in the second stanza she substitutes a feminine pronoun: "My God has done great things for me: Holy is Her Name!"[4] Winter's 1987 version uses feminine language for God without falling into patriarchal feminine gender stereotypes. By changing pronouns, we can continue to use the canticle in Christian worship.

Translation, then, is one method of adapting scripture and liturgical traditions to provide nonpatriarchal language for worship. At best, it casts the words of scripture and tradition in language that is not patriarchal, while otherwise staying as close as possible to original meanings. Because traditional texts are common language through which the contemporary church stays in connection with the church of the past, translation is an important way to provide language to speak of the God who seeks all people in love and grace.

---

4. Winter 1987, 219. The 1989 *United Methodist Hymnal*, hymn 198, changed the line "Holy is her name" to "Holy is this name."

Just as recasting traditional texts calls for a method of translation, so creating new words for worship calls for creative ritualization — the next method we will consider.

THE METHOD OF CREATIVE RITUALIZATION

I have worked extensively adapting hymn texts for inclusive language, especially in two hymn collections, *Because We Are One People* (Ecumenical Women's Center 1974) and *Everflowing Streams* (Duck and Bausch 1981). Sometimes a hymn can be successfully translated into inclusive language by changing a word or two. Other hymns require more extensive changes; for example, I wrote a new stanza for "Be Thou My Vision," referring back to a psalm to which the original text alluded. But at times the central metaphor of a hymn is no longer helpful for Christian worship. My first original hymns grew out of failed attempts to rewrite an old hymn. "Lead On, O King Eternal" was so full of royal and military imagery that all my attempts to adapt it seemed inadequate. Spontaneously, as if by a gift of the Spirit, the words to "Lead On, O Cloud of Presence" came to me, using the first words and tune of the old hymn and making the Exodus metaphor (present but less predominant in "Lead On, O King Eternal") more central. This experience of mine illustrates the limits of translation as a method of providing alternative liturgical language and the need for new work, using the method of creative ritualization.

In the following prayer, called the "Song of Anna," Mary Jo Stirling has imaginatively amplified Luke 2:25–38, which includes the Song of Simeon but mentions the Song of Anna without quoting it:

> I praise you, O God,
> For I have seen the Redeemer of Israel,
>   the Liberator of Jerusalem!
> Many years have I been fasting and praying,
> But now I will leave the temple and proclaim the Word for all.
> For it is written,
>   "Rejoice, rejoice, daughter of Zion,
>   shout aloud, daughter of Jerusalem."

(Duck 1981, 25–26)

Through creative actualization, Stirling lifted up Anna's role as a prophet and preacher in Luke's Gospel. A text may be amplified through storytelling, song, or dance.

The terms "creative ritualization" and "creative actualization" come from the work of Elisabeth Schüssler Fiorenza. Through creative *actualization*, women's participation in the biblical story is recovered (Schüssler Fiorenza 1984, 15). Creative *ritualization* recovers the participation of women in worship (Schüssler Fiorenza 1985). Through creative ritualization women share the same liturgical freedom exercised by men in the patriarchal church:

> In legend and apocryphal writings, in liturgy and sacred hymns, in feast days and liturgical cycles, the patriarchal church has ritualized certain aspects and texts of the Bible as well as celebrated the "founding fathers" of biblical religion. A feminist interpretation of creative ritualization reclaims for women-church the same imaginative freedoms, popular creativity, and liturgical powers. (Schüssler Fiorenza 1985, 135)

Through creative ritualization, women amplify biblical stories, rewrite patriarchal prayers, and remember their sisters of the past. Through this method, both women and men develop new ways of naming in worship beyond the patriarchal biases of the past. The experience of women, as well as men, shapes the language of worship.

The patriarchal church has excluded women from planning and leading worship, as well as from public theological reflection. Women were not part of the fourth-century church councils that so greatly influenced the language of Christian worship. Women's religious communities are the major exception to this general rule; Hildegard of Bingen preached publicly, and Egeria probably influenced the celebration of the liturgical year in Spain.[5] But

---

5. Caroline Walker Bynum, in her book *Jesus as Mother*, tells the story of three thirteenth-century women mystics, Gertrude of Helfta, Mechtild of Hackeborn, and Mechtild of Magdeburg, who were related to Helfta, a religious community of women founded in 1229 in Saxony (Bynum 1982, 170–262). These women used both maternal and paternal imagery of God. They composed prayers for the use of their own community, influenced the development of eucharistic piety, and counseled both women and men. At times, Gertrude of Helfta and Mechtild of Hackeborn were authorized by communications from God to give absolution to other sisters when a priest was not available, so that the sisters could partake in communion. These women supported the growing

by and large, the voices of women have been silenced in public worship. Gerda Lerner has observed that patriarchy excluded women from "symbol making," the process of interpreting human life and history through public speech, writing, and ritual. She has argued that women could acquiesce in their own domination by men because, excluded from symbol making, they could not form a collective historical identity (Lerner 1986, 6, 219). She writes, "Ultimately, it was men's hegemony over the symbol system which most decisively disadvantaged women" (219). Women must participate in the process of developing language for worship if it is to express and form the faith of the whole community. It is not enough simply to place women alongside men in church leadership roles, while expecting them only to speak in the language and think in the patterns developed by men. Women's experience in Christian community must be honored as a source for liturgical language. Through creative ritualization, the voices of women are finally heard in the church.

I recognize that feminist theorists have widely debated such terms as "voice" and "experience." The voice or experience of one woman or of women in one social context cannot be universalized as if they spoke for all women's experience; nor is there such a thing as an interiorized voice unaffected by culture. Yet the freedom to shape language growing out of our own Christian experience must not be denied by limiting women to the language of scripture and Christian tradition, most of which has been generated by men. Women and others who are marginalized in patriarchal society must become a part of the process of shaping the language of Christian worship, through free witness to their faith.

In her book *Women-Church*, Rosemary Radford Ruether claimed that "Women-Church represents the first time that women collectively have claimed to be church and have claimed the tradition of the exodus community as a community of liberation from patriarchy" (Ruether 1985, 57). She says that women now have taken "the shaping of the symbolic universe into their own hands" (2). The first Women-Church gathering in November 1983 was not literally the first time church women moved toward

---

priestly dominance of the church without challenging the exclusion of women from the priesthood, yet they themselves exercised priestly roles at times.

liberation from patriarchy and shaped their own symbols (66). The Women Exploring Theology gatherings at Grailville, Ohio, were beginning these activities more than a decade earlier (refer to Morton 1985, 155–157). However, the growing numbers of women clergy in Protestant churches and the Women-Church movement in the Roman Catholic church are signs that women are now shaping Christian worship in ways virtually unprecedented in Christian history after the second century. Even such women as the nuns of Helfta, who composed prayers and exercised priestly roles, did not understand themselves to be in exodus from patriarchy; they deferred to the sacramental ministry and theological leadership of the male priesthood and hierarchy (Bynum 1982, 170–262).

In recent decades, as women have taken a larger role in shaping Christian worship and theology, they have raised questions about liturgical language. Feminist objections to the language of worship create tensions that call forth creativity in the church (Troeger 1987, 8–9). The concern to provide hymnody that is gender inclusive has inspired the creativity of hymn writers such as Thomas H. Troeger, Susan Savell, Miriam Therese Winter, Brian Wren, and myself (refer to Grindal 1987). Such persons as Ruether and Winter have developed Women-Church rituals, and others have developed gender-inclusive worship resources for use in denominational churches. As women take part more fully in shaping worship, questions and tensions surface about the received language of worship, calling forth much creativity in the church.

Creative ritualization takes seriously the presence of God among women and men as they seek to build a discipleship community of equals that moves beyond patriarchal forms and expressions. Creative ritualization includes and also goes beyond remembrance or dynamic equivalence to incorporate women's experience into Christian worship. It assumes the continuing revelatory presence of God among women and men. Miriam Therese Winter describes the struggle, creativity, and debate in the early church that gave birth to the New Testament. Then she asks why the experiences of community today, like those of biblical times, cannot also serve as "vehicles of grace":

These human experiences became vehicles of grace in a celebration context, in turn impressing upon the community the
importance of its beliefs. Why must only past experience be
authoritative? We who live with the Holy Spirit as inspiration
within and among us surely have every right to add our piece to
the deposit of faith. It is the function of the canon to act as cura-
tor of tradition. Liturgy's role is to add to that tradition, evoking
meaning, inspiring commitment, encouraging all of us to carry
on. Underlying the rituals of *WomanPrayer, WomanSong* is this
understanding of liturgy. (Winter 1987, 9)

Creative ritualization is based on the claim that the Holy Spirit
continues to move within the church, calling forth appropriate
human witness and response in every age. Winter draws on the
traditional Roman Catholic affirmation of a "deposit of faith"
that grows through the centuries as an authority alongside scriptures. Reformed Christians find a similar resource in Calvin
himself, who affirmed the continuing presence of the Holy Spirit
in the church as a complement to the witness of scripture to God's
revelation (Battles 1980, 13; Calvin Book 1, Chapter 7 [1960],
80–81). A method of creative ritualization takes seriously the
presence of the Spirit in the church, specifically, but not only,
among women of faith.

Because the range of images in scripture and church tradition
is quite broad, creative ritualization does not necessarily bring
forward ways of talking about God that have never been used before. However, it recognizes the present and the experiences of
women as sources for the language of Christian witness and response to God. The test for adequacy of the language of Christian
worship is not whether it has been used before, but whether it is
appropriate for praising and responding to the God made known
in Jesus Christ. As the witness and liturgical leadership of women
emerge, new religious language may emerge beyond that which
can be retrieved or translated from tradition. McFague writes,
"We will not find religious language relevant unless we are freed
from the myth that in order for images to be meaningful they
must be traditional" (McFague 1982, 145). Instead, the method
of creative ritualization is based on what Letty Russell has called
"the authority of the future." She explains that phrase as follows:

In this sense, then, feminists appeal to the future as the source
of authority. They appeal to God's future action in creating

the world as a household where both humanity and nature can live in a community of responsibility and freedom, and they claim that this future is already present in the action of God through the people of Israel and through Jesus Christ. . . . Such an appeal to the future is not a flight from present reality but a commitment to contribute to the actualization of hope. (Russell 1987, 20)

Language discovered through the method of creative ritualization is shaped by hope for God's new creation "where both humanity and nature can live in a community of responsibility and freedom." Although the language of Christian worship should always be appropriate to respond and witness to the God made known in Jesus Christ, it need not always repeat past traditions. Instead, language itself becomes a means of emancipatory transformation as the Spirit "anoints to speech" and "blesses women with voice" (Chopp 1989, 53; refer also to Procter-Smith 1990, 111–115).

Marcia Falk, a Jewish feminist who has written new blessings based on traditional Jewish *berakoth*, describes the limits of seeking equivalent language for traditional terms:

The search for theological imagery is a journey whose destinations are rarely apparent at the outset. As many feminists have discovered, it is not merely a matter of changing male images to seemingly equivalent female ones: the relatively simple (though still courageous) act of "feminizing" the male God has proved, to many of us, to be inadequate and absurd. For a feminized patriarchal image is still patriarchal, though now in transvestite masquerade. The process has been instructive, however, in clarifying our theological concerns: in translating the king into a queen, for example, we realize that images of domination are not what we wish to embrace. (Falk 1987, 42)

Remembrance and translation of images developed in patriarchal religious traditions are not by themselves adequate to express the feminist hope for a just future. Falk continues:

We find instead that our search for what is authoritative leads us to explore more deeply what is just, and that the results of these explorations are not well represented by images of a monarch, either female or male. And so we find that we must create new images to convey our visions. (Falk 1987, 42)

Falk's method calls for seeking images for God that are appropriate both to the activity of God described and to the human occasion where the blessing is to be spoken. Thus (in English translation from the Hebrew):

> Blessed are you, Lord our God, king of the world,
> who brings forth bread from the earth.

becomes

> Let us bless the source of life
> that brings forth bread from the earth.
>
> (Falk, 1987, 50)

The image 'ayin (English "source," "well," or "wellspring") replaces melek ("king," "ruler"). Falk felt that the activity of "bringing forth bread" was more related to nurturing than ruling activity, and that 'ayin expressed the welling up from earth of life through God's nurturance. The method of translation might have led to the image "Ruler" or "Queen," because these images are nonmasculine ways of translating "king" (melek). However, Falk judged that these images reflect domination of some persons by others rather than just social relationships. Thus, through a method of creative ritualization, she chose the image "wellspring" as a new image for God in the prayer she was adapting.

Falk's observations ring true when I consider my own process of reflection around parental imagery for God. For many years, I avoided using gendered imagery when referring to God. Later, I noticed that it is quite possible to speak aloud of God using nongendered imagery, while privately still imagining God to be masculine. I decided to use some feminine and masculine language as a way to expand my imagination and enrich liturgical language. I began searching for feminine images appropriate to my own faith experience. "Mother" was readily available through remembrance of its use in tradition and through translation of the predominant "Father" image. But I soon realized that I needed to keep searching, even while occasionally using "Mother" as an image for God in hymns and prayers. Trying to replace the predominant "Father" image with "Mother" images reveals the inadequacy of parental images in general. Not only do parental metaphors depend on associations with very human parents; they also implicitly emphasize the childlike dimensions of faith. Such images must be complemented with images that emphasize Christian maturity and responsibility in covenant with God, to encourage Christians to grow in faith and discipleship in the world. It will take imagination, and not just repeating the past, to develop a system of metaphors diverse enough to witness to the varied dimensions of God's nature and of human experience with God. Baptismal liturgies in particular may do well to call up images emphasizing Christian maturity if baptism is to be recovered as "sacrament of Christian vocation" (Gunnemann 1985/1986, title) and not only a rite of passage to celebrate the birth of a new child.

A method of creative ritualization complements the methods of remembrance and translation by drawing on contemporary imagination and spirituality to surface ways of addressing and describing God. Women, laity, and other historically marginalized groups must be free to call upon their particular experiences and creative imaginations as daughters and sons of God in Jesus Christ as they take part in shaping worship. As Rebecca Chopp writes, this calls for "a new profusion of images, metaphors, songs, and visions" that push the limits of tradition (Chopp 1989, 84-85). Creative ritualization makes it possible to shape the language of worship contextually, developing common language appropriate for particular communities out of their life and work. For, as Marcia Falk writes, "tradition is not just what we inherit from the past; it is also what we create and pass to the future" (Falk 1987, 49). Methods of suspicion, remembrance, translation, and creative ritualization complement each other in developing a language of Christian worship that moves beyond patriarchy. This reformulated language will draw on a rich diversity of images from scripture, tradition, and contemporary experience.

We must consider the whole liturgical context of the words we shape for Christian worship. As we begin the process of seeking alternatives to the trinitarian baptismal formula, we must first consider the larger liturgical context — baptism — and its theological meaning. To that question let us now turn.

CHAPTER 5

THE MEANING OF BAPTISM

Remember and rejoice,
who, washed in floods of grace,
still bear the sign of Jesus Christ,
that time cannot erase.

In life, in death, we trust
in God's most holy name,
forever traced by water sign,
and sealed by Spirit-flame.*

My own baptism by confession of faith at age thirteen was a powerful experience. My parents asked our Methodist pastor to baptize me by immersion, so we went with Christian friends to College Avenue Baptist Church, which had a large baptismal font. I can still remember the whoosh of the water, but even more I can remember the strong sense I had of God's presence. We sang, "Where he leads me, I will follow"; and at the moment I was claimed as Christ's disciple. At the Easter vigil, the ministers of the water proclaim, "Remember your baptism and rejoice." Although many Christians cannot literally remember their baptisms, all who are baptized can rejoice in God's gracious call they received in baptism.

Because my own baptism was such a powerful experience, I have appreciated the rich imagery in scripture about baptism. Now, in the late twentieth century, many churches are recovering this rich imagery in their orders for baptism, a movement I can only applaud. The World Council of Churches document *Baptism, Eucharist, and Ministry* (BEM), highlighted five main dimensions of baptism in scripture and church tradition: dying and rising with Christ; conversion; the gift of the Spirit; incorporation into the church; and the sign of the kingdom. In exploring

---

*Words by Ruth C. Duck, copyright 1988.

the meaning of baptism, I will use these categories from BEM and interpret them drawing on the work of feminist and liberation theologians.

PARTICIPATION IN CHRIST'S DEATH AND RESURRECTION

Christians participate in the death and resurrection of Christ, thus mirroring Jesus' own baptism in "solidarity with sinners" (Matt. 3:15, Faith and Order 1982, par. 3). Christians closely identify baptism with the death of Jesus and of those who, like him, are faithful to God to the death (Luke 12:50; Mark 10:35-45; Brand 1975, 14-15). Paul, too, says that in being baptized, Christians are baptized "into the death of Jesus":

> What then are we to say? Should we continue in sin in order that grace may abound? By no means! How can we who died to sin go on living in it? Do you not know that all of us who have been baptized into Christ Jesus were baptized into his death? Therefore we have been buried with him by baptism into death, so that, just as Christ was raised from the dead by the glory of the Father, so we too might walk in newness of life. For if we have been united with him in a death like his, we will certainly be united with him in a resurrection like his.
>
> —Romans 6:1-5

Baptism represents a death to the old life estranged from God and entry to relationship with God through Christ. One's sinful self is "crucified" and "new life in the power of the Spirit" begins (Beasley-Murray 1962, 132). Rising from the water, Christians rise with Christ to live in new ways. Dying and rising with Christ involves identifying with Jesus Christ's death and resurrection, entering a new relationship with God, and turning from sin to a new way of life. Rising with Christ means being "raised here and now to a new life in the power of the resurrection of Jesus Christ" (Faith and Order 1982, par. 3). At the same time, rising with Christ is not complete in the here and now, for Christians wait in eager expectation of the full liberation of humanity and the whole creation (Rom. 8:18-25).

Immersion in and emergence from the water act out dying and rising with Christ. The ancient practice of baptizing at the center of paschal celebration also highlights the meaning of baptism as dying and rising with Christ (Schmémann 1974, 55).[1]

Sallie McFague's perspective on the death and resurrection of Jesus gives a basis for a feminist interpretation of baptism as dying and rising with Christ. Rather than interpreting the death of Jesus "as the King's sacrifice, in the mode of his Son, for the sins of the world," she calls it "a paradigm of God's ways with the world" (McFague 1987, 55). Jesus shows God's love for all people over against the hierarchies of this world, manifesting "in his own life and death that the heart of the universe is unqualified love working to befriend the needy, the outcast, the oppressed" (55).

Thus the way of the cross is the way of "radical identification with all," which is likely to bring punishment from those who reserve power for a privileged few (McFague 1987, 55). Or, as J. Russell Chadran has expressed it from a Third World perspective: "The manner in which Jesus worked out the implications of the solidarity of his baptism led him to the cross" (Chadran 1984, 117).

The appearance stories are paradigmatic of "God's permanent presence in our present," empowering life based on an understanding of "the Christian gospel as a destabilizing, inclusive, nonhierarchical vision of fulfillment for all of creation" (McFague 1987, 59, 60).

Under McFague's model, to die with Christ would be to participate with Jesus Christ in living in "radical identification with all," especially "the needy, the outcast, the oppressed" (McFague 1987, 55). To rise with Christ would be to know God as a permanent presence empowering the fulfillment of all creation.

CONVERSION: A NEW ETHICAL ORIENTATION

Second, baptism means conversion to a new way of life, to "a new ethical orientation" (Faith and Order 1982, par. 4). According

---

1. I urge the recovery of immersion as a powerful sign-act in baptism, though I do not argue that immersion is necessary for the sacrament to be valid. Kavanagh says that "baptism into Christ demands enough water to die in" (Kavanagh 1978, 179). Orthodox churches immerse infants, though among Western churches, mostly believer baptists practice immersion.

to Mark, John's baptism was a "baptism of repentance for the forgiveness of sins" (Mark 1:4). In Acts, Peter told those who were moved by his witness to the death and resurrection of Jesus the Christ: "Repent, and be baptized every one of you in the name of Jesus Christ so that your sins may be forgiven; and you will receive the gift of the Holy Spirit" (Acts 2:38). The passage from Romans quoted above continues:

> We know that our old self was crucified with him so that the body of sin might be destroyed, and we might no longer be enslaved to sin.... So you also must consider yourselves dead to sin and alive to God in Christ Jesus.
>
> —Romans 6:6, 11

Washing by water in baptism expresses God's forgiveness, which empowers human repentance and turning from sin. The washing away of sin has been emphasized as a meaning of baptism through much of Christian history. In fact, because of the idea (developed especially by Augustine) that baptism effected the washing away of original sin, at times the gift of God's forgiveness offered and received in baptism has overshadowed other meanings of baptism.

The acts of renunciation and adherence in the order for baptism also act out turning away from the ways of this world to new life in Christ (Schmémann 1974, 29).

The church has often interpreted repentance, washing, and conversion in individualistic ways, whether in terms of "salvation insurance" by pedobaptists or in terms of personal decision and confession by "believer baptists" (Brand 1975, 36). Conversion is not only a new relationship with God; it also means turning around to a "new pattern of relationship" with humanity (Farley 1975, title). This begins with participation in the life of the Christian community but is realized fully only in radical identification with all people (McFague 1987, 55). Thus conversion actually is a movement away from individualism in the sense of living only for oneself.

In baptism, God offers forgiveness, which candidates receive in faith. This does not mean that old ways will no longer attract; it does represent "a new ethical orientation" (Faith and Order 1982, par. 4). Writing from the perspective of Christian communities in Latin America, Gutiérrez says that conversion is both a break with one's former life and the beginning of a new path of discipleship.

> Conversion is not something that is done once and for all. It entails a development, even a painful one, that is not without uncertainties, doubts, and temptations to turn back on the road that has been travelled. (Gutiérrez 1984, 95)

Conversion is both the beginning of a new life in community and a process.

Ruether has provided a feminist interpretation of conversion in *Sexism and God-Talk: Toward a Feminist Theology* (1983, chap. 7), which she relates specifically to baptism in her book *Women-Church: Theology and Practice* (1985, 77, 125–130). According to Ruether, conversion is disaffiliation with realities recognized as evil, particularly patriarchal ways of thinking and acting. Baptism, then, symbolizes overcoming oppressive patterns of relationship and reclaiming "one's authentic potential for human life" in the context of a liberating community (1985, 77). This means rejecting internalized ideologies that allow persons to participate in exploiting themselves and others. For women, conversion means turning around to discover themselves as persons, "as centers of being upon which they can stand and build their own identity" (1983, 186). For men, conversion means "entering into real solidarity with women in the struggle for liberation" (1983, 190), no longer letting cultural definitions of masculine gender determine their identity. If this means losing certain privileges, it will also mean "receiving a grounded self" no longer based on the oppression of self and others (1983, 191). Baptism represents conversion from patriarchy to a new order: "Baptism signifies our disaffiliation from patriarchy and all its claims to social necessity and divine legitimacy, and our commitment to a new order" (1985, 125). Conversion is possible because of the support of a community that articulates and seeks to live out an alternative way of being in the world (1983, 184). In *The Color Purple*, Celie could refuse victimization and seek new ways to live, with Shug's support (D. Williams 1986, 231). In the same way, the church may provide the base of support for conversion, which is not a solitary process.

If conversion means turning away from victimization and awakening to new possibilities beyond cultural gender roles, it also means facing one's role in the whole patriarchal pyramid of power. For the privileged, both women and men, it means recognizing one's responsibility for structural injustice and turning toward solidarity with the poor in bonds of friendship and love (Gutiérrez 1984, 99, 104).

Conversion, then, means turning away from sinful patterns of relationship; it is "liberation into a new humanity in which barriers of division whether of sex or race or social status are transcended" (Faith and Order 1982, par. 2). From a feminist perspective, transcending divisions occurs through repatterning relationships so that all women and men turn from exploitation toward new ways based on justice and respect for the personhood of all. Through baptism, by the power of the Holy Spirit, persons and communities turn away from sin toward new patterns of relationship.

THE GIFT OF THE HOLY SPIRIT

In baptism, the Spirit is both giver and gift. The Spirit "brings the graces of God, ... gives a place for the sacraments among us, and makes them bear fruit" (Calvin Book 14, Chapter 17 [1960], 1293). Because the Spirit is at work in the church when it baptizes, baptism may be a sign and seal of grace. As David Royer writes, through the Spirit, baptism is a work of God:

> Baptism is in the Name of ... the Triune God who unites the sacramental sign with saving grace. The water itself does not save; God saves, forgives, renews, and sanctifies. The benefits of Christ are bestowed through *the action of the Holy Spirit* through the sacramental action. God gives and faith receives. (Royer 1986, 47, emphasis added)

The Spirit, giver and gift in baptism, reveals God as permanent empowering presence (suggested by McFague 1987, 59, 60). The Spirit is a gift of the risen Christ (John 20:22) and the giver of gifts for ministry (1 Cor. 12). Thus invocation of the Holy Spirit is an essential part of an order for baptism (Schmémann 1974, 48; Brand 1975, 54). The BEM document calls baptism "the Gift of the Spirit" (Faith and Order 1982, par. 5) and speaks of the Spirit as an active presence before, during, and after baptism (Faith and Order 1982, par. 5). The anointing and promise of the

Holy Spirit is given to all baptized persons: "God bestows upon all baptized persons the anointing and promise of the Holy Spirit, marks them with a seal and implants in their hearts the first installment of their inheritance as sons and daughters of God" (Faith and Order 1982, par. 5). The Spirit is an active presence in the lives of Christians, in baptism and always.

Liturgical actions in baptism that symbolize the giving of the Spirit include anointing and laying on of hands (refer to Faith and Order 1982, par. 14). Anointing represents empowerment of all the baptized for the priestly ministry of signifying God's love in the world (White 1983, 99; Wainwright 1969, 71). The laying on of hands has been described as commissioning for ministry drawing on images of military commissioning (Schmémann 1974, 126); as a blessing by the bishop (Fisher 1965, 21); or as an acted-out prayer for the baptized (Banks 1980, 83).

> Baptism is a call to ministry for all the baptized: [Baptism is] a call to share in and continue Jesus' ministry of reconciling and redemptive love. The call is addressed not only to the community as a whole but also to each member of it.... All are called to represent Christ in a real and significant way, to each other in the community, and to all others in the world. (Cardman 1984, 87)

Empowerment for ministry through the Spirit takes place in the context of the baptizing community. Ministry, like conversion, is possible through the support of the Spirit-filled community.

It is at the point of community recognition and support for ministry that a feminist perspective concerning baptism as the gift of the Spirit is necessary, for the church has not usually acted out of the belief that all baptized persons receive the anointing of the Holy Spirit. Instead, church leadership has usually been shared mainly among men, often of more privileged social status. The gifts of others are overlooked:

> The gifts [of the Spirit] that persons receive in order to contribute to the life of Christian communities are often overlooked because of prejudice stemming from racism, classism, sexism, or heterosexism. (Russell 1979, 100)

White writes, "Baptism is the foundation for justice within the church. It is the sacrament of equality" (White 1983, 96). This is expressed in Galatians 3:27, 28, a baptismal text:

As many of you as were baptized into Christ have clothed your-
selves with Christ. There is no longer Jew or Greek, there is no
longer slave or free, there is no longer male and female; for all
of you are one in Christ Jesus.

—Galatians 3:27, 28

According to the feminist interpretation of Schüssler Fiorenza,
this passage refers to egalitarian leadership styles through which
all Christians have access to positions of authority: "Within the
Christian community no structures of domination can be tolerated" (Schüssler Fiorenza 1983, 286–287). Equality goes beyond
equal worth before God to sharing the tasks of ministry, not
according to gender roles, but by the empowerment of the Spirit:

Women and men in the Christian community are not defined by
their sexual procreative capacities or by their religious, cultural
or social gender roles, but by their discipleship and empowering
with the Spirit. (Schüssler Fiorenza 1983, 212–213)

Women as well as men are charismatically gifted, and both women
and men "are prophets and leaders of worship in the community" (Schüssler Fiorenza 1983, 285). Thus, for example, to
deny women ordination is to deny their baptisms. Says White:
"Churches that refuse ordination to women, if they were consistent, would also deny them baptism" (White 1983, 99). All the
baptized, male and female, lay and ordained, share both the responsibility and the gifts of the Spirit for the ministry of the
church. If churches truly recognized that baptism is the gift of the
Spirit, they could not deny that all persons are gifted for ministry.
According to Luke's Gospel, Jesus received the empowerment of
the Spirit at his baptism and immediately began to speak in a
prophetic way "to bring good news to the poor, ... to proclaim
release to the captives, ... to let the oppressed go free ... " (Luke
4:16–21). Although the church often overlooks gifts in the community because of prejudice, God empowers the outcast to speak
prophetically:

God clearly does raise up persons from every "nation" or human
grouping and often God uses those who are outcasts to call
us back to our new focus in the gospel message of God's love.
(Russell 1979, 100)

The gift of the Spirit to baptized persons then means in part that God will empower them to proclaim "liberation into a new humanity in which barriers of division whether of sex or race or social status are transcended" (Gal. 3:27, 28; 1 Cor. 12:13) (Faith and Order 1982, par. 2). The implication of this last statement, in a feminist interpretation, may be much greater than the drafters of *Baptism, Eucharist, and Ministry* intended (cf. Faith and Order 1982, Section on Ministry, par. 18 and commentary, and par. 54).

INCORPORATION INTO THE CHURCH

Another meaning of baptism is incorporation into the church. Baptism is "the sign of the initiation by which we are received into the society of the church" (Calvin Book 15, Chapter 1 [1960], 1303). Baptism is an act of Christ in the church (Stookey 1982, title) by which the church is constituted, through the action of the Holy Spirit.

Incorporation into the church, as an aspect of the meaning of baptism, points to the context of baptism and of Christian identity in the Christian community. Baptism is normally administered by a representative of the church in the context of Christian worship. It is not a private act between God and an individual and is never self-administered (Barth 1969, 49). Baptism is sign and seal of relationship with God in the covenant community. "It is from within the community of the covenant that we respond to God" (Stookey 1982, 31), and covenant with God implies covenant among all in the community of faith. In baptismal liturgies from the time of Justin Martyr up to the present, the newly baptized have often been welcomed and introduced to the community (Searle 1980, 127). Indeed, Schmémann calls the procession of the newly baptized to join the rest of the faithful in the Eucharist an "essential part of the baptismal liturgy" (Schmémann 1974, 111).

Local communities provide the context for the faith and Christian life of the baptized; but baptism as a sign of the corporate nature of Christian faith goes beyond local communities, for baptism is a sign of Christian unity throughout the world. Those who are united with Christ through participation in the death and resurrection of Christ are thereby united with one another. All who belong to Jesus Christ also belong to one another:

> For just as the body is one and has many members, and all
> the members of the body, though many, are one body, so it is
> with Christ. For in the one Spirit we were all baptized into one
> body — Jews or Greeks, slaves or free — and we were all made
> to drink of one Spirit.
>
> —1 Corinthians 12:12–13

This understanding of the unity of all baptized Christians has
been important to the ecumenical movements of the twentieth
century (Faith and Order 1982, par. 6; Consultation on Church
Union 1984, 25). *The COCU Consensus* states it this way:

> Baptism effects or signifies the union of the baptized with
> Christ, and in Christ, with all members of his body, the universal
> church. Thus our baptism is a basic bond of unity. (Consultation
> on Church Union 1984, 25)

Union with Jesus Christ in baptism entails incorporation into
the universal church, Christ's body. In this sense, the church is
one, despite its structural divisions and diversity in theology and
practice.

Nevertheless, Christian communities have often compromised the "basic bond of unity" when they fail to accept one
another's theology and practice of baptism:

> The inability of the churches mutually to recognize their various
> practices of baptisms as sharing in one baptism, and their actual
> dividedness in spite of mutual baptismal recognition have given
> dramatic visibility to the broken witness of the church. (Faith
> and Order 1982, par. 6, commentary)

Because different Christian communities differ about what constitutes the church and baptism, baptism has not provided a
simple means of church unity. What Wainwright wrote in 1969
is just as true today: "There has been no simple, unclouded relation between the 'one baptism' and the 'one Church' as long
as there has been disunity among Christians" (Wainwright 1969,
69–70). To say that Christian unity is based on common baptism
into Christ is both a theological claim that unity already exists
and also a statement of hope that a fuller unity will be possible
in the future.

The reality of sexism, racism, and classism in the churches clouds the relation between one baptism and one church. The commentary in *Baptism, Eucharist, and Ministry* says:

> The readiness of the churches in some places and times to allow differences of sex, race, or social status to divide the body of Christ has further called into question genuine baptismal unity of the Christian community (Gal. 3:27–28) and has seriously compromised its witness. (Faith and Order 1982, par. 6, commentary)

This is a strong statement of the way racism, sexism, and classism cause division. However, this statement is compromised by the lack of a similarly strong stand on the ordination of women, in the Ministry section that says that differences on the issue "must not be regarded as a substantive hindrance for further efforts toward mutual recognition" (Faith and Order 1982, Section on Ministry, par. 54). A report from the Sheffield Commission on the Community of Women and Men in the Church of the World Council of Churches expressed hope for a new community in which all persons would be respected, a community without domination and subordination (World Council of Churches Community of Women and Men in the Church 1983, 109). Such a community would embody baptismal unity rather than divisions based on sex, race, social status, age, or physical ability.

If church union is to be more than an agreement on paper signed by members of dominant groups, truly reconciling Christians of the uniting denominations, sexism in the church must be addressed. A Consultation on Church Union (COCU) "alert" warned that increasing numbers of women and men can no longer accept the sexism of Christian language and leadership styles. By ignoring this challenge, the alert warned, the Consultation may achieve church union while alienating so many of its members in a few years that

> unity has become a gentlemen's agreement within the dominant group, rather than an agreement of partners who have struggled together toward true mutuality in every expression of their personal and institutional lives. (COCU 1980, 55–56)

As this statement warns, seeking Christian unity based on common baptism while failing to address the masculine bias in

Christian liturgy endangers the future of unity. For, as Janet Cawley, a pastor in the United Church of Canada, argues in a statement about the baptismal formula, true "unity cannot be founded on injustice":

> If a strong consensus develops that the trinitarian formula does indeed represent a sexist understanding of God, then the United Church is likely to declare that it cannot be required, even if the ecumenical cost is painful. We have never believed that the unity of the churches can be founded on injustice. (Cawley 1988, 74)

When patriarchal values determine the leadership styles and liturgy of the church, this undermines baptismal unity. Such is the witness of feminist Christians.

THE SIGN OF THE NEW AGE[2]

The BEM document calls baptism "the sign of the kingdom" and says, "Baptism initiates the reality of the new life given in the midst of the present world" (Faith and Order 1982, par. 7). God calls the church, in the here and now, to live out a new pattern of relationships. Through baptism, persons become a part of the Christian community called and commissioned to live in newness of life (Rom. 6:4), and to be a sign of joy, love, peace, and justice among humanity. Beasley-Murray says, "Baptism is ... an entry into the eschatological order of the new creation" (Beasley-Murray 1962, 292). Life is now to be lived in a new pattern of relationships with a new hope: "The baptized lived in hope of the new creation and of the time when God will be all in all" (Chadran 1984, 112).

The community of the baptized live in the time between the resurrection of Jesus Christ and God's promised future (Barth *CD* IV/1, 725–739). Christian hope is not idle, but active; for to be baptized is to be counted among those who in the here and now seek to live out God's intention for humanity. Indeed, the baptized are the "avant-garde of the new creation under the conditions of the old world and history" (Schüssler Fiorenza 1983, 184). In

---

2. "Kingdom" has masculine, hierarchical, and geographical connotations. Although no one term can replicate other rich associations of the word, "new age" is an appropriate substitute in a discussion of baptism as a sign of the kingdom. I do not intend association with the human potentialist New Age movement.

the life of the community, the baptized experience a foretaste of God's new age. The Christian community is called to embody God's intention for life in the midst of human history with its possibilities and limits.

Baptism should be a one-time event in a Christian's life, but conversion is a process never finally complete:

> This revolutionary transformation [conversion] cannot be done once and for all.... To be human is to be in a state of process, to change and to die.... Each new achievement of livable, humane balances will be different, based on new technologies, belonging to a new moment in time and place. It is a historical project that has to be undertaken again and again in changing circumstances. (Ruether 1983, 255)

The community of the baptized points to and embodies God's new age in ever-changing contexts.

Baptism as participation in the new age has been symbolized in many ways in baptismal liturgies; for example, by taking off old clothes and putting on a white robe. When, at the conclusion of the rite, the newly baptized and the rest of the Christian community share the meal of thanksgiving, the life of the new age is initiated (Schmémann 1974, 115–121); Jesus' table sharing with all, especially the outcast, is remembered. The church anticipates the day when a reconciled humanity will share at table.

Ecumenism and feminism share the common goal of reconciling all humanity in an inclusive community. Feminists, however, seek to ensure that the reconciled community would be "a community of equals, signed with a common discipleship" (Cardman 1984, 87). This would include recognizing the call of each and all to shared ministry, ordered through mutuality and not domination and subordination. Most Christian feminists do not, however, seek universal conversion to Christian faith, as implied by BEM (Faith and Order 1982, par. 7; cf. Ruether 1983, 250).

Further, feminists such as Ruether have argued that Christian hope is not a flight from history, either in life beyond death or in a future age of perfection on earth. According to Ruether, Christian hope should be sought "within the mortal limits of covenantal existence":

> By "turning around" we discover the blessedness and holy being within the mortal limits of covenantal existence. This is the

Shalom of God that remains the real connecting point of all our existence, even when we forget and violate it. Redemptive hope is the constant recovery of that Shalom of God/ess that holds us all together, as the operating principle of our collective lives. It is the nexus of authentic creational life that has to be reincarnated in social relationships again and again in new ways and new contexts by each generation. (Ruether 1983, 256)

A feminist interpretation of the new age would differ from BEM to the extent that "the life of the world to come" (Faith and Order 1982, par. 7) is understood in BEM primarily to refer to life beyond history. Although not necessarily denying the possibility of life beyond death, feminist interpretations emphasize hope directed at renewed life in this world.

Baptism, then, is a sign of the new age God seeks to bring to being among humanity. BEM states: "Through the gifts of faith, hope, and love, baptism has a dynamic which embraces the whole of life, [and] extends to all nations" (Faith and Order 1982, par. 7). As a sign of the new age, baptism points to the hope that all peoples may live in peace and justice. Through baptism, Christians become a part of the community that seeks in the here and now — under the conditions of human life with its limits and possibilities — to live out God's intention for humanity.

THE MEANING AND IMPORTANCE OF BAPTISM

Baptism is a central and formative event in the life of the church and of individual Christians. Dying to their old lives of separateness and rising to a new life in relationship with God and humanity, the baptized turn around to a new ethical orientation. They share in common life and ministry, through the power of the Spirit. The promise of baptism is often undermined as Christians succumb to the old ways of the world, rather than embrace new life in Christ. But the liturgy of baptism, and particularly the pivotal words spoken during the administration of water, must express the hope of new life in Jesus Christ and not the old ways of patriarchy. Baptism is so important to Christian liturgy and life that the words we use in baptism should grow out of our deepest and best theological reflection.

CHAPTER 6

THE HISTORY OF THE BAPTISMAL FORMULA

Only after eight centuries of the Christian Era was the baptismal formula "in the name of the Father and of the Son and of the Holy Spirit" used in Christian baptisms throughout the world. Almost as many centuries passed again before the Western church explicitly required the formula. The frequent assumption that all churches have used the present trinitarian formula from the beginning is not based in fact. Let us then trace the historical evidence about the words Christians have spoken during the administration of water.

BAPTISMAL FORMULAS IN THE NEW TESTAMENT

The New Testament gives few hints about the words used during Christian baptisms in the first century. However, I will consider three forms that scholars have identified as "baptismal formulas."[1] Of course, when speaking of the New Testament period, "baptismal formula" refers to a grouping of words characteristically used at baptism, not certain inalterable words that make baptism effective. In fact, only two of the three "formulas" occur more than once in the New Testament, and then they appear in varied forms. Of the three, the formula occurring most frequently in the New Testament occurs in Acts 2:38:

> "Repent, and be baptized every one of you in the name of Jesus Christ...."

---

1. Cullmann also believes that the Ethiopian eunuch's question "[See, here is water!] *What is to prevent my being baptized?*" represents a liturgical formula asking whether anyone knew of anything to hinder a person from being baptized (Cullmann 1950, 71–80). Other New Testament passages have been called baptismal professions, hymns, or formulas (for example, Rom. 10:9–10; Eph. 4:4–6; 2 Tim. 2:8–13; refer to Deiss 1979, 46–49).

Another formula appears three or four times and occurs in its fullest form in Galatians 3:26-28:

> (26) For in Christ Jesus you are all children of God through faith. (27) As many of you as were baptized into Christ have clothed yourselves with Christ. (28) There is no longer Jew or Greek, there is no longer slave or free, there is no longer male and female; for all of you are one in Christ Jesus.

(Note that verse 27 may also be an example of the formula "baptizing into [the name of Jesus] Christ.") The formula used by most churches today appears only in Matthew 28:19-20:

> Go therefore and make disciples of all nations, *baptizing them in the name of the Father and of the Son and of the Holy Spirit,* and teaching them to obey everything that I have commanded you. And remember, I am with you always, to the end of the age. (emphasis added)

The different formulas may represent different stages of development, or they may have been used in different regions. We can only guess whether they are theological descriptions of what happened or actual liturgical texts. Only the repeated use of these phrases (either in or beyond the New Testament) justifies the term "formula." Words used during baptism apparently varied from place to place; uniform practice had not yet emerged.

Baptism in the Name of Jesus

Many commentators hold that the oldest baptismal formulas referred only to Jesus Christ, in varying ways (Conzelmann 1969, 49). In Acts, baptisms are "in the name of Jesus Christ" (2:38, 10:48); or "in the name of the Lord Jesus" (8:16, 19:5). Paul asks, "Do you not know that all of us who have been *baptized into Christ Jesus* were baptized into his death?" (Romans 6:3, emphasis added). Paul also says, "But you were washed, you were sanctified, you were justified in the name of the Lord Jesus Christ and in the Spirit of our God" (1 Cor. 6:11b).

Scholars have argued that the form "in the name of Jesus Christ" was adequate as long as those being baptized were of Jewish heritage (Schaberg 1982, 10-11, reviewing literature on the subject). Church leaders would have assumed that Jews were monotheistic, and would ask them only to confess Jesus as Christ. A triadic formula may have been developed for use by Gentile converts to Christianity (Schaberg 1982, 10, citing G. F. Moore and Hans Konsmala).

Galatians 3:28 and Related Passages

Galatians 3:26-28 probably paraphrases or quotes a baptismal formula known to Paul and used in early Christian communities (Schüssler Fiorenza 1983, 205-241; Bouttier 1976, 1-19; Swidler 1979, 322-323). Because Paul switches from first person plural in verse 25 to second person address in verse 26, it appears that he has inserted verses 26-28 as a well-known expression that supports what he has just said. Neither baptism, gender, nor slavery has been the subject up to this point. The concept "slavery" appears in chapters 4 and 5, but it is used analogically; master-slave relationships as such are not discussed. Variations on the "formula" appear in 1 Corinthians 12:13 and Colossians 3:10-11, giving further support to the idea that Paul is quoting a liturgical phrase. Although these last two passages lack the couplet "male and female," they are otherwise similar in structure and content. Further, Swidler reports that a number of manuscripts for Colossians 3:11 do include "male and female" at the head of the list (Swidler 1979, 323). Schüssler Fiorenza believes that 1 Corinthians 7, which discusses relationships between men and women, slaves and masters, and Jews and non-Jews, elaborates on the baptismal formula to which Galatians 3:26-28 and 1 Corinthians 12:13 allude (Schüssler Fiorenza 1983, 220-226). In parts of 1 Corinthians, however, Paul appears to modify the theology and practice represented by the formula in Galatians 3:26-28 and 1 Corinthians 12:13, out of concern for decency and order; for example, he limits the participation of married women in worship (233).

Schüssler Fiorenza conjectures that the baptismal words that Paul knew and paraphrased were something like the following:

i. 3:26a   For you are all children of God
ii. 3:27a   For as many as were baptized into Christ
   b   have put on Christ

iii. 3:28a There is neither Jew nor Greek
    b   There is neither slave nor free
    c   There is no male and female
iv. 3:28d For you are all one

(Schüssler Fiorenza 1983, 208)

Although this reconstruction of the formula is plausible, the actual words probably varied from place to place.

As Schüssler Fiorenza argues, the formula in Galatians 3:28 should not be interpreted to refer only to the future age. It does not speak only of equal access to salvation. Gnostic androgyny denying biological distinctions is certainly not implied. The words of the formula do imply common sharing in grace and a common destiny as Christians, but they also speak of relationships within the community. As a part of the baptismal liturgy, the words affirm that those who have formerly been separated by social barriers are reconciled in Christ (Bouttier 1976, 10). They signal a radical equality and sharing of leadership between men and women, slaves and free persons, and people of diverse religious or cultural backgrounds. Christian masters were expected to free their slaves, and the church was expected to buy the freedom of slaves serving non-Christian masters (Schüssler Fiorenza 1983, 209, 214–215). Thus these words, used in baptism, expressed and shaped the eschatological Christian community marked by freedom, reconciliation, and egalitarian leadership styles.

Schüssler Fiorenza has documented the process through which the Christian community first modified, then abandoned, the hope for egalitarian community expressed by Galatians 3:28 and related passages (Schüssler Fiorenza 1983, 204–284). This formula may have been used mainly in the Hellenistic Christian communities with whom Paul ministered. In any case, patriarchalized churches would hardly have continued using this egalitarian formula in baptismal liturgies. On the other hand, churches that are moving past patriarchy might well use words like Galatians 3:26–28 at some point in the baptismal liturgy, perhaps as part of an alternative trinitarian formula.

Baptism in the Name of the Father, the Son, and the Holy Spirit

In scripture, baptism "in the name of the Father and of the Son and of the Holy Spirit" appears only in Matthew 28:19. This verse, quoted above, appears in the context of Jesus' final resurrection appearance in Matthew, in which he commissions the eleven to "go and make disciples of all nations."

A word about the dating and provenance of the Gospel is in order. The Gospel is commonly dated around 80-90 C.E., though some commentators argue for an earlier or a later date (Meier and Brown 1983, 15). Most scholars place its origin in Syria (Goulder 1974, 142; Brown 1984, 128; Kingsbury 1985, 613). Some, but not all, commentators specify Antioch of Syria (Kingsbury 1985, 613; Meier and Brown 1983, 22).

Eduard Schweizer holds that the original form of Matthew 28:19b said "baptizing them in *my* name" rather than "in the name of the Father and of the Son and of the Holy Spirit" (Schweizer 1975, 530). The main early evidence to support this theory comes from Eusebius, the church historian (c. 262-339 C.E.), who quoted Matthew 28:19 sixteen times with "in my name" rather than the triadic form (Schaberg 1982, 27). According to this theory, the churches edited all manuscripts either to reflect baptismal practice or to support orthodox trinitarian solutions achieved after Eusebius wrote. No New Testament manuscript evidence supports the idea (27). However, H. Benedict Green, who believes the original form was "in my name," explains the lack of manuscript evidence by arguing that it was changed very early before many manuscripts traveled outside Syria (Green 1975, 230-231). Green speculates that because Eusebius lived in Caesarea not far from the area where the Gospel probably originated, he may have known an early manuscript in which Matthew 28:19 said only "in my name."

Some scholars hold that the phrase "in the name of the Father and of the Son and of the Holy Spirit" reflects Matthew's own writing or editing. For example, Patte argues that through the triadic phrase, Matthew was recalling the baptism of Jesus, when "the Father" called Jesus "Beloved Son" and the Spirit descended (Patte 1987, 401).

Other biblical scholars hold that the phrase "in the name of the Father and of the Son and of the Holy Spirit" reflects the baptismal practice in Matthew's community (Schaberg 1982, 29). Among them are Jane Schaberg, who believes that the triadic phrase in Matthew 28:19b was drawn by the evangelist from contemporary liturgical sources, which in turn drew on Jewish apocalyptic and midrash.[2] In her opinion, the words have a particular relationship to Daniel 7:9-14:

> As I watched in the night visions,
> I saw one like a human being
>   coming with the clouds of heaven.
> And he came to the Ancient One
> and was presented before him.
> To him was given dominion and glory and kingship,
> that all peoples, nations, and languages
>   should serve him.
> His dominion is an everlasting dominion
>   that shall not pass away,
> and his kingship is one
>   that shall never be destroyed.
>
> —Daniel 7:13–14

The human being, in midrash on this passage, receives access to the heavenly court. The triad in this passage is "Ancient One," "One like a human being," and the angelic host mentioned in Daniel 7:10. Schaberg presents evidence that such a triad is common in apocalyptic literature, including apocalyptic midrash on scriptures such as Daniel 7; and over time, the phrase "spirits" or "the Spirit" tends to be interchangeable with "angelic hosts." The triad "Father [or God], Son [or Jesus Christ, or Lamb], and angels" is found in several New Testament passages (Mark 8:38, Rev. 1:1-2; 1 Tim. 5:21; Matt. 24:36). In his *First Apology*, Justin Martyr (not cited by Schaberg) follows a similar pattern, here in the form of a quarternity:

> Both him [the true God, who is the Father of justice and charity]
> and the son who came forth from him and taught us these things,
> and the host of other good angels who follow and are made like

---

2. Schaberg's thesis has met with mixed reviews; refer to Viviano 1984, Burnett 1984, and Evans 1985.

to him, and the prophetic Spirit, we worship and adore. (quoted in Lohse 1966, 43)

Other common features between Daniel 7 and Matthew 28 are the giving of *exousia* (authority, dominion) to the human being; the universal scope of that dominion ("all nations"); and its extension in time. Matthew ends with the words translated "the end of the age" (28:20); Daniel ends similarly with "the end of the days" (12:13). Matthew's depiction of the exalted Christ appearing on the mountain may represent the appearance of the throne of God on earth (Dan. 7:9). In Matthew 28:19, then, "the Father, ... the Son, and ... the Holy Spirit" may reflect baptismal practice influenced by Jewish apocalyptic, and especially the book of Daniel.

Some scholars hold that the original form of Matthew 28:19b was "baptize in my name." Others hold that it was a Matthean composition reflecting his theology and purposes. Still others hold that the phrase (included in the original edition of the Gospel of Matthew) comes from the baptismal practice of the early church. These are the three main positions held by biblical scholars who apply historical-critical method in discussing the source of the triadic phrase in Matthew 28:19b. These scholars do not argue that the words "in the name of the Father and of the Son and of the Holy Spirit" came from Jesus. Persons who accept historical-critical scripture scholarship would find it difficult to support the idea that the trinitarian baptismal formula must be used because it represents the words of Jesus.

Even if Matthew 28:19b originally read "in the name of the Father and of the Son and of the Holy Spirit," it is "triadic," not "trinitarian," if by "trinitarian" we mean a fully developed trinitarian theology. Further, we cannot assume that the phrase was actually spoken in baptismal liturgies, or that it represented set, inalterable usage at this stage (Schaberg 1982, 16–23).

Clearly, the idea that we must baptize with the formula "in the name of the Father and of the Son and of the Holy Spirit" because of its presence in Matthew 28:19b is not adequately supported by the evidence.

THE HISTORY OF GROWING USE OF THE TRIADIC FORMULA

An early nonscriptural reference to Christian baptismal practice in the West appears in the *First Apology* of Justin Martyr, writing in Rome around 150 C.E. Justin reports a washing in water "in the name of God the Father and Master of all, and of our Savior Jesus Christ, and of the Holy Spirit":

> Those who are persuaded that and believe that the things we teach are true, and promise that they can live accordingly, are instructed to pray and beseech God with fasting for the remission of their past sins, while we pray and fast along with them. Then they are brought by us where there is water, and are reborn by the same manner of rebirth by which we ourselves were reborn; for they are then washing in the water in the name of God the Father and Master of all, and of our Savior Jesus Christ, and of the Holy Spirit. (*First Apology* in Richardson et al. 1970, 282)

If Justin means that the presider speaks the trinitarian formula as such (perhaps doubtful in light of later evidence), it may be in adapted form. Apparently, Justin considers naming God "Father and Master" to be a circumlocution rather than a pronouncement of the divine name. For, a bit later in the passage, he says:

> So that we should not remain children of necessity and ignorance, but . . . of free choice and knowledge, and obtain remission of the sins we have already committed, there is named at the water, over him who has chosen to be born again and repented of all his sinful acts, the name of God the Master and Father of all. Those who lead to the washing the one who is to be washed call on [God by] this term only. For no one may give a proper name to the ineffable God, and if anyone should dare to say there is one, he is hopelessly insane. (*First Apology* in Richardson et al. 1970, 282–328)

Richardson and his colleagues say that Justin here was condemning the use of the divine name ("Yahweh") of Hebrew scripture as a magical intonation — which use Jews would have also condemned (283). In the *First Apology*, Justin also says: "and after we have washed him that is persuaded and *declares his consent*" (Holeton 1988, 70; emphasis added by Holeton). Holeton suggests that this statement means that the presider questioned candidates about their faith, without using a declarative formula (70). This would mean that Justin's testimony agrees with that of Hippolytus, to which I now turn.

The *Apostolic Tradition*, attributed to Hippolytus, was written in Rome about sixty-five years after Justin wrote the *First Apology* (Whitaker 1965b, 1). It provides a more detailed account of Christian baptismal rites. By this account, the following dialogue took place between candidates for baptism, while standing in the water, and those who administered the rite:

> — Do you believe in God the Father almighty?
> — I believe.
> — Do you believe in Christ Jesus, Son of God born by the Holy Spirit of the Virgin Mary, who was crucified under Pontius Pilate, who died, was raised on the third day, living from among the dead, who ascended to the heavens, who sits at the right hand of the Father, who will come to judge the living and the dead?
> — I believe.
> — Do you believe in the Holy Spirit,
>   in the holy Church,
>   in the resurrection of the flesh?
> — I believe. (Deiss 1979, 141–142, rubrics omitted)

Each time, after answering "I believe," the candidate was immersed in the water. No other words accompany the administration of water. Similar accounts with variations in wording are found in Ambrose's account of baptism, in the sixth century *Gelasian Sacramentary*, and in the *Stowe Missal*, a Gallican document dated around 800 C.E. (Whitaker 1965b, 1, 7). Further, comments about baptism that assume threefold immersion and questioning (with no mention of a declarative formula) appear in the canons of the Council of Carthage, in Tertullian's writings, and in other documents of the Western church (Whitaker 1965b, 3). According to Whitaker, in no Western sources until 667 C.E. is there evidence for the liturgical use of the actual words "I baptize you in the name of the Father and of the Son and of the Holy Spirit" (Whitaker 1965b, 4). Yarnold concludes, after reviewing the evidence from Hippolytus and Tertullian: "Evidently the early Church did not believe that fidelity to Mt. 28:19 required the minister to quote Christ's words as we do today at the moment of baptism" (Yarnold 1971, 27).

Ambrose's baptismal instructions support Yarnold's contention. Although Ambrose says, "We must baptize in the name of the Father and of the Son and of the Holy Spirit," he applies this to the invocation over the water and reports only a three-fold questioning and immersion at the point of actual baptism (Yarnold 1971, 114, 117). Yarnold's contention also finds support in the *Tractatus de Baptismo* ascribed to Maximus of Turin, who reports a threefold questioning and immersion similar to that in Hippolytus, and then says, "This we did in accordance with the command of our Lord Jesus Christ, who gave commandment saying: 'Go and baptize all nations in the name of the Father and of the Son and of the Holy Ghost'" (Whitaker 1965b, 5).

In surviving Western church orders, the form of the interrogations was consistently like that found in the *Apostolic Tradition*. A separate question was always asked for each person of the Trinity, with exact wording varying considerably within and among regions (Fisher 1965, 16, 32, 50, 97).

Geographical Spreading

It is likely that Syrian churches were the first to baptize with a declarative trinitarian formula. The Gospel of Matthew and the *Didache*, the earliest sources that speak of baptizing "in the name of the Father and of the Son and of the Holy Spirit," do not specify whether these words were actually spoken in baptism. However, both documents probably were written in Syria, perhaps Antioch, in the second half of the first century. (The dating and source of Matthew was documented above; refer to Cross and Livingston 1983, 401; Schweizer 1975, 17; and Deiss 1979, 73, for scholars' views on the dating and source of the *Didache*.) This area later provides us with the first clear evidence that the words were actually spoken in liturgy, as we shall see. The account of baptism in the *Didache* begins as follows:

> Now about baptism: this is how to baptize. Give instruction on all these points, and then baptize in running water in the name of the Father and of the Son and of the Holy Spirit. (*Didache* 7:1; in Richardson et al. 1970, 174; quotation marks supplied

by Richardson et al. may be misleading and have been omitted here.)

The author states a preference for running water, or at least for cold water, but adds, "If you have neither, then pour water on the head three times in the name of the Father and of the Son and of the Holy Spirit" (*Didache* 7:3; in Richardson et al. 1970, 174). Later the document says, "You must not let anyone eat or drink of your Eucharist except those baptized in the Lord's name" (Richardson et al. 1970, 175). Thus, the *Didache* may document baptizing both "in the name of the Lord" and "in the name of the Father and of the Son and of the Holy Spirit." It is uncertain whether this represents two layers of liturgical tradition or whether both passages refer to the same act and not to specific liturgical words.

Many documents originating in Syria speak of baptizing in the name of the Father and the Son and the Holy Spirit without stating that the formula was actually spoken (Whitaker 1965b, 5). The *Testament of our Lord* (a late fifth-century Syrian document) reports a threefold questioning and immersion apparently without use of the trinitarian formula (Whitaker 1965b, 1), as does the baptismal catechesis of Cyril of Jerusalem, written around 348 C.E. (Yarnold 1971, 76). However, some Syrian literature specifically mentions use of one baptismal formula or another:

> The *Acts of Xanthippe and Polyxena*, which was written in the middle of the third century, contains the passage: "And Paul said, 'We baptize thee in the name of the Father and of the Son and of the Holy Spirit.'" Similarly, in the *Acts of Paul and Thecla*, written in the middle of the second century, Thecla is represented as baptizing herself and saying, "In the name of Jesus Christ do I baptize myself for the last day." (Whitaker 1965b, 5–6)

Whitaker believes that when Syrian documents speak of baptizing "in the name of," the formula is not a theological summary, but a spoken liturgical word (Whitaker 1965b, 5–6). Chrysostom, probably speaking shortly before 397 C.E. in Antioch (Yarnold 1971, 155–156), provides more specific evidence. He says the bishop pronounces the words "N. is baptized in the name of the Father and of the Son and of the Holy Spirit," plunging the candidate's head in the water three times (Yarnold 1971, 168).

Theodore of Mopsuestia, probably speaking between 383 and 392 C.E. in Antioch, reports the same practice and uses it in his homily as a basis for consideration of trinitarian doctrine (Yarnold 1971, 200).

Thus, at least by the third century, some Syrian baptismal liturgies included the triadic baptismal formula. By the late fourth century, the formula may have been used in most Syrian baptismal liturgies, at least in Antioch (given the evidence from Chrysostom and Theodore).

Whitaker believes that what he calls "the Syrian formula" traveled to the West by way of Alexandria (Whitaker 1965b, 11). Third- and fourth-century sources from Alexandria attest to the use of the interrogatory formula (Whitaker 1965b, 7). The *Canons of Hippolytus*, a fourth-century Egyptian adaptation of the *Apostolic Tradition*, adapts the primitive text by instructing the officiant to say "I baptize you in the name of the Father and of the Son and of the Holy Spirit" after each interrogation and immersion (Whitaker 1965b, 3). Use of the formula became common there sometime between the late fourth century and the late fifth century (Whitaker 1965b, 11).

The next evidence for liturgical use of the triadic formula in baptism comes from Spain, by the year 650 C.E. in Toledo at the latest, and perhaps as early as the year 538 C.E. (Whitaker 1965b, 10). It appears in Spanish and Gallican liturgical books by the year 700 C.E. (Whitaker 1965b, 9). However, as noted above, one Gallican liturgical book included a threefold interrogation without the formula as late as 800.

Whitaker says a letter of Pope Gregory II to Boniface in the year 726 contains the first evidence for the liturgical use of the formula in Rome. The letter makes it seem that the formula has been adopted at Rome rather recently (Whitaker 1965b, 9). The formula only began to appear in liturgical books with the *Gellone*, a Frankish-Roman hybrid, and the supplement to the Gregorian sacramentary known as the *Hadrianum*, which comes from Frankish sources. From that time, use of the triadic formula at baptism became more and more prevalent in Western churches.

According to Dix and Wainwright, in the ninth century, Pope Nicholas I accepted baptisms that were administered "in the name of Jesus" or "in the name of the Holy Trinity" (Wainwright 1969, 100; Dix 1982, 275, n. 3). Peter Lombard, the twelfth-century theologian, wrote in his *Sentences* that "baptism in the name of Christ" should be accepted, provided that no denial of "the mystery of the Trinity" was intended (Lombard, excerpted in Rogers 1976, 89). Quoting Ambrose in support, he says:

> From the above you have understood clearly that baptism can be administered in the name of Christ; whence it seems no less to be implied that true baptism can be administered in the name of the Father alone, or of the Holy Spirit alone, provided he who baptizes holds the faith of the Trinity, which Trinity is signified by any one of these names. (Lombard, excerpted in Rogers 1976, 90–91)

Thomas Aquinas, like Lombard, quoted Ambrose and held that baptism in the name of Christ is acceptable, because "in the name of Christ the whole Trinity is implied and therefore the form which Christ handed down in the gospel . . . would at least be preserved with implicit integrity" (Aquinas *Summa Theologica*, iii/66/6 [1975], 29). However, Aquinas also held the trinitarian formula to be the normative, if not exclusive, form of baptism. By this time, the scholastic definition of sacraments centered on the form (characteristic words) and the matter (physical element). This definition shaped the teaching of the Council of Florence (1439) on baptism: "The matter of [baptism] is true and natural water. . . . The form is 'I baptize you in the name of the Father and of the Son and of the Holy Spirit'" ([Catholic Church] 1955, 269).

Unlike the Council of Florence, the Council of Trent did not provide a positive definition of baptism, but Canon 690 says: "If anyone says that baptism, even that given by heretics in the name of the Father, and of the Son, and of the Holy Spirit, with the intention of doing what the church does is not true baptism: let him be anathema" ([Catholic Church] 1955, 270). So far as I have been able to determine, neither Council specifically discussed "baptism in the name of Jesus" or "of Christ." It appears that in the approximately two centuries between the writing of Aquinas's *Summa Theologica* and the Council of Florence, baptism in the name of the Father, and of the Son, and of the Holy Spirit had become normative and universal in the Western church.

The emphasis in scholastic theology on these words as the form of baptism may well have contributed to this shift.

Why the Declarative Formula Came to Be Used

What was the reason for the change from threefold questioning and immersion to the use of a declarative formula, especially "I baptize you [you are baptized] in the name of the Father and of the Son and of the Holy Spirit"? Certainly, as Whitaker suggests, this form would have been more fitting for infant baptism (Whitaker 1965b, 12; refer also to Wainwright 1969, 13). However, the baptismal catecheses of Theodore and Chrysostom, among the first clear evidence for the liturgical use of the formula, assume adult baptism as the norm. Whitaker also notes that another clear piece of evidence shows the formula being used with conditional baptism (Whitaker 1965b, 12). Some may have considered the declarative form ("If you have not already been baptized, I baptize you") to be better suited to conditional baptisms than threefold questioning.

It is likely that the trinitarian controversies influenced the spread of the trinitarian baptismal formula, just as it influenced increasing prayer to God as Father, Son, and Holy Spirit. Although I cannot establish a causal connection, the formula appears to have spread into new areas as they became embroiled in christological or Arian controversies. Although Basil assumes use of the formula, he may have influenced its growing use throughout Syria and Asia Minor (refer to Jungmann 1959, 193–194; and Kelly 1960, 45). The use of the formula in Alexandria is documented around the fifth century, when that city was embroiled in the Arian and *Theotokos* disputes. It appeared in Spain during the sixth and seventh centuries, when orthodox Catholics were struggling with their Arian Teuton rulers for control of the country. A national council at Toledo in 583 anathematized those who would not say the doxology *Gloria et honor Patri et Filio et Spiritu Sancto*, because Arians held that doxologies spoken only "through Jesus Christ" supported their subordinationist beliefs (Jungmann 1962, 27). Another council in Toledo in 589 established the use of the Nicene-Chalcedonian creed in the Mass (Jungmann 1962, 21). Jungmann has documented other references to God as Father, Son, and Spirit that entered the Spanish liturgy in the sixth and seventh centuries (Jungmann 1962, 15–32). The first references to liturgical use of the trinitarian formula in baptism also appear in the sixth and seventh centuries. Gaul, the next place where such references appear, was also ruled by Arians during the sixth and seventh centuries, though for a shorter time than in Spain, and with less bitter controversy (Jungmann 1962, 19).

Rome, which was never much embroiled in Arian controversies, only introduced use of the trinitarian formula in baptism in the eighth century. Jungmann writes: "Outside the Spanish-Gallic sphere, that is in the realm of the Roman Church, almost all signs are lacking of the devotional attitude having been forged in the heat of creedal wars" (Jungmann 1962, 31). The trinitarian formula may have been used liturgically in baptism as early as the late first or early second century in Syria. Then, creedal wars may have accelerated its spread to other parts of the East, including Alexandria, and to Spain and Gaul.

The Donatist controversy may also have influenced increasing use of the trinitarian formula in baptism. Kelly reports that Optatus argued against the Donatists that "baptism is a gift of God, not any human minister" so that "while the minister may be changed the trinitarian formula must be inviolate"; Basil made similar arguments (Kelly 1960, 424–425). As Schüssler Fiorenza has noted, when church leaders prohibit or condemn a practice, it most surely is occurring or otherwise prohibition would not be needed (Schüssler Fiorenza 1983, 30). Thus, we can guess that some may not have been using the trinitarian formula in the way Optatus thought they should. Through the influence of those opposing the Donatists, its use may have become more standard.

Historically, the liturgical use of the trinitarian formula in baptism may have grown partly out of creedal controversies and other factors such as the increase in infant or conditional baptisms. Like the use of masculine and paternal imagery for God in general, the use of the formula developed due to historical factors, rather than by Jesus' command or other theological necessity. Still, there is good theological reason to baptize in the name of the triune God and not only "in the name of Jesus" or "in the name of Christ." To consider this theologically, we must consider the meaning of the phrase "in the name of," and then the meaning of trinitarian affirmations.

CHAPTER 7

THE STRONG NAME OF
THE TRINITY

> I bind unto myself today
> the strong name of the Trinity
> by invocation of the same,
> the Three in One and One in Three.

This Celtic hymn expresses the faith that to invoke the Trinity is to invoke a strong name. Its concluding blessing expresses faith that this invocation affects not only a liturgical moment, but indeed every day and night:

> Christ be with me, Christ within me,
> Christ behind me, Christ before me,...
> Christ beneath me, Christ above me,
> Christ in quiet, Christ in danger,
> Christ in hearts of all that love me,
> Christ in mouth of friend and stranger.

The hymn refers to the baptism of Jesus and seems as if it might have been written as a baptismal hymn.

In many cultures, invoking the name of the deity means calling on the power of the one named; it is more than a simple designation (Bietenhard 1967, 243). In such an understanding, knowing the name of a deity is essential, but sometimes the name is shrouded in secrecy. Only by calling on the deity by name can one hope that a prayer will be granted. Cross-cultural studies indicate that to pray or carry out ritual acts calling on God through a specific name may mean to call on the energy and power of the God so named.

The sense of "name" and "name of God" in the Hebrew scriptures shares some of the characteristics just described. Alan

Richardson says that the Hebrews shared the sense of others in the ancient world that a name bears the nature of its bearer:

[A] name does not merely distinguish a person from other persons, but is closely related to the nature of its bearer. Particularly in the case of such powerful persons as deities, the name is regarded as part of the being of the divinity so named and of his character and powers. (Richardson 1957, 157)

To bless a congregation using God's name was to bestow God's power on them (Richardson 1957, 157). In some cases, the "name" signifies God's self or God's presence: "Be attentive to him and listen to his voice; ... for my name is in him" (Exod. 23:21). Jews came to avoid using the sacred name *Yahweh*, at first replacing it with *'ădona(y)* and later (in rabbinic Judaism) by *haššēm* ("the name") (Bietenhard 1967, 268). Thus "name" became a circumlocution of the secret name of God (*Yahweh*).

To the extent that this Hebrew sense of the name of God is operative, "to baptize in the name of" may mean a baptism "into" God. This interpretation would emphasize the sense of the Greek preposition *eis*, used in some but not all baptismal texts in the phrase translated "in the name." *Eis* refers to location in space, calling for the English translation "into." Grant Osborne explains the difference between "in the name" and "into the name" by saying that

"In the name" generally refers to the ceremonial rite invoking the name of Jesus while "into the name" speaks of the results of the act, namely incorporation "into" the fellowship of the Godhead. (Osborne 1976, 81)

In other words, "in the name" identifies the context of the liturgical act, whereas "into the name" describes the relationship that is entered and its fruits.

Another interpretation draws on use of the phrase *eis tò 'ónoma* in nonbiblical Greek texts. In texts written during the New Testament period, this phrase often referred to financial transactions. Money deposited "in the name of" someone went to that person's account. By this interpretation, to be baptized "in the name of" is to be transferred into the ownership of the one into whose name she or he is baptized. Lars Hartman and Jane Schaberg report this idea with reserve, thinking that the phrase more likely draws on Hebrew and Aramaic meanings than on this restricted Greek usage (Hartman 1973/1974, 432; Schaberg 1982, 19).

Indeed, it may be more fruitful to regard *eis tò 'ónoma* as the translation of the Hebrew term *lešem* (or Aramaic, *lešum*) which combines the noun root meaning "name" with a prepositional prefix meaning "to" of "for." This Hebrew to Greek translation is found in the Septuagint, though the prepositions *epi* and *en* (also translated "in" in English) more frequently translate the prepositional prefix of *lešem* (Bietenhard 1967, 262). Some rabbinic materials also translate *lešem* as *eis tò 'ónoma* — even in regard to proselyte baptism "in the name of the covenant" (268). If derived from Semitic usage, *eis tò 'ónoma* probably means "with respect or regard to" in the sense of purpose or intention (275). Barth holds that "in the name of " speaks of the goal of baptism: "Baptism is a going forth to Jesus Christ" (Barth *CD* IV/4, 94).

Barth's review of New Testament texts where activities other than baptism are done "in the name of Jesus" is instructive. Such activities include healing (Acts 3:6), casting out demons (Mark 9:38), preaching (Luke 24:47), and receiving children (Mark 9:37), as well as enduring the hatred of non-Christians (Mark 13:13, 1 Pet. 4:14). The author of Colossians tells Christians: "Whatever you do, in word or deed, do everything in the name of the Lord Jesus" (Col. 3:17a). These passages bear the sense of "by the authority of Jesus" or "because of Jesus," and often occur in the context of spreading of faith in God through Jesus Christ into new parts of the world (Barth *CD* IV/4, 93–95). In the case of healing and exorcism, "in the name of Jesus" may also mean "through the power of Jesus' name." These passages suggest that "baptism in the name of " means "baptism by the power of " motivated "because of " the one named.

Although not accepting the emphasis of Barth and Bietenhard on the goal or purpose of baptism, Hartman agrees that *eis tò 'ónoma* derives from the Hebrew-Aramaic *lešem-lešum*. Pointing out that *lešem* is used in a variety of ways in rabbinic texts, Hartman argues that to baptize into the name of Jesus means to baptize "with respect to" or "with reference to" Jesus, in the sense of qualifying or defining the ritual action. Thus the phrase separated Christian baptism from John's baptism, not only in the negative sense ("not John's baptism"), but also in the positive sense ("this baptism refers to Jesus") (Hartman 1973/ 1974, 440).

Schaberg agrees with Hartman that the phrase "in the name of" qualifies the rite, without denying that the phrase might bear some of the sense of God's name found in Hebrew scripture (Schaberg 1982, 1622).

Drawing on these interpretations, one can say that, at the least, to speak of baptism "in the name of" identifies the ritual act by reference to the one named. It may also have the sense of "by the power or authority of" or "because of." Finally, drawing on traditions in which the sacred name is equated with the presence and power of the deity, to baptize "in the name of" could have the sense of empowering a person to enter into a new relationship with God and the church. This last interpretation is consistent with the theology of baptism articulated in Chapter 5, particularly as Christian baptism empowers persons to participate in the death and resurrection of Jesus Christ and to be incorporated into the church.

Having considered the meanings of "name" and "in the name of" from a historical-linguistic standpoint, I now consider the phrase in a thematic way.

A name is often *denotative*, giving information about its bearer. In scripture, the name often reveals the being, the essence of a person, or indeed of God. Changes in names accompany changes in persons. Naomi, whose name meant "pleasant," called herself Mara ("bitter") when she lost her husband and sons (Ruth 1:20). Simon became Peter ("rock"), a bold witness to Jesus the Christ. To baptize "in the name of Jesus Christ" defines the ritual act by reference to Jesus Christ. To baptize "in the name of the Father and of the Son and of the Holy Spirit" means that the ritual act refers not to some vague deity, but precisely to the God made known through Jesus Christ in the power of the Spirit.

Naming is connected with *power*. To act in someone's name is to act in that person's power or authority; the Sanhedrin asks Peter and John about a healing: "By what power or by what name did you do this?" (Acts 4:7). The name in which we baptize is also the authority by which we baptize. The One in whose name the a person is baptized empowers that person.

A name implies *relationship;* my name "Duck" is so rare that when I encounter it I can assume distant blood relationship. In naming, we know other people and are made known to them. To be baptized "in the name of the Lord Jesus" or "the name of the Father and of the Son and of the Holy Spirit" is to enter into relationship with both the one named and the community who call upon the name. The most important meanings of "in the name of" appear then to be these:

1. To identify the reference of the act of baptism in a denotative and delimiting way;
2. To indicate through whose authority and power the baptism takes place;
3. To imply initiation into relationship with God so named.

Given these meanings of "in the name of," it is possible to examine how baptizing "in the name of the Father and of the Son and of the Holy Spirit" is different from baptizing "in the name of Jesus."

THE MEANING OF TRINITARIAN AFFIRMATIONS

The trinitarian solutions of the fourth century affirmed that Father, Son, and Spirit were of the same being, one yet distinguishable, coeternal, together and equally worthy to be praised. Understandings that subordinated the Son to the Father or the Holy Spirit to the Father and the Son were rejected. Understanding the three "persons" as mutually, interdependently, and equally related to one another was affirmed. Baptizing with trinitarian naming rather than in Jesus' name came to reflect this interrelationship.

The church developed trinitarian affirmations primarily to clarify the status of Jesus Christ in the context of belief in one God. These statements affirmed that in Jesus Christ and in the Holy Spirit God is revealed correctly and trustworthily (Barth *CD* II/1, 210). Jesus Christ is God's *self*-revelation in a human life. If there is more to God than mere human beings can understand or articulate, that "more" does not contradict what we know about God in Jesus Christ. Therefore those who receive Jesus Christ as God's self-revelation can trust in God as one who compassionately loves all people, without fear of some hidden God who is hostile or indifferent to humanity.

God's compassion toward humanity was revealed through the life, death, and resurrection of Jesus Christ. Jesus, as "a paradigm of God's ways with the world," is "genuinely revelatory of God" (McFague 1987, 55). In ministering to and sharing table with those ignored or exploited by the pious and the powerful, Jesus revealed God's all-encompassing love that seeks and saves the lost, the neglected, and the oppressed. Through building solidarity among these "lost" ones together with more privileged persons, Jesus built a new community that sought to embody God's all-encompassing love. Unshaken in commitment to this new community and its people, Jesus accepted death at the hands of those who were threatened by "the Christian gospel as a destabilizing, inclusive, nonhierarchical vision of fulfillment for all of creation" (McFague 1987, 59, 60). God's permanent presence as all-encompassing love is made known in every age through the work of the Spirit in the church and the world.

Baptism "in the name of Jesus Christ" identifies Jesus as the Messiah or "anointed one" and does not directly indicate Jesus' status in relationship to God. Baptism "in the name of the Lord Jesus" may say a bit more, because to call Jesus *kyrios* after the resurrection speaks of his continuing authority in the church (Fuller 1965, 156).

In the delimiting sense of naming, baptism in the name of the "Father, the Son, and the Holy Spirit" says more clearly than baptism "in the name of Jesus" or "the Lord Jesus" that Jesus is God's self-revelation. It does this by calling on the Father-Son metaphor. As discussed in Chapter 3, this metaphor perhaps originally pointed to Jesus' intimate relationship with and knowledge of God, like the knowledge of a father by a son. The title "Son of God" that was applied to Jesus also had royal and messianic connotations (Ps. 2:7). Later, "the Son of the Father" became a way of affirming that Jesus was God's self-revelation in a human life. Still later, the terms "Son" and "Father" became shorthand for the developed trinitarian and christological affirmations of the fourth and fifth centuries.

Baptizing in the name of "the Father and the Son and the Holy Spirit" also expressed relational and authoritative aspects of naming. This triadic naming affirmed that God as Father, Son, and Holy Spirit is the main actor in baptism. Baptism is participation in the death and resurrection of Jesus Christ. The Holy Spirit is both giver and gift in baptism, through which Christians receive their calling and are empowered to fulfill it. Yet Jesus

Christ and the Holy Spirit do not act separately from "the Father." Calling on the "Father," as well as the "Son" and "Spirit," made it clear that the church was invoking the full authority and power of God, and that persons were entering into relationship with God understood as Father, Son, and Spirit.

The Trinitarian Formula and the Immanent Trinity

I have argued, based on Jungmann's research, that the resolution of trinitarian and christological controversies may have led to more widespread use of the trinitarian formula in baptism. Also, through these controversies, the terms "Father, Son, and Holy Spirit" became closely associated with orthodox trinitarian doctrine, and a new focus on the interrelationships and distinctions of God as Father, Son, and Spirit emerged. Later, theologians referred to God as self-related with the term "immanent Trinity," in contrast to God as revealed in the history of salvation ("economic Trinity").

Those who oppose any revision of the trinitarian formula generally argue that other forms (such as "in the name of the Creator, Redeemer, and Sustainer") do not adequately express trinitarian faith. They argue that "Father, Son, and Holy Spirit" has become a shorthand expression implying orthodox doctrine about both the immanent and economic Trinity. Because this concern is at the heart of many objections to the revision of the formula, it is appropriate to discuss the basic points in the trinitarian solutions.

The trinitarian solutions of the fourth and following centuries can be summarized in four main points:

1. The persons of the Holy Trinity are coequal with one another.[1]
2. The persons of the Holy Trinity can be distinguished from one another.
3. The persons of the Holy Trinity are interrelated with one another.
4. The persons of the Holy Trinity subsist in a unity of being and acting, and indeed comprise one God.

Let us consider these affirmations one by one.

---

1. In order to make discussion less cumbersome, I use the term "person" for God as Father, Son, and Spirit, although as will be discussed in the next section, this term should not be assumed to indicate separate consciousnesses.

Coequality.[2] To say that the persons of the Holy Trinity are coequal denies the idea that one is subordinate to the other; for example, it denies the idea that Jesus Christ is divine, but subordinate to the Father. Affirmation of the coequality of the three persons of the Trinity also denies the idea that the Son and Spirit are creatures of the Father; instead, all three persons are said to be "of one substance" (Nicene-Constantinopolitan Creed; Lohse 1966, 64). Coequality also involves coeternity, lest it be thought that Father, Son, and Spirit were differentiated only in time as salvation history evolved. Further, all three persons are equally to be "worshiped and glorified" as God by Christians (64). Baptism in the triune name has come to imply the coequality of the three persons.

Distinguishability of persons. All three persons of the Holy Trinity are equally to be worshiped. Mainstream Christian tradition has also insisted that the persons can be distinguished, in contrast to the modalist position that "Son and Spirit were only appearances of the One God" (Lohse 1966, 44). Basil of Caesarea called distinctions in the Trinity "particularizing characteristics" or "identifying peculiarities," and named them "paternity," "sonship," and "sanctifying power" (Kelly 1960, 265). Gregory of Nyssa and Gregory of Nazianzus named the characteristics "ingenerateness," "generateness," and "procession" (265). The distinct characteristics are not, however, distinct centers of consciousness, as the term "person" now implies: "There are not three consciousnesses; rather, the one consciousness subsists in a threefold way" (Rahner 1970, 107).

Rahner attempts to articulate the "distinct manners of subsisting" of the Father, Son, and Spirit in terms that grow out of the economy of salvation. God the Father is the "generating principle" or "source of the whole Godhead," as Rahner writes: "This unoriginate God is experienced as the *Father of the Son*, as 'generating principle,' as source, origin, and principle of the whole Godhead" (Rahner 1970, 61). God the Son is God's self-communication, and only the Son (also called Logos or Word) is God's self-communication historically as a human being (86). The

---

2. The works by Barth, Boucher, Farley, Kelly, LaCugna, Lohse, Moltmann, Oxford-Carpenter, Rahner, and Ramshaw in the reference list lie behind this interpretation of the Trinity, as do single works by the following authors: Russell (1979), Wainwright (1980), and Wilson-Kastner (1983).

Spirit "brings about the acceptance by the world (as creation) in faith, hope, and love of this self-communication" (86). These distinct manners of subsisting are revealed in salvation history. They are proper to each person and cannot be exchanged. Note that we could draw the expression "Source, Word, and Spirit" from Rahner's explanation of the Trinity. This is one way of naming the Trinity in nonmasculine, nonfunctionalist, yet traditional terms that are not primarily philosophical but metaphorical. Baptism in the triune name implies the distinctions of persons in God.

Interrelation. To speak of distinctions within the Trinity is not, however, to speak of any separation of persons, but rather of mutually related and interpenetrating persons who share one life.

Patricia Wilson-Kastner has said that "if one images God as three persons, it encourages one to focus on interrelationship at the core of divine reality" (Wilson-Kastner 1983, 122). Traditional trinitarian formulations have drawn on the Father-Son metaphor as an image of the mutual relation of the divine persons (with the Spirit sometimes explained as the bond of relation itself; for example, Augustine, "On the Holy Trinity" 6.5.7.). Augustine used the terms "Lover," "Beloved," and "Love" as a way of expressing the mutual relationship of persons within the Trinity. He also used the analogy of memory, knowledge, and will within the same person as a way of describing the distinguishability and interrelatedness within the Trinity (9.2.2. and 10.12.19.). Many other terms have been proposed suggesting the intimate and intrinsic relations between persons of the Trinity.

Mutual relationship in the Trinity entails acting in concert; it is not as if each "person" were in charge of a different department of salvation history with separate and mutually exclusive job descriptions. For example, though creation is assigned or "appropriated" to the first person of the Trinity, the Word and Spirit also take part in creating (John 1; Genesis 1). Names such as "Savior" refer to both the first and second persons of the Trinity (LaCugna 1989, 243, n. 16; she cites Luke 1:47; John 4:42; Acts 5:31; and 1 John 4:14). The Son suffers on the cross, but the Father suffers with the Son in the compassion of a shared life. The Spirit is both the gift of the risen Christ and the Spirit of the risen Christ. The interrelation of divine persons means that they act in concert, so in some cases the names that describe God's actions can be used interchangeably between each member of the Trinity.

Two images of the mutual relations within the Trinity have intrigued Christian feminists. One of these images, borrowed from the thought of John of Damascus, comes from the Greek word *perichoresis*, which literally means "a dance around." Patricia Wilson-Kastner describes the attraction of this image as follows:

> Because feminism identifies interrelatedness and mutuality — equal, respectful, and nurturing relationships — as the basis of the world as it really is and as it ought to be, we can find no better understanding and image of the divine than that of the perfect and open relationships of love. In its divine dancing together, the Trinity of persons manifests the harmony and beauty of such a relationship; the unity of body, mind, and movement and sound in dance provide an engaging and comprehensive metaphor for the unity, comprehensiveness, and cooperative diversity in the divine life. (Wilson-Kastner 1983, 127)

Wilson-Kastner admits that the metaphor of dancing together is "imperfect and breaks down if pushed too far," but argues that this image is more appealing and inclusive than others such as "two seated males and a dove" (Wilson-Kastner 1983, 127). The unity of common movement in a dance is one image for the shared life of the Trinity.

Another suggestive image is that of the Trinity as a "community of persons" in contrast to a monarchical, isolated image of God. Barbara Brown Zikmund writes that through belief in a triune God, persons understand God as "dynamic community." She writes:

> Trinitarian theology asserts that relationship is fundamental to God and that community is the foundation of God's interaction with the world. Instead of an unmoved mover, God as community calls us to shared responsibility. (Zikmund 1987, 356)

The image of coequal community implies shared decision making and acting rather than domination and subordination. It implies the interdependence of a shared life rather than life characterized by separation, independence, or dependence. As such, the image of God as community of persons is a good model for relationships within the "discipleship community of equals" (Schüssler Fiorenza 1984, 74–75). Indeed, the movement away from trinitarian theology in white, Western modern thought can be regarded as a denial of diversity and a capitulation to monarchical ways of thinking (Thistlethwaite 1989, 122).

Baptismal naming that is trinitarian implies a shared life, a dancing together, at the heart of divine reality. Further, it implies an invitation for human beings to share in life with God, to become "partners in the divine dance" (Catherine M. LaCugna, class lectures, summer 1986). Wilson-Kastner states: "Through the being of Christ, God's trinitarian life is extended to creation, inviting it to share in the very divine life itself" (Wilson-Kastner 1983, 128). The openness of persons to one another in the triune God is not a closed system; it opens out in love to the whole creation. Joining in the dance through the invitation of Jesus Christ, the community of the baptized may call on God in the terms of intimate personal relationship.

Unity. The three coequal, distinct, and interrelated persons of the triune God are one God. To affirm a triune God is not to deny monotheism, but to affirm a specific approach to monotheism. Father, Son, and Holy Spirit are not three gods but one God. The classical trinitarian formulations clarify the status of Jesus Christ in the context of belief in one God, by affirming that the one God is triune and by identifying Jesus Christ with the second person of the triune God.

Some have argued that in the baptismal formula, the singular "name" rather than "names" implies the unity of Father, Son, and Holy Spirit (for example, Barth *CD* IV/4, 96). This may depend too much on a dubious grammatical point. The trinitarian formula reinforces the affirmation of the unity of God more by association than dictionary definition. For example, baptism "in the name of Hecate, Demeter, and Persephone" might well imply the equality, distinction, and mutual relationship of the three, but not necessarily their unity. However, the Nicene Creed says that Jesus Christ is "true God from true God, begotten not made, *of one being with the Father*" (English translation by the International Consultation on English Texts, as printed by the English Language Liturgical Consultation 1987, 4; emphasis added). Other creeds and hymns speak of the unity of the Father, Son, and Holy Spirit. The well-known hymn "Come, Thou Almighty King" addressed God as King and Father, Incarnate Word, and Comforter and Spirit, then continues with the words "To thee, great One in Three, eternal praises be." Other hymns are even more direct in calling Father, Son, and Holy Spirit one. Thus, by association, the trinitarian baptismal formula reinforces the affirmation of the unity of God.[3]

BAPTISM IN THE NAME OF THE FATHER AND OF THE SON AND OF THE HOLY SPIRIT

Laurence H. Stookey has said that "the Trinitarian formula is an amazing kind of theological shorthand" (Stookey 1982, 200). One may be more optimistic than Stookey about the possibility of revising the formula so that it will be gender inclusive. However, it is true that the phrase "I baptize you in the name of the Father, and of the Son, and of the Holy Spirit" has been a shorthand affirmation of classical trinitarian doctrine with its complexity. Thus Christians affirm "Father, Son, and Holy Spirit" as coequal, distinct, and interrelated persons of one God. To baptize "in the name of the Father and of the Son and of the Holy Spirit" is to identify and authorize the act of baptism by reference to this trinitarian understanding of God. To baptize in this name is to call on the full power of God to work within the life of the community of the baptized. To baptize "in the name of the Father and of the Son and of the Holy Spirit" is to extend the circle of those who share in a relationship with God, dancing together in a community of love.

The Role of the Baptismal Formula

From a liturgical standpoint, all the meanings of "in the name of" describe the role of the formula. The formula identifies the reference of the act of baptism; it indicates through whose authority and power the act takes place; and it implies initiation into relationship with God as named in the formula. Through its trinitarian naming, it summarizes Christian faith, including the status of Jesus Christ in relation to God. Thus, it is a statement of the church's identity. The classical trinitarian formula has been understood to imply the coequality, the distinguishability, the mutual relations, and the unity of the Trinity. Therefore,

---

3. Refer to Bennett's discussion of the influence of creeds and hymns on the interpretation of biblical statements, and their influence on Christian communities; 1987, esp. 548–549.

willingness to use the trinitarian formula has come to be a test of Christian orthodoxy.

The baptismal formula has also come to be seen as the word spoken at baptism, which, with the physical symbol of water, forms the heart of the sacrament. Roman Catholics have considered the formula to be the "form" and the water to be the "matter" of the sacrament (Whitaker 1965a, 6). Protestants have emphasized the source of the formula in the early Christian witness or in the actual words of Jesus (in which case they call it part of his institution of the sacrament).

Speaking the formula and administering the water form the dramatic center of the baptismal rite. Revised Roman Catholic and Protestant baptismal rites in recent years have emphasized the communal aspect of baptism and discouraged private baptisms. The depth and breadth of scripture references in these rites have increased, and in many Protestant rites, chrismation (baptismal anointing) has been restored. Rubrics advise pouring the water quite visibly and audibly, and placing the font at prominent places in the church. All these reforms prevent a minimalist focus on speaking the formula and administering the water, but these acts still form the dramatic center of the rite. For example, use of the formula, administration of water, and prayer asking for the gift of the Spirit are the main elements included in the United Church of Christ (USA) baptism order under the heading "The Act of Baptism" (United Church of Christ 1986, 142-143).

The texts and ceremonies for the sacrament of baptism have varied greatly throughout history. For example, whereas some denominations have not practiced baptismal anointing, others have had one or two anointings before and/or after baptism, with a variety of interpretations. Some baptism rituals have been very elaborate, whereas emergency baptisms have been extremely short and simple. Sometimes those who have administered baptism have been well educated; sometimes they have not been able to read. Some medieval priests reportedly used variant formulas not for theological reasons, but because they couldn't read and didn't learn the formula correctly. Even the water has been administered in various ways — through immersion, pouring, and sprinkling.

Given this diversity, and also given the commendable reluctance of most churches to rebaptize those who have already been baptized, the church needed some means to determine what constitutes baptism. It became important to identify what words and actions were absolutely necessary to consider that a person had been baptized, and what could be left out or done differently. This question was necessary both within a communion, in case an officiant made mistakes or omissions, and among communions, if they were to recognize one another's baptisms. The identification at which most, but not all, churches arrived is summed up in this phrase from *Baptism, Eucharist and Ministry*, already quoted: "Baptism is administered with water in the name of the Father, the Son, and the Holy Spirit" (Faith and Order 1982, par. 17). The intention of the person who administers baptism has also been considered important; for example, baptism done in jest or playacting would not be considered valid. The basic requirements — formula, water, and intention — made it possible to ensure that a baptism was valid and to allow people within or among denominations to recognize it.

Using the formula connected churches of different times and places, and connected baptism with the rest of Christian worship. The baptismal language of "Father, Son, and Holy Spirit" has echoed through Christian worship from the solemn declaration through the eucharistic prayer to the closing blessing. Any new language for the formula should be appropriate for the whole worshiping life of the church.

The words spoken at the act of baptism have summarized Christian faith, identified baptism, and linked local congregations with the church throughout time and space. Though part of a whole order now restored with rich scriptural associations and the baptizing community, the baptismal formula is pivotal. With the administration of water, it forms the theological and liturgical center of baptism. What is said at this sacramental moment matters.

Because it matters what the church says at the moment of baptism, language reflecting patriarchal values is not appropriate. Use of the baptismal formula "in the name of the Father and of the Son and of the Holy Spirit" conflicts with an adequate theology of baptism, because baptism represents turning around to become part of a new egalitarian order of relationships (Gal. 3:28).

By contrast, the use of predominantly masculine language in the baptismal formula represents the old patriarchal patterning of reality. In the very words that define and focus the rite and that summarize Christian faith, the language of this world and its patriarchal systems appears. Using imagery that exalts a more privileged group and excludes a less privileged group contradicts participation in the death and resurrection of Jesus Christ through solidarity with suffering humanity. Using paternal imagery in the formula in patriarchal society contradicts solidarity with some of its most vulnerable members — children who are victims of abuse. Images that reflect cultural gender biases contradict conversion to new life in egalitarian community and subvert openness to the gifts of the spirit.

The formula must be revised; the trinitarian formula presently used is not adequate to serve as the theological and liturgical center of the rite of baptism. The moment when the water and the word come together is a key moment in the sacrament of baptism and of all Christian worship. This moment of worship, of all times, should reflect worship theology at its best.

Because changing the formula is so challenging ecumenically and theologically, denominational leaders delay providing alternatives. But this contradiction at the heart of Christian worship — the masculine, paternal imagery in the pivotal words of the baptismal liturgy — must be faced and healed. It matters what we say. Revision of the formula is necessary, yet it cannot be taken lightly. Those who seek nonpatriarchal alternatives must proceed carefully, considering the meaning and purpose of the words spoken at the font.

The Naming of God

The words said during administration of water in baptism come from the community's characteristic way of addressing God. Robert W. Jenson has expressed it quite well:

> The function of naming God in initiation, in baptism as elsewhere, is to address the initiate to new reality, to grant new access to God. In the community of the baptized, therefore, the divine name spoken in baptism is established as that by which the community has its particular address to God. (Jenson 1982, 16)

Because the naming of God in baptism is appropriately the community's characteristic address to God, this naming should be as theologically adequate as possible. The way God is named through any alternative to the present trinitarian baptismal formula must at least make it known that the baptism takes place through the God of Jesus Christ. This may not necessarily involve explicit reference to a developed doctrine of the economic and immanent Trinity. Certainly, however, what is said as part of the act of baptism must provide a clear theological focus to the rite.

Theological adequacy is at stake in moving past predominantly masculine language in the formula. Words spoken with the act of water baptism represent the "community's particular address to God." Jenson argued that this fact means that alternatives to the traditional trinitarian formula should not be sought (Jenson 1982, 16–17); to the contrary, that is exactly why alternatives must be sought! Use of predominantly masculine language in this central act of Christian worship suggests that the community characteristically names God using masculine imagery. Alternatives must be free of such gender bias. At this point in history, alternatives using both masculine and feminine imagery may be desirable, because nongendered language tends to evoke masculine imagery. However, gendered language is not inherently preferable to nongendered language, in the baptismal formula or elsewhere in Christian worship.

Although revised practice should make it known that baptism takes place through the God of Jesus Christ, all naming of God is necessarily metaphorical. With Justin one may deny that the "proper name of God" may be known once and for all. The divine name "Father, Son, and Holy Spirit" is metaphorical, as any alternatives will be. Though the desire for mutual recognition may predispose churches to seek only one way of naming God in the formula, the tendency of people to forget that set, unalterable phrases are not the final word about God should also be taken into account.

Liturgical Function

Any proposed alternative must provide a dramatic center of baptism that can be readily identified. Some spoken word must accompany the administration of water and witness to the meaning of this act. Further, although a statement such as "I baptize you" was seemingly not a part of Western baptismal rites when the interrogations were still used, something similar may be desirable to announce that baptism is actually taking place. Further, the phrase must be "appropriate for doxological use" (Kasper 1986, 246). Judgments about what is appropriate for doxological use will differ, reflecting the diverse traditions and cultural contexts of churches. However, our exploration of liturgical language has provided some ways of measuring appropriateness. The metaphors used should be alive, rich in associations, and accessible to the whole community of faith. Thus, for example, whether or not Rahner's term "distinct manners of subsisting" may be theologically acceptable in speaking of the persons of the Trinity, it is not apt for liturgical use because it is neither metaphorically alive nor widely accessible in meaning (Rahner 1970, 109). As words that accompany an action, they probably should be relatively brief and easy to memorize or repeat.

The language used to summarize the meaning of baptism is a part of the language of praise and thanksgiving used in Christian worship as a whole. Thus it should resonate with and be reflected by the language used whenever the community gathers to worship.

Scriptural Resonance

Erik Routley's concept of scriptural resonance applies to evaluation of a baptismal formula. Although the baptismal formula might not directly quote scripture, it should resonate with the witness of Christian scripture through paraphrase or allusion. Through scripture resonance, the church's worship stays in continuity with the church throughout time and space. Witness to Jesus Christ remains central. The words, "I baptize you in the name of the Father and of the Son and of the Holy Spirit" are, of course, rooted in Matthew 28:19b, in the account of Jesus' commissioning the disciples. Any other words used to focus the meaning of baptism should ground the rite appropriately in scripture, especially in the New Testament witness to Jesus Christ.

The words with which the BEM document begins discussing baptism provide a context in which to consider the scriptural resonance of any baptismal formula: "Christian baptism is rooted in the ministry of Jesus of Nazareth, in his death and in his resurrection" (Faith and Order 1982, par. 1). Most historical-critical theories locate the origin of the words "baptizing them in the name of the Father and of the Son and of the Holy Spirit" (Matt. 28:19b) in early Christian communities, and not in Jesus' actual words. Based on this scholarly consensus, Matthew 28:19b need not have privileged status over other New Testament passages that refer to baptism. However, as BEM states, baptism is rooted in Jesus' ministry, death, and resurrection. Words that focus the meaning of baptism do well to indicate this rooting, drawing on one or more texts from the Christian Testament. Because of its likely place in the baptismal practice of the early church, Galatians 3:26–28 is among the scripture passages with which an alternative formula could resonate.

Ecumenical Identification

To be acceptable ecumenically, a revised formula must name God as adequately as possible, fulfill its liturgical role well, and resonate with scripture, as a primary source for common language. Resonance in church tradition may also be important for many ecumenical partners.

Concern for the role of baptism in ecumenical relations also means providing alternatives that can cross lines of language, culture, and denomination. Any alternative to the present formula should be capable of being translated into a great variety of cultural contexts and languages. The Father-Son metaphor may mean different things in different cultures, but in every human society there are fathers and sons. To be useful in a worldwide context, metaphors used in alternatives to the formula must resonate with the experience of human beings around the globe. Alternatives that are relatively brief and simple may be easier to translate and use in a variety of contexts.

It seems to me, however, that an overemphasis on validity based in correct words should be avoided. Concerns about validity center on the formula and the method of administering water, and they grow out of emphasis on baptism as a means to overcome original sin. Overemphasis on validity, sin, and grace can eclipse other meanings of baptism, such as dying and rising with Christ and moving toward new life in community. Alexander Schmémann, the Greek Orthodox theologian writes: "To reduce baptism to the principle of 'validity' only is to make a caricature of Christ's teaching" (Schmémann 1974, 45). For example, though the moral character of the officiant and the baptizing community do not affect the validity of baptism, they do influence whether baptism is fulfilled in human lives, for communities nurture Christian faith and life (45). Discovering a uniform formula to ensure validity and mutual recognition, without concern for the quality of life in the churches, may not necessarily lead toward genuine Christian reconciliation. Instead, the churches should leave some room for one another to witness to their faith in diverse ways, in the words of the act of baptism as elsewhere. The *Baptism, Eucharist, and Ministry* document encourages churches to accept the different ways they administer the water. Cannot some diversity of words also be tolerated?

Although the words said during administration of water are important, they need not bear the whole burden of helping us recognize one another as Christians. When one set of metaphors becomes a test of Christian orthodoxy, it becomes a literalized definition and its metaphoric power is endangered. As LaCugna has written:

> The ultimate criterion of orthodoxy (= right praise) is the lived expression of what we undertake and undergo in baptism.... The fullest expression of orthodoxy is to be found in the life of individuals and communities.... The community glorifies God when it gathers together in the Spirit in whom all differences are acknowledged and embraced. (LaCugna 1988, 68)

Participation together in shared life in the Spirit is a more adequate way to recognize one another as Christians than to demand that all churches summarize their faith through one literalized metaphor.

True Christian reconciliation requires respect for the various ways in which Christians witness to their faith. Yet mutual respect also entails communication about theological and liturgical concerns to remove unnecessary barriers to Christian unity and to find common ground if possible. Thus those seeking alternatives to the trinitarian formula should search, through thought and dialogue, for options that are not merely parochial but that can cross lines of language, culture, and denomination.

Revision of the trinitarian baptismal formula is urgently needed. Alternatives must be evaluated in terms of their naming of God, their liturgical function, and their scriptural resonance, as well as their viability across the lines of denomination and language. We turn now to evaluate some alternative baptismal formulas that have been offered in the last two decades.

CHAPTER 8

ALTERNATIVES

A number of people have offered alternatives to the trinitarian baptismal formula, though significantly no official denominational worship books have done so. Some alternatives use a method of remembrance, others a method of translation, and still others a method of creative ritualization. All grow out of the conviction that predominantly masculine language is not adequate in the formula, and some also avoid parental metaphors. Let us consider these alternatives one by one.

THE METHOD OF REMEMBRANCE

Several alternatives to the trinitarian baptismal formula use a methodology of remembrance. These approaches seek to draw on the resources of a common past to provide direction for a common future.

Baptism in the Name of Jesus or in the Name of Christ

I have already observed that baptism "in the name of Jesus" or "in the name of Christ" has been a persistent alternative to baptism "in the name of the Father and of the Son and of the Holy Spirit." These forms were accepted by the Roman Catholic Church until at least the thirteenth century and are still used in some churches today, including some Pentecostal churches (Davies 1986, 71). Some persons who are concerned about inclusive language have turned to this alternative as a way of retrieving past traditions to use in inclusive, egalitarian Christian community. For example, John W. Riggs of the United Church of Christ has designed a baptismal liturgy using this formula (Duck 1985, 102–103). Riggs wrote concerning the alternative:

> Despite ecumenical concerns, the trinitarian baptismal formula, which cannot be made adequately inclusive, and which imposes a certain theological view on a congregation, has been dropped in favor of the more apostolic form, "in the name of Jesus." (Duck 1985, 103)

Riggs's exact form was "*Name*, I baptize you in the name of Jesus, our Christ" (Duck 1985, 103).

Baptism "in the name of Jesus" or "of Christ" meets many of the criteria considered here. Certainly these alternatives provide a dramatic center for the liturgy with clear scriptural resonance. They are easy to translate and remember. They have promise for ecumenical recognition because of their strong precedence in church tradition. Also, because "baptism in the name of Jesus" is presently practiced by some churches, discussion of this alternative is already on the ecumenical agenda.

One question that we must address concerning this alternative to the baptismal formula is whether it names God and expresses Christian faith adequately enough.

Baptism in the name of Jesus does not directly indicate Jesus' status in relationship to God. In fact, all three baptismal formulas in scripture appeared before the church began to articulate this relationship precisely, though Matthew 28:19b uses language later identified with trinitarian affirmations.

Must the status of Jesus Christ in relation to God be articulated clearly in Christian worship, and specifically in the baptismal formula? If this question is understood to refer to trinitarian dogma as articulated in the fourth century, the answer might be "no." However, "baptism in the name of Jesus" does not make it clear that the full presence, authority, and power of God are sought as the means and fulfillment of Christian baptism. "Baptism in the name of Christ" may make a somewhat stronger claim by pointing to the risen Christ; for, as Wilson-Kastner says, "the Christ" points to the Eternal Word of God:

> The Christ we are considering is, after all, the living Christ, not simply a Palestinian rabbi of the first century. This Christ is the Incarnation of the eternal Word of God, in whom all things came to be, the center of the cosmos, who became human at

a particular place and time to manifest God's love among us.
(Wilson-Kastner 1983, 91)

Already in New Testament times, "Christ" as a title for the incarnation of the word was being used to refer to the risen and living
Christ present and embodied in the community (Fuller 1965, 184–
185). Although popular piety often refers to the risen Christ as
"Jesus," the term can serve equally well to refer to a Palestinian
rabbi.

"Baptism in the name of Christ" also is a more gender-
inclusive term than baptism either "in the name of Jesus" or
"in the name of the Father and of the Son and of the Holy
Spirit." Because the Christian community is called the body of
Christ, "Christ" includes not only the historical Jesus, but also
all members of the Christian community. Through the centuries,
Christian leaders have often expressed christology in sexist ways,
lifting up Christ not as the redeemer of all, but as the savior of humanity defined as normatively male (Wilson-Kastner 1983, 77).
Focusing on the term "Jesus" or even "Jesus Christ" as a male
human being in the crucial point of the baptismal formula may
risk calling forth such associations that even have been used to
exclude women from the priesthood.

Considering "baptism in the name of Jesus" or "the name of
Christ" from a feminist perspective raises questions of christology — a disputed issue among Christian feminists. One approach
has been to portray Jesus as a prophet who championed the oppressed over against patriarchal values (Ruether 1983, 119–122).
Brock argues that this image is individualistic: "Few prophetic
images connote receptivity toward, listening to, or interaction
with a community of support" (Brock 1988, 65). Thistlethwaite
also warns that portraying Jesus as a feminist in contrast to
his Jewish contemporaries risks anti-Semitism (Thistlethwaite
1989, 94–97). Wilson-Kastner's approach is to emphasize the
risen Christ in contrast to the historical Jesus, but Brock has
pointed out that this universalized Christ appears to deny human
particularity even as it makes unique claims for "one human
form" (Brock 1988, 63). In my opinion, neither the prophet-
feminist nor the universalized Christ by itself is adequate, because
the first appears to deny or de-emphasize Jesus Christ's participation in the divine life, and the second denies or de-emphasizes

the incarnation. Thus I find Brock's third alternative to be promising. She proposes relocating the Christ "in the community of which Jesus is one historical part," which she calls "Christa/community" (69). The name "Christa/community" alludes to the female crucifix by the artist Edwina Sandys originally at the Cathedral of St. John the Divine in New York City; and it points beyond any one individual male or female to the life of community (113–114). She argues that Christa/community includes the historical Jesus, but it "is not limited to the historical Jesus, even in his lifetime" (68). Thus redemption occurs in the context of community rather than through one isolated individual.

Given this christological understanding, "baptism in the name of Christ" would be clearly preferable to "baptism in the name of Jesus," because the church is called "the body of Christ," but not the "body of Jesus."

Some Christians may argue that trinitarian doctrine, being postbiblical, is not essential to Christian faith (Johnson 1987, 534–535). However, most churches worldwide would not agree. Some Christian groups might expect that trinitarian faith would be explicitly expressed in any baptismal formula if it were to name God adequately. Even in expressing concern about the traditional trinitarian formula in their responses to BEM, the United Church of Christ, the Anglican Church of Canada, and the United Methodist Church appeared to assume that any revised formula would express trinitarian faith in other words.

Baptism in the name of Christ might be ecumenically accepted if churches agreed that this form need not contradict a trinitarian faith, which, perhaps, could be expressed elsewhere in the rite of baptism. Or the formula could be augmented to express trinitarian faith, for example: "in the name of Jesus Christ, and by the power and authority of the triune God." Some U.S. Presbyterians have included a blessing with laying on of hands immediately after the act of baptism (Horace Allen, interview with the author, July 1988). This triadic blessing came from scripture: "And may the love of God, the grace of the Lord Jesus Christ, and the communion of the Holy Spirit be with you" (2 Cor. 13:14). The formula "I baptize you in the name of Christ" could be augmented with the blessing "May the love of God, the grace of Christ, and the communion of the Holy Spirit be and abide with you" as a way of affirming trinitarian faith (Allen July 1988).

"Baptism in the name of Christ" finds scriptural resonance in some Pauline passages that allude to baptism (for example, Gal. 3:27). It is a short, memorable formula that can be easily memorized. It is more gender inclusive than baptism "in the name of the Father and of the Son and of the Holy Spirit." Therefore "baptism in the name of Christ" merits some consideration as an alternative baptismal formula, especially when augmented with a triadic blessing.

Augmenting the Formula with Feminine Language

At New York City's Riverside Church, these words are used for the formula in all baptisms: "I baptize you in the name of the Father and of the Son and of the Holy Spirit, One God, Mother of us all." Because the persons who proposed this formulation did so appealing to the writings of Julian of Norwich, I categorize this approach as a method of remembrance.

In the early 1980s, a committee at Riverside Church had been working on inclusive language in worship. The pastoral staff, led by William Sloane Coffin, discussed the language used in baptism. They decided in 1982 to modify the formula for the sake of inclusive language, administering baptisms in the name of "God the Creator, Christ the Redeemer, and the Holy Spirit our Constant Companion" (Kay, letter to Eugene Laubach, April 5, 1982; Eugene Laubach, letter to the author, May 1988). Christopher Morse, a United Methodist clergyperson and professor at Union Theological Seminary, objected. He mentioned his concern to James F. Kay, then a Ph.D. student and tutor in systematic theology at Union Seminary. Kay questioned the validity of baptisms administered with the revised formula. Eugene Laubach, minister of parish life, was at first angry at this response, which he considered "hair-splitting," and he challenged Morse to offer a better alternative (Laubach May 1988). Kay provided the alternative. He wrote to Dr. Coffin expressing his objections to the alternative formula. He argued that the new formula was not equivalent to the traditional one, for it abandoned orthodox trinitarian doctrine:

Such a formula cannot be equated in meaning with the designation "In the Name of the Father and of the Son and of the

Holy Spirit" since "Creator" and "Redeemer" pertain equally
to all three Persons of the Holy Trinity on the basis of the axiom that the *ad extra* works of the Trinity are indivisible. Only
on the basis of the doctrine of appropriation have these titles
ever been restricted to any single Person of the Godhead, and
such a restriction, to my knowledge, has never been used before
with reference to the baptismal formula probably for obvious
soteriological reasons. Perhaps, more seriously, is the restriction of the designation "God" by the new Riverside formula to
the first Person of the Trinity, a view repudiated by Christianity
at Nicaea in A.D. 325. (Kay 1982, 1)

After expressing his concern, Kay offered an alternative formula
based on the writings of Julian of Norwich:

In the fourteenth century [Julian] proposed that Jesus exer-
cises the office of Mother towards us in his redemptive work.
On the basis, then, of the Trinitarian axiom that the work of
the Trinity towards us cannot be divided, Julian also could call
the Father and the Spirit "Mother" as well. Baptism "In the
Name of the Father and of the Son and of the Holy Spirit, One
God — our Mother" might, on the basis of Julian's insight, be
an alternative baptismal formula that would remain Trinitarian without slighting the maternal dimension to the Christian
experience of salvation. (Kay 1982, 1)

The pastors accepted Kay's suggestion, changing the wording to
the present form: "In the name of the Father and of the Son and
of the Holy Spirit, One God, Mother of us all" (Eugene Laubach,
letter to the author, May 1988).

Laubach, in response to questions about the process of introducing the new formula, said that the ministers had acted on
clerical authority, without consulting the Public Worship Council
(Eugene Laubach, letter to the author, May 1988). They simply
began using the formula and did not explain the change in a sermon, newsletter, or other public forum. Laubach believes that
this was the only way that they could have successfully initiated
the change. He writes that "occasionally a traditionalist asks if
we can use the old formula — we say no" (Laubach May 1988).
Members have generally accepted the new formula very well, and
visitors (of which Riverside has hundreds) are fascinated and
usually comfortable with it.

Riverside's alternative, augmenting the formula with feminine language, meets most of the criteria developed here. The formula continues (with the administration of water) to provide the dramatic center of the baptismal liturgy. It is resonant with scripture, both through using Matthew 28:19b and through use of maternal imagery for God. It should be easy to translate and memorize.

There is ample precedence in church tradition for augmenting the formula so that it makes theological affirmations important to a particular tradition. Some believer baptists emphasize the importance of individual faith by the way they augment the formula. For example, the Christian Church (Disciples of Christ) uses this form: "By the authority of our Lord Jesus Christ, in whom you have confessed your faith, I baptize you, (N), in the name of the Father, the Son, and the Holy Spirit" (Davies 1986, 64). Presbyterians often add "child of the covenant": "(N), child of the covenant, I baptize you in the name of the Father and of the Son and of the Holy Spirit" (Presbyterian Church, U.S.A., and Cumberland Presbyterian Church 1985, 38). When they do this, they express the belief that children of believing parents are baptized because they are included in the covenant community through God's promise (Calvin Book 4, Chapter 16 [1960], 1324–1359). Riverside's addition of "One God, Mother of us all" also makes an important theological affirmation. It makes clear that the baptizing community is repudiating patriarchal notions of God and seeking new patterns of relationship. It avoids the impression that exclusively masculine language must be used to legitimate baptism. The addition of "One God" indicates that the "Mother" image is intended to refer to all three persons of the Trinity, and gives explicit expression to the unity of persons. Only those who reject outright the use of feminine or maternal imagery for God could say this addition to the formula is less acceptable than the Presbyterian and Baptist/Disciples additions.

Unfortunately, however, the Riverside formula is relatively inadequate in naming God. In the first place, there are two masculine images and only one feminine image, thus keeping masculine imagery central. However, because "Mother" refers back to all three persons, this would not seem to be a serious problem.

Second, the Riverside formula names God inadequately because it continues to keep parental imagery central. Earlier I questioned the wisdom of solving the problem of "Father" and "Son" imagery by adding "Mother" imagery for God. Although not arguing that parental imagery should be completely eliminated from Christian worship, I believe that such imagery should lose its privileged place in Christian worship. Thus I question whether parental imagery ought to be used in the formula as the characteristic naming of God to be repeated throughout Christian worship.

The formula "I baptize you in the name of the Father and of the Son, and of the Holy Spirit, One God, Mother of us all" is also limited as a way of naming God because it does not avoid the risk of subordination inherent in the "Father-Son" metaphor.

One possible way to address the paternal imagery in the formula would be to augment it with a metaphor that would be in tension with the "Father" metaphor: "I baptize you in the name of the Father, the Son, and the Holy Spirit, one God and Sister of us all." Because the first person of the Trinity is called "our Father" in Christian worship, "Father" in the formula has the connotations of referring both to God as "Father of the Son" and God as "Father of Christians." To call God both "our Father" *and* "our Sister" relativizes both the literalistic identification of God with male persons and the patriarchal associations of "Father." Still, naming God "Father" in such a key part of the liturgy as the baptismal formula is risky in a patriarchal society, no matter what feminine imagery we might add.

The Riverside formula is certainly an improvement over the unaugmented formula. Some communities may use an augmented formula as a good first step toward making the baptismal formula more inclusive. Because there is precedent for augmented formulas in church traditions, an augmented formula may be accepted ecumenically more immediately than any other alternative, except perhaps baptism in the name of Christ. For these reasons, we should not dismiss out of hand the option of augmenting the formula. However, in my opinion, other options are preferable.

Restoration of Threefold Questioning in Place of the Formula

In many recent books of worship, candidates or their parents or sponsors are asked whether they renounce Satan and/or the unjust and sinful ways of this world. They are then asked three questions through which they affirm their faith in the triune God (one question for each "person"). Such questions are asked in the Consultation on Common Texts' Liturgy for Baptism (Consultation on Common Texts 1987, 18–22) immediately before the water is administered while a declarative baptismal formula is spoken. This revives ancient Western practice, though adding a declarative formula to the questions.

Drawing on these past traditions, David R. Holeton, an Anglican active in ecumenical dialogue about worship, has argued that baptismal interrogations would be sufficient as an alternative to the declarative trinitarian formula (Holeton 1988, 70). In this model, separate questions about each person of the Trinity would be asked of the candidates and/or their sponsors. The first question could be something like, "Do you believe in God, creator of heaven and earth?" Although the ancient questions spoke of God as "Father" as well as "Creator," Holeton argues that this was necessary to rule out the Valentinian heresy that the Father of Jesus Christ was not the creator of this evil world. Because this heresy is not a threat today, Holeton regards "Creator of heaven and earth" to be an adequate naming of the first person of the Trinity. In ancient interrogations, the second question bore the weight of clarifying the status of Jesus Christ vis à vis God. (For example, the second question in Hippolytus' order called Christ Jesus the Son of God, and affirmed the true humanity and exaltation of Christ Jesus.) If the interrogations were restored as an alternative for the baptismal formula, then, argues Holeton, the second question could be, "Do you believe in the child [son] of God, Jesus Christ?" with some further elaboration. The third question could elaborate the relationship between the Holy Spirit and the other two persons of the Trinity. This is something baptismal creeds have not attempted in the past, even though some claim that the "Father" and "Son" language cannot be changed because it articulates the relationship between the first and second persons of the Trinity.

In situations where all or most candidates for baptism were believing adults, they could answer the questions. Where infants were the only candidates for baptism, sponsors and the whole congregation could profess their faith by answering the questions. This would acknowledge that "the faith being expressed is that of the whole church" (Holeton 1988, 71) and would be quite appropriate to the theology of many traditions. If this solution were not considered acceptable for infant baptism, the questions could then take an assertive form. For example:

> *Name*, you are baptized in the Name of God,
> the creator of heaven and earth.
> You are baptized in the name of Jesus,
> the Son/Child of God,
> and so on
>
> (Holeton 1988, 71; I omit the rubrics indicating that candidates are dipped after each statement.)

As these examples show, replacing the formula with threefold interrogation makes it possible to summarize Christian faith using a few more words than does the trinitarian formula.

Holeton believes that the threefold interrogation is a viable alternative to the trinitarian baptismal formula, because it is based on the practice of the Western church for roughly half of its history. However, he admits that the practice might be less acceptable to Eastern churches, which have experienced intense trinitarian controversies and used declarative formulas longer. He suggests that using feminine images such as "birthing" might be another way to make baptismal liturgies more gender inclusive (Holeton 1988, 71).

More than other options explored thus far, return to a threefold questioning in place of the present baptismal formula provides a new opportunity to name God in ways that are trinitarian and also inclusive. Perhaps Stookey is correct that at this point in history it is difficult to say all the trinitarian formula says both inclusively and briefly (Stookey 1983, 168). Use of the interrogatory form reduces the pressure to say so much in so few words.

Holeton has not attempted to develop definitive questions; each example is tentatively offered. Still, it is possible to reflect on the wording he offers. First, let us consider the naming of the first person of the Trinity ("Creator of heaven and earth"). In his letter to the pastors at Riverside, James Kay objected to "Creator" as naming for the first person of the Trinity. Although creation has been "appropriated" to the first person of the Trinity, all three persons participate in creation. Some object to naming one person of the Trinity in terms of activity shared by all. Thus it might be better to use metaphors that identify the first person of the Trinity as the unoriginate source of created things from whom the second and third person process (but in more accessible language). Another objection to calling the first person of the Trinity "Creator" is that, because in the traditional formula "Father" was understood to mean "Father of the Son," the implication is the idea that the second person of the Trinity is a creature of the first. This view, held by Arius, was rejected by the fourth-century councils. By saying "Creator of heaven and earth," Holeton attempts to avoid this second difficulty.

Next, let us consider Holeton's naming of the second person of the Trinity. "Child" presents a problem because it has two primary meanings; it can mean either a preadolescent human being or the son or daughter of a parent. "Son" or "daughter" is more often used to refer to an adult than "child"; "child" does not usually connote an adult person. Further, in worship, "child" has traditionally been used of Jesus mainly in reference to the baby Jesus in the Christmas story. Therefore, by association, "child of God" suggests that Jesus is not an adult; thus it tends to subordinationism even more than "son of God." Thus "Child" has limited usefulness as a characteristic title for the second person of the Trinity. On the other hand, "Son" is a masculine metaphor. Therefore, especially if the other images were gender neutral, some other way of designating Jesus as (adult) child of God would be desirable. Or, if designating the internal relationship of the first and second person of the Trinity were not deemed essential in the formula, perhaps Justin's form "our Savior Jesus Christ" could be augmented with "true God, true human."

The limitations of Holeton's questions related to the first and second persons of the Trinity might be overcome through further work. He has not offered a specific form for the question about the Holy Spirit. Although the interrogatory method holds promise, more intensive work must be done on the wording of the questions to find language that is fully trinitarian and inclusive. The possibility of using both feminine and masculine language for God should be explored.

Words comparable to "I baptize you" could be added to declare that baptism is actually taking place. Orders like the *Apostolic Tradition* fulfilled the declarative function by introducing the

newly baptized to the community. However, communities accus-
tomed to hearing the words "I baptize you" might prefer to have
a declarative statement following the interrogations, administration of water, laying on of hands, and/or chrismation. Perhaps an
adaptation of Galatians 3:26-28 could serve this function, with
wording such as the following:

> You have been baptized into Jesus Christ;
> you are now a child/children of God;
> you have put on Christ.
> There is no longer Jew nor Greek,
> there is no longer slave nor free,
> there is no male and female,
> for we are all one.

(Adapted from Schüssler Fiorenza 1983, 208)

Communities could adapt this statement to reflect actual differences in their human histories as the first Christian communities
did (cf. Gal. 3:26-28, 1 Cor. 12:13, and Col. 3:10, 11; Bouttier
1976, 9).

The interrogatory form makes it possible to draw from Christian scriptures more extensively than the traditional trinitarian
formula has done. The threefold questioning resonates with
Matthew 28:19b, and allusions to other scriptures can also be
made.

A further advantage of this proposal is that not only clergy, but
some combination of candidates, sponsors, and congregation participate in saying the key baptismal words, thus demonstrating
mutuality between clergy and laity.

The greatest difficulty with the proposal to replace the trinitarian formula with a threefold questioning seems to concern the
identifying function of the formula. Through the precedent of
several centuries of church history, Western churches might allow
that a declarative formula is not necessary, so long as interrogatory affirmation of trinitarian faith is part of baptism. However,
the same precedent does not exist for the Eastern churches.
Eastern churches have a longer history of using the trinitarian
baptismal formula than do the churches of the West. Some Syrian
churches may even have used the formula liturgically in baptism
as early as the first century. The fact that one major segment

of the church did not share in the practice compromises this alternative's claim to acceptability based on ancient tradition.

The longer the questions, the less helpful the alternative of interrogation would be for mutual recognition. Longer questions might be more difficult to agree upon, translate, or memorize, unless perhaps they were based on a widely used creed or were direct scripture quotations.

The dialogical affirmation of faith provides an excellent opportunity to use language that is not exclusively masculine or parental. Rather than augmenting or adapting the existing formula, this option makes a fresh start on wording possible. Linda Clark has observed that the more familiar a hymn is, the more resistance there will be to changing it (Linda Clark, letter to the author and Michael Bausch, 1981). The same thing may apply here. Because few phrases are more familiar in modern Christian worship than "in the name of the Father and of the Son and of the Holy Spirit," an option in a different form may seem less to tamper with familiar language than other options using the same form.

For this option to be useful, very careful work must be done in developing the questions, and they must be kept brief. Despite the difficulty of the task, this approach has much to commend it theologically.

THE METHOD OF TRANSLATION

Perhaps a method of translation, attempting to reword the trinitarian formula with nongendered terms has been the most commonly practiced alternative to baptism "in the name of the Father and of the Son and of the Holy Spirit." One fairly common attempt to recast the formula into inclusive language has been "Creator, Redeemer, Sustainer."

People who are opposed to or cautious about changing the trinitarian formula to make it gender inclusive almost always single out "Creator, Redeemer, Sustainer" for criticism.[1] The frequent criticism is probably a response to frequent use of "Creator, Redeemer, Sustainer" as a substitute for "Father, Son, and

---

1. Wainwright 1980, 353; Stookey 1982, 198–200; Erickson 1985, 208; LaCugna 1988, 68; Ramshaw 1986b, 492; cf. Kay, letter to Laubach, April 5, 1982, and Laubach, letter to Duck, May 1988.

Holy Spirit" (refer to Schüssler Fiorenza 1983, 60). "Creator, Redeemer, Sustainer" appears as an alternative baptismal formula in two books by United Methodist pastors Sharon and Thomas Neufer Emswiler. In *Women and Worship* (Neufer Emswiler and Neufer Emswiler 1984, 93)[2] it appears in a list of alternatives:

> Maker (Creator), Christ (Jesus), Holy Spirit
> Creator, Redeemer, Sustainer
> Creator, Savior, Healer
> Source, Servant, Guide
> Three in One, One in Three

In *Wholeness in Worship* they present two alternatives: "I baptize you in the name of the Father/Mother, the Christ, and the Holy Spirit"; and "I baptize you in the name of the Creator, Redeemer, and Sustainer" (Neufer Emswiler and Neufer Emswiler 1980, 134).

A service authored by UCC pastor Mitzi Eilts uses the formula "We baptize you in the name of the Creator, Sustainer, and Redeemer" (Duck 1981, 7). Eilts used this unusual order to emphasize the coequality and unity of persons in the Trinity. She believes the unchanging order ("Father, Son, Spirit") has tended to impose a hierarchy among persons, and that the church has overemphasized distinctions in the Trinity at the expense of the unity. Further, she believes the order "Creator, Sustainer, and Redeemer" is better for oral communication (Mitzi Eilts, letter to the author, August 1988).

The order for baptism by Mary Ann Neevel and Paul J. Flucke, drawn from practice at Plymouth Church (UCC), Milwaukee, Wisconsin, has the formula: "(Child's name), I baptize you in the name of God the Creator, Jesus Christ the Redeemer, and the Holy Spirit who sustains us" (Duck 1981, 8). This uses "God" only in the first term, thus becoming subject to the interpretation that "Christ" and "Spirit" are considered to be less than God.

Because the naming "Creator, Redeemer, and Sustainer" appears in some printed sources, provoking considerable criticism,

---

2. In the original edition of *Women and Worship*, only the alternatives "Creator, Redeemer, and Sustainer" and "Creator, Christ, and Holy Spirit" were offered (Neufer Emswiler and Neufer Emswiler 1974, 24).

I will evaluate adaptation of the baptismal formula through considering this particular naming and its variations. Naming its limitations and possibilities can point the way to other ways of adapting the formula that church leaders will receive more favorably.

Some criticisms of the formula "in the name of the Creator, Redeemer, Sustainer" are rather easy to dismiss. I have already advanced arguments against the idea that "Father" and "Son" are "revealed" names of God, unlike other metaphors used in scripture and Christian tradition. Another criticism that is easy to counter is concern that "Creator, Redeemer, Sustainer" contains no gender reference, and to forfeit "sexual language is to risk falling into an impersonal neuter" (Wainwright 1980, 353). Unless male-female relationships with emphasis on sexual or gendered aspects are regarded as the only possible human relationships, this concern seems to be misplaced. Is "friendship" an "impersonal" relationship because the word is not gender specific?

Stookey argues that the "intimate biological and psychological relationship of parent and child expresses in a unique way the unity of purpose that exists in all that God does" (Stookey 1982, 199). Although it is true that "an intimate biological and psychological relationship" often exists between parent and child, it does not follow that this relationship is one of "unity of purpose"; conflict often exists between parents and children.

As Holeton suggests, the insistence that the intratrinitarian relationship between Father and Son must be expressed in the formula is suspect, because the formula has never articulated the relationship between the Spirit and the other persons. Of course, language in the formula ought not contradict trinitarian understandings, for example, by implying that the second person of the Trinity is created by the first.

Although some arguments against it are difficult to support, there are genuine — though perhaps not insurmountable — difficulties with using "Creator, Redeemer, Sustainer" as a substitute for "Father, Son, Holy Spirit." Gail Ramshaw went too far when she called the naming "Creator, Redeemer, Sustainer" a "reincarnation of modalism" (Ramshaw 1986b, 492). Wainwright is more to the point when he says, "The constant use of 'Creator, Redeemer, Sustainer' might push the understanding of the Trinity in an unacceptably modalist or economic direction" (Wainwright 1980, 353).

Although great diversity of imagery and naming of God is desirable, language at baptism should name God with particular care. To call God "Creator, Redeemer, Sustainer" relies on the doctrine of appropriations — the idea that though the persons of the Trinity act in concert, some activities are more directly attributable to one person than another. As LaCugna has argued, this risks overemphasizing distinctions in the life of God at the expense of unity; for all persons participate in creating, redeeming, and sustaining, and each is more than these "functions" (LaCugna 1989, 243–244). Erickson and LaCugna argue that "economic" or "functional" language — defining persons of the Trinity by what they do in the economy of salvation — inadequately expresses the relational nature of God as grounded in the inner life of God (LaCugna 1988, 68; Erickson 1985, 208).

One response to concerns that the phrase "Creator, Redeemer, Sustainer" does not adequately refer to the immanent Trinity is that Christian worship is precisely worship and praise in response to who God is for us in the economy of salvation (as LaCugna herself argues, 1986). Considering the immanent Trinity can help to overcome misunderstandings in Christian theology, affirming that the inner life of God and the way God has been revealed to us are utterly consistent. However, it is questionable whether philosophical distinctions about the immanent Trinity must be central in the language of Christian worship, even though they may help us evaluate worship.

The formula "in the name of the Creator, Redeemer, and Sustainer" has been criticized because it uses functional terms for God rather than names (for example, Erickson 1985, 208). To respond to this concern, those who seek to adapt the formula might well choose metaphors closely identified with each person of the Trinity that more closely approximate names than functions. Although "Redeemer" has been appropriated to describe the work of the second person of the Trinity, the whole Trinity participates in redeeming. By contrast, "Christ" is specifically identified with the second person of the Trinity, the incarnation of God. However, because both "names" and "functional terms" are metaphors for God, the difference between the two may not be as great as some have argued. In my opinion, exaggerated separation of who God is from what God does belongs to a static rather than a dynamic understanding of the divine-human relationship.

Neufer Emswiler and Neufer Emswiler say that some of the alternatives for the trinitarian formula they have suggested are "descriptive." Although they admit that such descriptive terms may "tend to limit our view of that aspect of God to that particular function" they may also "help us discover new understandings of the meaning of the Trinity" (Neufer Emswiler and Neufer Emswiler 1984, 93).

Indeed, although the phrase "Father, Son, and Holy Spirit" may refer to both the economic and immanent Trinity, constant use reduces its metaphoric and revelatory possibilities. Yet careful evaluation of alternatives is certainly in order. For example, metaphoric language more resonant with scripture and contemporary life than "Creator, Redeemer, and Sustainer" could be sought. Even "Creator, Redeemer, and Spirit" or "Creator, Christ, and Spirit" would be somewhat better, though perhaps these phrases risk the idea that the Christ or Savior is created by the Creator. An adapted formula can name God in more metaphorically rich and lively ways than the traditional trinitarian formula can after centuries of exclusive use.

Perhaps the most telling criticism of "Creator, Redeemer, Sustainer" is made by Gail Ramshaw. She says that it fails to answer the central question in trinitarian naming: "Who is Jesus in relation to God" (Ramshaw 1986b, 492). "In the name of the Creator, Redeemer, and Sustainer" arguably says less about the status of Jesus Christ than baptism "in the name of Jesus," because nothing in the formula reveals that the "Creator, Redeemer, Sustainer" has anything to do with Jesus Christ. The terms "Father" and "Son" have come for Christians to be identified with the God made known in Jesus Christ, though this identification is not intrinsic; for example, Osiris and Horus are father and son in the cult of Isis. The terms "Creator, Redeemer, and Sustainer" are not necessarily identified with the Christian tradition.

Admitting the limitations of "Creator, Redeemer, and Sustainer" as a substitute for "Father, Son, and Holy Spirit" is not the same thing as ruling out adaptation of the formula as a way of addressing its masculine language. Instead, it is an impetus to seek better alternatives. Future attempts to adapt the formula should take care to balance any functional understanding of the Trinity with some expression of the unity of God and with some clear sign that the sacrament refers to the God of Jesus Christ. Those adapting the formula should consider providing some suggestion of the intratrinitarian relationship. They should seek metaphors that resonate with scripture and human experience. These metaphors might well come from human relationships.

Finally, then, let us consider how the alternative of adapting the formula measures up against the criteria I have articulated.

"Creator, Redeemer, Sustainer" names God without using gender specific language, and in that sense it is adequate naming for God. However, some critics consider this formula to be inadequate otherwise in naming God. It is fair to say that it is not a close equivalent to "Father, Son, Holy Spirit," whatever the intent of those who proposed it. However, other adaptations may yet be found that name the God made known in Jesus Christ more adequately. Rahner's explanation of the Trinity (1970) has suggested one possibility: "I baptize you in the name of God, the Source, Word, and Spirit."

"Creator, Redeemer, Sustainer" meets the other criteria fairly well. It continues to fulfill the function of focusing the liturgical act, though "Creator, Redeemer, Sustainer" is not the most lively metaphoric language. It draws on scriptural descriptions of God, though an adaptation such as "Creator, Christ, and Spirit" would have a broader base in scripture. As a means of ecumenical identification, "in the name of the Creator, Redeemer, and Sustainer" would be relatively easy to translate and memorize. However, initial responses suggest that some churches will not find it to be an adequate summary of Christian faith.

The alternative of adapting the formula, then, has the possibility of fulfilling all the criteria rather well, though the most popular approach to date, "Creator, Redeemer, Sustainer," is not without difficulties. The content, number, and vehemence of responses to this formula indicate how great a challenge it is to provide alternatives that are considered equivalent to well-known language.

THE METHOD OF CREATIVE RITUALIZATION

The two options I categorize as "creative ritualization" are quite different from one another. One is part of a baptismal liturgy suggested by Ruether for Women-Church gatherings; the other is part of the most recent United Church of Christ baptismal order.

Rosemary Ruether's Baptismal Order

In *Women-Church*, Ruether, a Roman Catholic feminist theologian, offers a baptismal ritual for Women-Church gatherings (Ruether 1985, 125-130). The ritual draws on ancient ceremony, including a litany of disaffiliation similar to the traditional renunciations. After the water rite, the baptized are clothed in a white garment, anointed, and given a candle and a stole. Then everyone shares a Eucharist of milk and honey.

These words are spoken each of three times when water is administered through pouring or immersion:

> Through the power of the Source, the liberating Spirit, and the forerunners of our hope, be freed from the power of evil. May the forces of violence, of militarism, of sexism, of racism, of injustice, and of all that diminishes human life lose their power over your life. May all the influences of these powers be washed away in these purifying waters. May you enter the promised land of milk and honey and grow in virtue, strength, and truthfulness of mind. And may the oil of gladness always anoint your head. (Ruether 1985, 130)

Baptism is here administered "through the power of the Source, the liberating Spirit, and the forerunners of our hope." Though there is a threefold washing, this order does not name the second person of the Trinity except as one among an indefinite number of forerunners of hope. This would seem to be in keeping with Ruether's christology articulated in an earlier work (Ruether 1983, 116-138).

The words Ruether proposes for use during administration of water are much like the trinitarian formula in their liturgical function. They clarify the meaning of water baptism theologically and liturgically. However, because they do not meet two of the criteria considered here, they are unlikely to be useful in many churches.

The naming of God in Ruether's baptism ritual is gender inclusive. The reference to sexism as something that diminishes human life keeps the lack of gender reference from disguising or evoking a hidden gender bias. The naming of God as "Source" is capable of referring to God as "Creator" and "Father," applying to both created and uncreated realities. However, because the baptism occurs through "the power of the Source, the liberating Spirit, and the forerunners of hope," the order avoids an affirmation of trinitarian faith as usually understood. Where affirmation of the second person of the Trinity has been made in past formulas, here an unspecified group, "the forerunners of our hope," is named. Ruether may here be alluding to a communal christology. This would, however, seem to be insufficient expression of faith in God through Jesus Christ to be useful across a wide spectrum of Christian churches.

By its length the formula defies memorization and translation. Because it apparently avoids expressing trinitarian theology, it would not do much to serve ecumenical identification. Ecumenical recognition aside, threefold repetition of such a long statement would seem to be more monotonous than dramatic.

Ruether's formula resonates with several scripture passages. "Liberating Spirit" calls to mind many scripture passages, including Luke 4:18-19 (parallels Isa. 61:1, 2, and 2 Cor. 3:17). The image of "milk and honey" is drawn from Hebrew scripture passages such as Deuteronomy 26:5-11; in the *Apostolic Tradition*, the newly baptized also received milk and honey (with the bread and wine) for the baptismal Eucharist. A correlation between scriptural meanings of conversion and the meaning of conversion in a contemporary context is drawn (refer especially to Luke 3:10-14). Ruether's alternative, then, shows how one may draw upon a broader range of scriptural associations than the historical trinitarian formula does.

Ruether is not seeking to create a separate denomination alongside others, but an Exodus community where for some years feminist women and men may bring to life the hope for liberated and liberating community (Ruether 1985, 57-74). Some members of this Exodus community may participate in existing Christian churches, and some may not. However, "unity" with and "mutual recognition" by Christian churches in their present patriarchal forms is not the concern of Women-Church. Thus, to judge Ruether's formula in terms of viability in an ecumenical context is to ask it to do something it does not seek or intend.

From Ruether's baptismal liturgy, churches can, however, learn how to ritualize the meaning of baptism in vivid ways that correlate Christian traditions with the process of liberation from patriarchal oppression. "Liberating Spirit" as a name for God in her formula is a case in point. Ruether's baptismal liturgy demonstrates the importance of feminist creative ritualization as a source for renewing Christian worship.

Balancing the Formula with Feminine Language Elsewhere in the Service

Another creative alternative to present baptismal practice uses the traditional trinitarian formula, but balances it elsewhere in the baptismal liturgy with feminine imagery for God. The editors of the United Church of Christ *Book of Worship* chose this option (1986, 142–143).[3]

To address the formula's use of masculine language for God, the 1986 UCC *Book of Worship* provides a feminine image for God in one option for the "Prayer for the Baptized" following baptism. It begins: "We give thanks, O Holy One, mother and father of all the faithful . . . " (United Church of Christ 1986, 143). This imaginative effort toward inclusivity falls short. By addressing God both as "mother and father," it augments but does not balance the masculine language of the formula. It is one of two options for the prayer, and may not be used anyway. Moreover, the *Book of Worship* mainly avoids gender references to God, except in the Prayer of Jesus. This may be a good way to introduce inclusive language where it had not been used before, because the metaphors used are familiar, even if some familiar metaphors are avoided. The United Church of Christ, the first denomination to provide a worship book characterized by a thoroughgoing commitment to inclusive language for God and humanity, may have been wise to exercise caution in this way. However, avoiding any gender reference to God limits rather than enriches liturgical language. Further, occasional use of feminine terms helps to free us from the habit of thinking of God as masculine, even when gender-free terms are used. More frequent use of feminine and

---

3. The present section incorporates some material from my article reviewing the UCC *Book of Worship* ("Baptism in the Church's Life: From the Periphery to the Center," *Prism* 3, no. 2 [Fall 1988]: 12–22).

masculine imagery for God throughout the book would have had advantages.

The UCC baptismal order is more adequate in its naming of God than it would be without the prayer using a feminine metaphor for God. It begins to move past predominantly masculine language for God, providing congregations with the experience of using a feminine metaphor for God. However, because it does not replace the traditional formula, the UCC *Book of Worship* does not adequately address the problem of gender bias in naming. Moreover, because the book rarely uses masculine metaphors for God elsewhere, the formula does not adequately represent the characteristic ways of addressing God in congregations that use this nonmandatory book. Use of the unaltered formula also contradicts the denomination's genuine efforts toward creating egalitarian community. On the other hand, the strength in naming of the traditional formula — its resonance with orthodox trinitarian solutions — is maintained.

The liturgical function of the formula as dramatic center of the rite is maintained. However, the use of feminine imagery is so exceptional here that it may not be very accessible to communities. The scripture rooting in Matthew 28:19b is well-defined and is complemented by rich and diverse scripture allusion in the rest of the service. Other denominations would have no difficulty in recognizing this ritual as the sacrament of baptism, even if they took exception to the feminine metaphor in one prayer.

The United Church of Christ's effort to address masculine language in the baptismal formula raises the question of context. The traditional trinitarian baptismal formula might be used in contexts in which God is described using mostly masculine language or little gender-specific language, or both feminine and masculine language. How does the context affect how the formula is heard? Using the traditional formula in a context where few gender-specific terms are used may give the impression that masculine language is needed to legitimate baptism. However, in a context in which both feminine and masculine images for God were used freely, and in which egalitarian leadership styles had been developed, the traditional formula might be used because of its historic and ecumenical significance. Continuing to use the traditional formula might be possible in contexts in which feminine imagery, and not only masculine or nongendered imagery, is used. Still, the baptismal formula is so important that I believe it is preferable to seek alternatives that do not give the impression of masculine bias. The United Church of Christ would do well to continue its exploration and ecumenical conversations concerning the formula.

COMPARISON OF ALTERNATIVES

Serious theological and ethical difficulties encumber the trinitarian baptismal formula "I baptize you [you are baptized] in the name of the Father and of the Son and of the Holy Spirit." Frequent use of paternal imagery for God may encourage violence against children, and it may be a barrier to effective Christian witness and faith response. Using paternal imagery infrequently — but then in such pivotal times of worship as the act of baptism — causes similar problems. Use of paternal imagery for God in the formula — especially in the absence of any feminine imagery for God — cannot be ethically justified. Masculine and paternal imagery has been so predominant in Christian worship and feminine imagery has been so lacking that masculine language has become literalized and idolatrous. So long as society is structured according to patriarchal patterning, "God the Father" will not be free from association with powerful and sometimes abusive patriarchs in home and society. Surely this association endangers the theological adequacy of this metaphor as a predominant name for God. In a patriarchal society, the "Father-Son" metaphor will also be associated with the subordination of son to father. The traditional trinitarian baptismal formula is unacceptable as characteristic naming for God.

Viable alternatives to the formula are available. In my opinion, most if not all of these alternatives are preferable to present practice. If no one of them is beyond criticism, neither is the traditional trinitarian formula, even apart from its masculine gender language. Justin spoke truly when he said that "no one may give a proper name to the ineffable God, and if anyone should dare say there is one, he is hopelessly insane" (*First Apology* in Richardson et al. 1970, 282–283). Although some language for God may be judged to be more adequate for God than other language, no way of speaking about God is without limitation. Of the alternatives that I have considered, adapting the formula and restoring threefold questioning seem most promising to me. These alternatives offer opportunities to explore the naming of God theologically and metaphorically, and to seek the most adequate naming.

The alternative presented by the United Church of Christ *Book of Worship* is not a very adequate alternative to present practice. It continues to keep paternal and masculine language for God at a privileged place in Christian worship, giving the impression that masculine naming is necessary to legitimate the sacrament of baptism. For those who believe that at present they must continue using the traditional formula but balance it with feminine imagery, the Riverside Church formula is a much better alternative with an immediate claim to ecumenical recognition. At one time, I would have called the Riverside Church formula the most attractive alternative. However, as my research progressed, I came to believe that neither "father" nor "mother" is fit as the characteristic Christian metaphor for God in a patriarchal society. Until patriarchal patterns are only a part of past history and not present reality, predominant use of parental imagery endangers children and endangers the faith response. Therefore I do not feel that this alternative is adequate, even though it moves toward balancing gender imagery and clearly affirms trinitarian theology.

The alternative presented by Rosemary Ruether is creative in its naming of God and its use of scripture. Nevertheless, it is not an adequate baptismal naming for Christian communities. Perhaps her intention was not so much to reject trinitarian naming for God as to provide a ritual of initiation that could be used in groups that include women who are not Christians. However, her triad of "the Source, the liberating Spirit, and the forerunners of our hope" appears to avoid affirming Jesus Christ's unique participation in the life of God. Therefore, it is not so useful for specifically Christian initiation. However, "Source" and "Liberating Spirit" are quite acceptable theologically as names for the first and third persons of the Trinity. Further, her wording "through the power of" may be more expressive than "in the name of," because the latter phrase does not have all the connotations in modern society that it did in ancient times. Thus Ruether will contribute to my own reconstruction of the trinitarian formula.

Baptism in the name of Christ does not rely on trinitarian naming to clarify the status of Jesus Christ in relation to God. Instead, it emphasizes the presence of the risen Christ in the Christian community. Used in the sacramental context of baptism, it implies that through Christ God is revealed. Although this formula antedates the trinitarian formulations, it does not necessarily contradict trinitarian faith. "Baptism in the name of Christ" is also fairly adequate in terms of gender-inclusive naming. Further, this formula is scripturally resonant, with a strong basis in church tradition. For all these reasons it is a fairly acceptable baptismal formula, especially when augmented with a triadic blessing.

Although baptism "in the name of Christ" is acceptable, a fuller expression of Christian faith that is gender inclusive would be better. Because adaptation and recovery of the interrogatory affirmation of faith provide this opportunity, they are the two best alternatives.

Further, these two alternatives provide the opportunity to seek a living language of faith. "Father" and "Father, Son, and Holy Spirit" have been used predominantly to the exclusion of other metaphors in Christian worship. Thus these metaphors for God have lost much of their power to evoke a faith response to God, especially for persons whose experience with human fathers has been unfortunate. The most adequate alternatives will go beyond simply translating these names through formal correspondence into other names. The most adequate alternatives will seek to name God in continuity with Christian tradition yet with living metaphors capable of forming and expressing the faith of present and future generations of Christians. To do less than this is to undertake the challenge but to miss the creative opportunity presented by the need to replace the traditional trinitarian formula for baptism. The particular alternatives I have called "creative ritualization" are limited in their usefulness, but developing good alternatives will certainly require creativity.

Adapting the formula makes it possible to seek living language produced by contemporary theological reflection. However, most present adaptations do not go far enough, because they seek to recast the formula at the level of words, not sentences, and to provide a one-to-one equivalent for "Father, "Son," and, perhaps,

"Spirit"; they translate through formal correspondence. A dynamic equivalent recasting of the formula might not even be in triadic form. However, a short, adapted declarative formula will need to be adequate for characteristic Christian naming of God in baptism and in all of worship.

All or most of the present adaptations have sought to find new ways of triadic naming. "I baptize you [you are baptized] in the name of [through the power of] [God], the Source, Word, and Liberating Spirit" is the best short triadic naming that I have been able to discover or conceive. I would argue that this triadic form uses names closely associated with each person of the Trinity. It avoids implication that the second person of the Trinity is created. It neither affirms nor contradicts understandings of the immanent Trinity. Each of the metaphors used is accessible to contemporary persons, though I believe that as creative persons continue to reflect, more lively language will be discovered.

Characteristic naming of God that is consistent with trinitarian faith is not necessarily triadic in form. For example, "I baptize you in the name of the God who has been made known through [or, embodied in] Jesus Christ" makes a stronger christological statement than "I baptize you in the name of the Creator, Redeemer, and Sustainer." The point is to discover a short declarative statement of Christian faith, not to duplicate the triadic form of the traditional trinitarian formula.

Coming up with a new and more adequate declarative formula would certainly be a good way to replace the baptismal formula. Yet at present, I feel a threefold questioning is even better. As Routley and Troeger have observed, this is an age when the theological ground is shifting and new ways of expressing Christian faith are emerging. At present, for many Christians it is a great challenge to find words to name God that do not perpetuate patriarchal patterns and that express faith in a lively way. Threefold questioning, though rather brief, is less compressed than declarative formulas have been. It provides the best opportunity to recast the language of faith in careful and evocative ways, so it is the option I will develop in my own constructive proposal.

CHAPTER 9

PROPOSAL FOR CHANGE

The words spoken as the water of baptism is administered focus its meaning. At this point in history, I believe that speaking these words in the form of three questions that affirm trinitarian faith is the best alternative. With strong historical precedent, threefold questioning provides the opportunity for inclusive and metaphorically rich naming of God.

My own baptismal order would begin with an opening statement rich in scriptural allusions, after which the candidates would be presented. A ritual of disaffiliation from the patriarchal powers of this world and affiliation in loving discipleship with the God of Jesus Christ would follow. Next, thanksgivings would be said over the water. The presider would ask candidates and congregation to join in affirming their faith by answering three questions. Then, after each response, the presider would administer the water. I propose the following questions and responses:

Do you believe in God, the Source, the fountain of life?
I believe.
Do you believe in Christ, the offspring of God embodied in Jesus of Nazareth and in the church?
I believe.
Do you believe in the liberating Spirit of God, the wellspring of new life?
I believe.

Laying on of hands with chrismation and a baptismal prayer would follow. Then the presider would say:

N, through the power of God you have been baptized into a new relationship with God and this community. You have put on Christ.
"Whoever is in Christ is a new creation.
The old has passed away, the new has come."
You have passed through the waters of new life.

Together we join in exodus from the injustice and sin of this world
toward God's new age.

The baptizing community would then welcome the newly baptized persons, and all would share in a eucharistic meal.

I believe the dialogue I propose for use during the administration of water is acceptable in its naming of God. It avoids
predominantly masculine language. Specific naming of the male
Jesus of Nazareth is put in the context of the whole church as
the body of Christ, following Brock's christology. Although some
feminists hold that "God" is masculine in connotation, I am unwilling to concede that "God" is a masculine term. I claim "God"
as a nongendered name for God, just as I claim "poet," not "poetess," as a name for myself. I decided not to avoid "God" because
I wanted through repetition of the word to emphasize the unity
and equality of God as Source, Christ, and Spirit.

My alternative is acceptable in its affirmation of trinitarian
faith. All three persons are named as God. Although using one
functional title ("the liberating Spirit"), I generally use metaphors that are specifically associated with one person of the
Trinity, without relying on the doctrine of appropriations. By
calling Christ the "offspring of God," I hint at traditional understandings of the inner relationship in the Trinity, while avoiding
the subordinationism and masculine language of the "Father-
Son" metaphor. It is enough to hint. The words spoken at baptism
witness to the way God has been made known in the economy
of salvation; they are not a doctrinal test or philosophical trea-
tise. I hint at but do not contradict traditional understandings
of the immanent Trinity. The phrase "in the church" assumes
that inner relationship in the Trinity is open to the life of the
world.

By using "fountain," "offspring," and "wellspring," I seek to
represent metaphorically the relationship among the persons of
the Trinity. These metaphors are related water metaphors, appropriate to baptism, and carried through in the phrase "you
have passed through the waters of new life" in the declarative
statement after the chrismation and prayer. They are more lively
than the overused "Father-Son" metaphor, while being resonant
with scripture and accessible to people in all or most parts of
the world. "Fountains" and "wellsprings" are even more pre-

cious in desert and arctic lands where they are less frequently found. I would want to complement these natural metaphors with personal metaphors elsewhere in the liturgy.

Certainly the naming of God in my proposed alternative provides a summary of Christian faith and specifies the God through whom the baptism is administered.

My proposed alternative acceptably fulfills its liturgical function. The words I have suggested accompany the act of water baptism with witness to the God made known in Jesus Christ and in the church. Together with the administration of water, they provide a dramatic center for the rite. The lively and accessible metaphors of this alternative are appropriate for doxological use throughout Christian worship.

The baptismal dialogue I have proposed is appropriate for use in Christian communities in process of becoming free from patriarchal patterns and of creating new patterns of relationship. The dialogical form undermines hierarchical assumptions by involving not just the presider, but the whole community in affirming Christian faith at the moment of baptism. The wording of the third question, "Do you believe in the liberating Spirit of God, the wellspring of new life?" explicitly affirms that baptism represents liberation into a new life.

It might seem that a threefold baptismal questioning would be more appropriate in liturgical function to baptisms in which the candidates could speak for themselves. In fact, I would encourage baptism by confession of faith as the norm for baptism, even while accepting infant baptism. Although infant baptism signifies incorporation into the church and witnesses to the grace of God, conversion from the patriarchal patterns of society toward new patterns of relationship awaits conscious decision. Administering baptism to those who cannot confess their faith appears to deny mutual relationship between the candidate and both God and the community of faith; the candidate is simply acted upon, rather than being an active participant in the sacrament. These concerns apart, however, I fail to understand why it is better for the presider alone to affirm faith during the administration of water. Because the community and not the candidate responds in faith to God's self-giving in infant baptism, it is arguably more important for the whole community to affirm faith during infant baptisms than during confessing baptisms.

I sought scriptural resonance through a number of strategies. "Fountain of life" comes from Psalm 36: "For with you is the fountain of life; in your light we see light" (v. 9). It is a metaphor for God as the unoriginate source of all things. "Do you believe in Christ, embodied in Jesus of Nazareth and in the church?" resonates both with John 1:14 ("the Word became flesh") and 1 Corinthians 12:27 ("you are the body of Christ"). "Wellspring" recalls John 4; and while Raymond Brown cautions against narrowly identifying the "spring of living water" (John 4:14) with the gift of the Spirit, he allows that this is one association of the metaphor (Brown 1966, 179–180). As discussed above in connection with Ruether's baptismal order, "liberating Spirit" has rich associations with many scripture passages. By juxtaposing this term with "the wellspring of new life," I hope to emphasize the meaning of baptism as sign of the new age. The triadic structure of my baptismal dialogue resonates with Matthew 28:19 in form if not content.

The declarative statement toward the end serves the dramatic function of announcing that the baptism has taken place. It serves the theological and ethical purpose of declaring that baptism is a sign of the new age and of entry into a new pattern of relationships. I paraphrase 2 Corinthians 5:17 (which may be another reference to the early baptismal formula of Gal. 3:26–28) to resonate with scripture and announce a new pattern of relationships. Then, saying that the candidate has "passed through the waters of new life," I imitate Ruether's imagery of exodus out of the unjust structures of patriarchy.

The alternative I have presented has good claim to ecumenical acceptance. It names God and summarizes faith in a way that should be recognizable to most Christians, partly because of its scriptural resonance. These questions are brief, and they resonate with scripture; thus they can easily be translated and remembered. The metaphors are lively and cross-cultural in association. For all these reasons, and because a baptismal dialogue was used throughout much of Western Christian history, my alternative stays in continuity with Christian tradition. At the same time, it addresses the problem of predominantly masculine language for God. As I have already argued, the church must deal with its sexism if Christian unity is to be authentic.

My baptismal order as a whole would incorporate all the meanings of baptism I articulated in Chapter 5. In the dialogue itself, the words "liberating Spirit" point to baptism as conversion and the words "wellspring of new life" point to baptism as a gift of the Spirit and sign of God's new age. In the baptismal pronouncement, I point to baptism as "incorporation into the church" through the words "you have been baptized into a new relationship with God and this community." Elsewhere in the service I would refer to baptism as dying and rising with Christ in solidarity with all people, especially the neglected and oppressed. Thus my alternative is consistent with the modern church's recovery of richer scriptural imagery for baptism.

In forming my alternative, I called upon all the methods outlined in Chapter 4. Through a method of suspicion, I identified the patriarchal bias of the traditional trinitarian formula. Through a method of remembrance, I called for restoration of the baptismal dialogue and drew upon "fountain of life" and "wellspring" as scriptural metaphors for God. Through the method of translation, I used the words "offspring of God" to hint at what "Son of God" has traditionally expressed. Through the method of creative ritualization, I drew on feminist theological insights to include the community of faith in christological understandings.

The dialogical affirmation of faith that I have offered as a substitute for a declarative trinitarian baptismal formula does not do everything I would have wished it to do. I earlier stated a preference for using both feminine and masculine language to revise the baptismal formula, but the images which came to me were not personal but natural. I would want to use both feminine and masculine imagery elsewhere in the liturgy to counteract the tendency to hear nongendered words as masculine. I use "offspring" both to hint at intratrinitarian relationships and carry through the water metaphor, but I have reservations about this implicit parent-child metaphor.

I realize that threefold questioning has less historical precedence in the East than in the West. However, it seems to me that this alternative makes theological adequacy more possible, because it does not require such a condensed statement of faith. Thus I am giving precedence to theological adequacy over traditional form, because in the long run I suspect that this will support ecumenical dialogue.

Church leaders ought not avoid discussion of the baptismal formula for fear that it will delay organic union or universal recognition of baptism. Several other substantive issues will have to be resolved before the church can realize either of these goals. The formula should be discussed along with these other issues, because there are already several variations in practice. I plead for a worldwide church that makes room for different traditions, even as it witnesses to shared faith and moves away from patriarchal patterns.

In the early stages of writing the dissertation on which this book is based, I was reluctant to choose and defend any one alternative. I realize now that I was resisting offering one model as the definitive answer that the church could follow for the next eight hundred years. Like most feminists involved in shaping liturgy, I have always hoped that local communities who build on my ideas and words will work with them until they are appropriate for their own worship life. Indeed, some churches may wish to develop affirmations of faith in consultation with each person being baptized or bringing children for baptism.[1]

I offer my proposal as a model for use in churches that are now moving past patriarchal patterns. I believe that the model I have developed has few of the weaknesses and many of the strengths of other proposed alternatives. I hope it will generate discussion and revised practice, leading to even better alternatives.

Presently no denomination in its recognized liturgies or official statements has mandated changing the baptismal formula. However, not all denominations explicitly require clergy to baptize "in the name of the Father and of the Son and of the Holy Spirit." The 1988 General Conference of the United Methodist Church rejected resolutions requiring the traditional formula for baptisms (United Methodist Church, 1988; Hoyt Hickman, letter to the author, November 1990). In fact, according to Hoyt Hickman, Director of Resource Development of the Section for Worship, United Methodist Church, it would have been an unprecedented departure from that church's tradition of local freedom in worship to require that "Father, Son, and Holy Spirit" be used in baptisms:

---

1. This intriguing idea was suggested by Janet Walton and Miriam Therese Winter at a meeting of the Feminist Liturgy study group of the North American Academy of Liturgy, January 1991.

Any action requiring clergy to use the words "Father, Son and Holy Spirit" in baptizing... would have been astonishing in view of our 200-year tradition of freedom in local church worship. While we have had an official Ritual, it has never been a requirement of church law that our clergy and congregations follow it. I know of United Methodist clergy who use other formulas in baptizing, and I have not heard anyone suggest that they were subject to discipline for doing so (Hoyt Hickman, letter to the author, November 1990)

The United Church of Christ, another denomination that raised questions about the masculine language of the formula, has a similar tradition of local freedom in worship. Those who officiate at baptisms in the United Methodist Church and the United Church of Christ have not only the freedom but also the responsibility to develop liturgies based on their best theological, liturgical, and ethical judgments.

All who are working for feminist reconstruction of liturgical language in local churches must develop contextualized strategies for the process of change. In most contexts, change will best come gradually, not all at once. I suspect that in most cases, words that have been committed to memory — such as the baptismal formula or the Prayer of Jesus — should be changed later rather than earlier in the process. But churches who generally use inclusive language in worship surely will want to seek alternatives, rather than have the baptismal formula be discordant with language used elsewhere in worship. Communities who are seeking to move beyond patriarchal patterns and to live out God's new order now will surely want to avoid patriarchal assumptions in words that mark persons' entry into the church. Churches who use nonpatriarchal language to express their baptismal faith can be the testing ground for revisions that may in time be accepted in larger ecumenical contexts.[2]

---

2. Horace T. Allen Jr. has suggested that denominations in which practice is already diverse might address the question of mutual recognition by declaring "in definitive language that whatever the language of the local liturgy, the intent is 'to do what the church has always done,' i.e., to baptize in the name of the Father, the Son, and the Holy Spirit" (letter to the author, January 1991). In other words, denominational leaders can reaffirm the intent toward continuity with Christian faith and tradition even when language (and I would add, theology) is being reformulated.

Certainly denominations in which practice is already diverse should press their ecumenical partners to discuss the language of the baptismal formula. Those who represent these denominations in ecumenical discussions about liturgy must not fail to raise questions coming from feminist concern for justice and new patterns of relationship. Such persons may represent a small percentage of the world's Christians. As North Americans, they can assume no prerogative for worldwide ecumenical leadership. Still, advocacy for the full inclusion of women in the liturgy and life of the church is theologically and ethically essential. Advocacy for women is an important contribution some ecumenical partners can bring to the life of the whole church. The United Church of Canada, although officially mandating use of "Father, Son, and Holy Spirit" in the baptismal formula, has fulfilled this role in the Canadian Council of Churches by asking for discussion of inclusive language, including the language of the trinitarian formula (Hallett Llewellyn, letter to the author, December 1990). Other denominations concerned about the masculine language of the formula and about mutual recognition of baptism should follow suit.

Francine Cardman, in an article entitled "BEM and the Community of Women and Men," observed that "the [BEM] text's lack of attention to the male language of the trinitarian baptismal formula" is "something of a time bomb," because it has already raised difficulties in some churches (Cardman 1984, 87). In reference to the ordination of women she asked:

> Why should the onus of continuing ecclesial division rest solely on the churches that ordain women, rather than being shared humbly and equally by those who do not? (Cardman 1984, 94)

She argues that the burden of division be shifted and shared, and that women's concerns be considered central to the project of seeking Christian and human unity.

Cardman's words about the ordination of women also apply to mutual recognition of baptism. In *Baptism, Eucharist, and Ministry*, baptism is called "liberation into new humanity" (Faith and Order 1982, par. 2), and churches are asked "wherever possible" to express recognition of one another's baptism (Faith and Order 1982, par. 16). Might not the onus be "shifted and shared" so that churches that continue to baptize "in the name of the Father and of the Son and of the Holy Spirit" might recognize agreed-upon variations to the formula as a "means of expressing the baptismal unity given in Christ" (Faith and Order 1982, par. 16)? Though some churches may not yet consider an alternative formula essential in expressing liberation into new humanity, they should leave room for churches who do believe it essential to use alternatives. Unity is not uniformity.

The theological issues involved in changing baptismal formula are as complex as they are important. Yet the churches may draw on a common past, even as the Spirit draws them toward a future of growing unity in which both women and men fully share. There are enough good alternatives that the church can find a way — even in the baptismal formula — to express its faith through metaphors that transcend masculine bias and welcome the coming of God's new day in our midst.

APPENDIX

BEM RESPONSES RELATED TO THE BAPTISMAL FORMULA

In 1982, the Faith and Order Commission of the World Council of Churches published a document, *Baptism, Eucharist, and Ministry* (BEM), which outlined the convergences the commission had identified on these subjects. One hundred forty-three official responses received from churches, councils of churches, and church leaders have been published in six volumes (Faith and Order 1986a, 1986b, 1987a, 1987b, 1988a, and 1988b). The document states: "Baptism is administered with water in the name of the Father, the Son and the Holy Spirit" (Faith and Order 1982, par. 17). Most of the responses either affirmed this statement or expressed no reservations about it, but some churches expressed reservations about the formula. The responses give an indication of baptismal theology and practice worldwide, though by no means did all denominations provide reports. For example, no churches identified as Pentecostal had responded, which is significant for this study because some of these churches baptize in the name of Jesus.

Some churches said that they recognize only baptisms administered in the name of "the Father, the Son, and the Holy Spirit." The Episcopal Church [USA] reported that they did not "acknowledge as Baptism" any baptisms that use formulas other than "in the name of the Father, the Son, and the Holy Spirit," but asked for discussion of the question (Faith and Order 1986b, 59). The Reformed Churches of the Netherlands stated that the Roman Catholic episcopacy had not recognized some baptisms by the Remonstrant Fraternity (a Reformation church in their country) because the trinitarian formula had not been used. What, if any, alternative formula was used was not identified in the response (Faith and Order 1987b, 102). The Bulgarian Orthodox church insisted that the difference between the Eastern and

Western forms of the formula "must be removed," but that Orthodox churches cannot change the form "*Name* is baptized..." (Faith and Order 1986b, 16). It seems safe to say that this church regards the difference between the passive and active formulas to be more than syntactical.

Four churches raised questions about the present form of the baptismal formula because of its use of exclusively masculine language for God. The United Church of Christ [USA] wrote:

> Many in our church who give full assent to the doctrine of the Trinity look to the day when the language used to express what that doctrine intends will be gender sensitive and inclusive. (Faith and Order 1986b, 328)

The United Church of Canada criticized the patriarchal tone of the document in general (Faith and Order 1986b, 285) and asked for further work by the Faith and Order Commission on the issue of masculine language in the trinitarian formula:

> The use of the Trinitarian formula in baptism seems to be fundamental to any ecumenical consensus. However in many churches, including our own, the formula is questioned as intrinsically "sexist." This is a problem that is critical for many Western churches like ours but barely exists as an issue for many churches elsewhere. As we, the United Church of Canada, struggle with the issue, we become aware that it is more complex than a question of language, but involves our basic understanding of God. We would urge further work by the Faith and Order Commission that would show sensitivity to the fact that the Trinitarian formula, while central to ecumenical consensus, is experienced by many Christians as a source of alienation. (Faith and Order 1986b, 279)

The Anglican Church of Canada asked for clarification about the baptismal formula and its use of masculine language:

> A question has been raised, in connection with the Trinitarian baptismal formula, which Faith and Order could clarify. Are we being asked to recognize as valid the baptism of persons baptized only with the particular wording "in the name of the Father, and of the Son, and of the Holy Spirit"? What of the request by some in the Anglican communion and elsewhere for a gender-free formula (Creator, Redeemer, and Sanctifier, for example)? What of the biblical formula, used by some Christians,

"in the name of Jesus"? Our relations with other denominations have sometimes been strained because of their baptismal
wording or liturgical practice. For a number of reasons, then, we
request that the question be more fully explored. We are not,
necessarily, asking for a change in the formula, but for some
guidance. (Faith and Order 1986b, 45)

The United Methodist Church [USA] also stopped short of
recommending a change in the formula:

Since the biblical and traditional form for baptism with water
includes the phrase, "in the name of the Father, the Son, and the
Holy Spirit" we do not urge abandoning or changing it. Nevertheless, with the heightened sensitivity to the disproportionate
masculinity of liturgical language, we are compelled to sense a
certain reserve about perpetuating this form of the trinitarian
name of the triune God. (Faith and Order 1986b, 184–185)

Although this United Methodist statement about the baptismal
formula is quite restrained, a section elsewhere advocated gender-
inclusive language and discussed it in more detail than did any
other report.

The Church of North India requested that baptisms administered in the name of Jesus be accepted because some churches use
that form. The National Council of Churches of the Philippines
also indicated that some of their member churches baptized "in
the name of Jesus" (Faith and Order 1988a, 189), though without
any hint of concern about the masculine language of the traditional baptismal formula. Finally, one report, from a leader of the
Evangelical Presbyterian Church of Ghana, appeared to question
the essentiality of the formula, saying that water is the "essential
symbol of baptism" (Faith and Order 1988b, 93).

REFERENCES

Aquinas, Thomas. [1975 edition]. *Summa Theologica*, vol. 3a. Translated by James J. Cunningham. New York: Blackfriars in conjunction with McGraw-Hill.

Atkinson, Clarissa. 1987. "Your Servant, My Mother: The Figure of Saint Monica in the Ideology of Christian Motherhood." In *Immaculate and Powerful: The Female in Sacred Image and Social Reality*, edited by Clarissa Atkinson, Constance Buchanan, and Margaret R. Miles, 139–172. Boston: Beacon Press.

Augustine, Bishop of Hippo. [1956 reprint of 1887 Schaff edition]. "On the Holy Trinity." In *A Select Library of the Nicene and Post-Nicene Fathers*, edited by Philip Schaff, translated by Arthur West Haddan, vol. 3, 1–228. Grand Rapids: Wm. B. Eerdmans.

Banks, Robert. 1980. *Paul's Idea of Community*. Grand Rapids: Wm. B. Eerdmans.

Barnstone, Willis. 1984. *The Other Bible*. San Francisco: Harper & Row, Publishers.

Baron, Dennis. 1986. *Grammar and Gender*. New Haven: Yale University Press.

Barr, Browne. 1987. "Prayers of Confession: Let's Get Unspecific." *The Christian Century* 104 (October 27): 844.

Barth, Karl. 1956. *Church Dogmatics* IV/1, paragraph 62, 725–739. Translated by G. W. Bromiley. Edinburgh: T. & T. Clark. (Original German edition, 1953).

———. 1957. *Church Dogmatics* II/1, paragraphs 26 and 27, 63–178 and 179–254. Translated by G. W. Bromiley. Edinburgh: T. & T. Clark. (Original German edition, 1940).

———. 1969. *Church Dogmatics* IV/4. *The Doctrine of Reconciliation* (fragment). Translated by G. W. Bromiley. Edinburgh: T. & T. Clark. (Original German edition, 1967).

———. 1975. *Church Dogmatics* I/1. Translated by G. W. Bromiley. Edinburgh: T. & T. Clark. (Original German edition, 1932).

Basow, Susan A. 1980. *Sex-Role Stereotypes: Traditions and Alternatives*. Monterey, Calif.: Brooks/Cole.

Battles, Ford Lewis, and John Walchenbach. 1980. *Analysis of the Institutes of the Christian Religion of John Calvin*. Grand Rapids: Baker Book House.

Beasley-Murray, G. R. 1962. *Baptism in the New Testament.* Grand Rapids: Wm. B. Eerdmans.

Bennett, Robert A. 1987. "The Power of Language in Worship." *Theology Today* 43 (January): 546–551.

Bietenhard, Hans. 1967. *"Onoma."* In *Theological Dictionary of the New Testament,* edited by Gerhard Kittel. Vol. 5 translated and edited by Geoffrey W. Bromiley, 242–283. Grand Rapids: Wm. B. Eerdmans.

Black, Max. 1962. *Models and Metaphors.* Ithaca, N.Y.: Cornell University Press.

Bloesch, Donald G. 1985. *The Battle for the Trinity: The Debate Over Inclusive God-Language.* Ann Arbor: Servant Publications.

Bohn, Carole R. 1985. "The Silent Partners: Religious Tradition and Domestic Violence." Unpublished paper delivered at the American Academy of Religion.

Boucher, Madeleine. 1983. "Scriptural Readings: God-Language and Nonsexist Translation." *Reformed Liturgy and Music* 17 (Fall): 156–159.

Bouttier, Michel. 1976. "Complexio Oppositorum: Sur les Formules de 1 Cor. 12:13; Gal. 3:26–28; Col. 3:10–11." *New Testament Studies* 23 (October): 1–19.

Brand, Eugene L. 1975. *Baptism: A Pastoral Perspective.* Minneapolis: Augsburg Publishing House.

Brock, Rita Nakashima. 1988. *Journeys by Heart: A Christology of Erotic Power.* New York: Crossroad.

Brown, Raymond E. 1966. *The Gospel According to John (i–xii),* 179–180. *The Anchor Bible.* Garden City, N.Y.: Doubleday & Co.

———. 1979. "Roles of Women in the Fourth Gospel." *The Community of the Beloved Disciple,* app. 2, 183–198. New York: Paulist Press.

———. 1984. *The Churches the Apostles Left Behind.* New York: Paulist Press.

Burnett, Fred W. 1984. Review of *The Father, the Son, and the Holy Spirit,* by Jane Schaberg. *Interpretation* 38 (July): 320, 322.

Bynum, Caroline Walker. 1982. *Jesus as Mother: Studies in the Spirituality of the High Middle Ages.* Berkeley: University of California Press.

———. 1986. "Introduction: The Complexity of Symbols." In *Gender and Religion: On the Complexity of Symbols.* Edited by Caroline Walker Bynum, Stevan Harrell, and Paula Richmond, 1–20. Boston: Beacon Press.

Calvin, John. [1960 edition]. *Institutes of the Christian Religion.* 2 vols. Library of Christian Classics XX. Edited by John T. McNeill; translated and indexed by Ford Lewis Battles. Philadelphia:

Westminster Press. (Based on 1559 Latin text and compiled with other editions 1536–1544).

Cardman, Francine. 1984. "BEM and the Community of Women and Men." In *The Search for Visible Unity*, edited by Jeffrey Gros, 83–95. New York: Pilgrim Press.

[Catholic Church]. 1955. *The Church Teaches: Documents of the Church in English Translation*, translated and edited by John F. Clarkson, John H. Edwards, William J. Kelly, and John J. Welch. St. Louis: B. Herder.

Cawley, Janet. 1988. "The United Church of Canada and the Trinitarian Formula." *Ecumenical Trends* 17 (May): 72–74.

Chadran, J. Russell. 1984. *"Baptism, Eucharist, and Ministry:* The Reception of the Text and Third World Concerns." In *The Search for Visible Unity*, edited by Jeffrey Gros, 107–124. New York: Pilgrim Press.

Chester, Barbara. 1987. "The Statistics About Sexual Violence." In *Sexual Assault and Abuse: A Handbook for Clergy and Religious Professionals*, edited by Mary Pellauer et al., 1–16. San Francisco: Harper & Row.

Chopp, Rebecca S. 1989. *The Power to Speak: Feminism, Language, and God*. New York: Crossroad.

Clark, John P. 1982. "Nature, Grace, and the Trinity in Julian of Norwich." *Downside Review* 100 (July): 203–220.

Clark, Linda J. 1978. "We Are Also Sarah's Children." *The Drew Gateway* 48 (Spring): 11–37.

―――. 1980. "In Christ There Is No East or West." In *Language About God in Liturgy and Scripture*, edited by Barbara A. Withers. Philadelphia: Geneva Press.

Collins, Mary. 1985. "Naming God in Public Prayer." *Worship* 59 (July): 291–305.

Cone, James. 1975. *God of the Oppressed*. New York: Seabury Press.

Consultation on Church Union (COCU). 1980. *In Quest of a Church of Christ Uniting: An Emerging Theological Consensus. Chapter VII: Ministry*. Princeton, N.J.: COCU.

―――. 1984. *The COCU Consensus: In Quest of a Church of Christ Uniting*. Princeton, N.J.: COCU.

Consultation on Common Texts. 1987. "A Celebration of Baptism: An Ecumenical Liturgy" (draft), edited by Frank Henderson and David Holeton. Unpublished photocopied draft given to the author by Horace T. Allen Jr., a Consultation member. 24 pages.

Conzelmann, Hans. 1969. *An Outline of the Theology of the New Testament*. Translated by John Bowden. London: SCM Press.

Coons, Philip M., Elizabeth S. Bowman, Terri A. Pellow, and Paul Schneider. 1989. "Post-Traumatic Aspects of the Treatment of Sexual Abuse and Incest." *Psychiatric Clinics of North America* 12, no. 2 (June): 325–335.

Cross, F. L., and E. A. Livingstone. 1983 [corrected and revised from 1957 and 1977 editions]. *The Oxford Dictionary of the Christian Church*. New York: Oxford University Press.

Cullmann, Oscar. 1950. *Baptism in the New Testament*. London: SCM Press.

Culpepper, Emily Erwin. 1987. "Contemporary Goddess Thealogy: A Sympathetic Critique." In *Shaping New Vision: Gender and Values in American Culture*, edited by Clarissa Atkinson, Margaret Miles, and Constance Buchanan. The Harvard Women's Studies in Religion Series, vol. 2. Ann Arbor: University of Michigan Research Press.

Daly, Mary. 1973. *Beyond God the Father: Toward a Philosophy of Women's Liberation*. Boston: Beacon Press.

Daly, Mary, in cahoots with Jane Caputi. 1987. *Websters' First New Intergalactic Wickedary of the English Language*. Boston: Beacon Press.

Daro, Deborah. 1988. *Confronting Child Abuse*. New York: Free Press.

Daro, Deborah, Kathleen Casey, and Nadine Abrahams. 1990. "Reducing Child Abuse 20% by 1990: A Preliminary Assessment." Working Paper 843. Chicago: The National Center on Child Abuse Prevention Research.

Davies, J. G. 1986. *The New Westminster Dictionary of Liturgy and Worship*. Philadelphia: Westminster Press.

Deiss, Lucien. 1979. *Springtime of the Liturgy*. Collegeville, Minn.: Liturgical Press.

Dix, Gregory. [1982 reprint]. *The Shape of the Liturgy*. New York: Seabury Press. (Original edition, London: Dacre Press, 1945).

Duck, Ruth C., ed. 1981. *Bread for the Journey: Resources for Worship*. New York: Pilgrim Press.

———. 1985. *Flames of the Spirit*. New York: Pilgrim Press.

Duck, Ruth C., and Michael Bausch, eds. 1981. *Everflowing Streams: Songs for Worship*. New York: Pilgrim Press.

Duck, Ruth C., and Maren C. Tirabassi, eds. 1990. *Touch Holiness: Resources for Worship*. New York: Pilgrim Press.

Ecumenical Women's Center. 1974. *Because We Are One People*. Edited by Sandra Amundsen, Ruth C. Duck, Susan Del Grande Dixon, Marcie Smith Edgerton, Judy Thomas, and Julie Less Wagstaff. Chicago: Ecumenical Women's Center.

English Language Liturgical Consultation. 1988. *Praying Together.* Nashville: Abingdon Press.

The Episcopal Church. 1977. *The Book of Common Prayer* (proposed). New York: Church Hymnal Corporation.

Erickson, Craig Douglas. 1985. "The Strong Name of the Trinity." *Reformed Liturgy and Music* 14 (Fall): 205–210.

Evans, Craig A. 1985. Review of *The Father, the Son, and the Holy Spirit*, by Jane Schaberg. *Journal of Biblical Literature* 104 (December): 731–732.

Faith and Order. Refer to World Council of Churches. Faith and Order Commission.

Falk, Marcia. 1987. "Notes on Composing New Blessings: Toward a Feminist-Jewish Reconstruction of Prayer." *Journal of Feminist Studies in Religion* 3 (Spring): 39–53.

Faller, Kathleen Coulborn. 1989. "The Role Relationship Between Victim and Perpetrator as a Predictor of Characteristics of Intra-familial Sexual Abuse." *Child and Adolescent Social Work* 6 (Fall): 217–229.

Farley, Margaret. 1975. "New Patterns of Relationship: Beginnings of a Moral Revolution." *Theological Studies* 36: 627–646.

Feinauer, Leslie L. 1989. "Comparison of Long-Term Effects of Child Abuse by Type of Abuse and by Relationship of the Offender to the Victim." *American Journal of Family Therapy* 17 (Spring): 48–56.

Ferguson, John. 1970. *The Religions of the Roman Empire.* Ithaca, N.Y.: Cornell University Press.

Finkel, Asher. 1981. "The Prayer of Jesus in Matthew." In *Standing Before God*, edited by Asher Finkel and Lawrence Frizzell, 131–170. New York: Ktav.

Fisher, J. D. C. 1965. *Christian Initiation: Baptism in the Medieval West.* London: SPCK.

Fitzmyer, Joseph A. 1985. "Abba and Jesus' Relation to God." In *Melanges Offerts à Dom Jacques Dupont*, 15–38. Paris: Les Editions du Cerf.

Fuller, Reginald H. 1965. *The Foundations of New Testament Christology.* New York: Scribner.

Gerhardsson, Birger. 1979. *The Origins of the Gospel Traditions.* Philadelphia: Fortress Press.

Golden, Daniel. 1988. "What Makes Mommy Run?" *Boston Globe Magazine* (April 24): 41–55.

Goulder, M. D. 1974. *Midrash and Lection in Matthew.* London: SPCK.

Grant, Frederick C., ed. 1957. *Ancient Roman Religion.* New York: Liberal Arts Press.

Gray, Kenneth. 1990. "Images of God in Contemporary Hymn Texts." M.Div. thesis, University of Emmanuel College, Saskatoon, Canada.

Green, H. Benedict. 1975. *The Gospel According to Matthew in the RSV*. New Clarendon Bible Commentary. London: Oxford University Press.

Green, Marty [pseud.]. 1987. "Liturgy for a Lost Childhood." *Daughters of Sarah* 13 (September/October): 20–21.

Grindal, Gracia. 1987. "Where We Are Now." *The Hymn* 38 (October): 22–26.

Gunnemann, Louis H. 1985/1986. "Baptism: Sacrament of Christian Vocation." In *On the Way* 3 (Winter): 12–19.

Gutiérrez, Gustavo. 1973. *A Theology of Liberation*. Maryknoll, N.Y.: Orbis Books.

———. 1984. *We Drink from Our Own Wells*. Maryknoll, N.Y.: Orbis Books.

Halsey, Peggy. 1984. "Abuse in the Family: Breaking the Church's Silence." New York: Office of Ministries with Women in Crisis, United Methodist Church.

Hamerton-Kelly, Robert. 1979. *God the Father: Theology and Patriarchy in the Teaching of Jesus*. Philadelphia: Fortress Press.

———. 1981. "God the Father in the Bible and in the Experience of Jesus: The State of the Question." In *God as Father?* edited by Johannes Baptist Metz and Edward Schillebeeckx, 95–102. Edinburgh: T. & T. Clark; New York: Seabury Press.

Handelman, Susan A. 1982. *The Slayers of Moses: The Re-emergence of Rabbinic Interpretation in Modern Literary Theory*. Albany: State University of New York Press.

Hardesty, Nancy A. 1987. *Inclusive Language in the Church*. Atlanta: John Knox Press.

Hartman, Lars. 1973/1974. "Into the Name of Jesus." *New Testament Studies* 20: 432–440.

Henderson, J. Frank. 1988. Work in progress on the use of paternal imagery in Christian worship. Unpublished computer printout, 82 pages.

Herman, Judith Lewis. 1981. *Father-Daughter Incest*. Cambridge: Harvard University Press.

Heyward, Isabel Carter. 1982. *The Redemption of God: A Theology of Mutual Relations*. Lanham, Md.: University Press of America.

Holeton, David R. 1988. "Changing the Baptismal Formula: Feminist Proposals and Liturgical Implications." *Ecumenical Trends* 17 (May): 69–72.

Jenson, Robert W. 1982. *The Triune Identity: God According to the Gospel.* Philadelphia: Fortress Press.

Jeremias, Joachim. 1965. *The Central Message of the New Testament.* New York: Scribner.

——. 1978. *The Prayers of Jesus.* Philadelphia: Fortress Press.

Johnson, Terence Elwyn. 1987. Letter in response to "The Trinity and Women's Experience" by Barbara Brown Zikmund. *The Christian Century* 104 (June 3–10): 534–535.

Jones, Major J. 1987. *The Color of God: The Concept of God in Afro-American Thought.* Macon, Ga.: Mercer University Press.

Julian of Norwich. [1978 translation]. *Showings,* translated by Edmund Colledge and James Walsh, with a Preface by Jean Leclercq. New York: Paulist Press. (Original c. 1373 C.E.).

Jungmann, Josef. 1959. *The Early Liturgy.* Notre Dame: University of Notre Dame Press.

——. 1962. *Pastoral Liturgy.* New York: Herder & Herder.

Kasper, Walter. 1986. *The God of Jesus Christ,* pt. 2, 133–316. New York: Crossroad.

Kavanagh, Aidan. 1978. *The Shape of Baptism.* New York: Pueblo.

Kelly, J. N. D. 1960. *The Early Christian Doctrines.* San Francisco: Harper & Row.

Kingsbury, Jack Dean. 1985. "Matthew, the Gospel According to." In *Harper's Bible Dictionary,* edited by Paul J. Achtemeier, 613–615. San Francisco: Harper & Row.

LaCugna, Catherine Mowry. 1986. "Making the Most of Trinity Sunday." *Worship* 60 (3): 210–224.

——. 1987. "The Baptismal Formula, Feminist Objections, and Trinitarian Theology." Paper given at the September, 1987 meeting of the North American Academy of Ecumenists, in Toronto, Ontario, Canada. Abridged in the *Journal of Ecumenical Studies* 26 (Spring 1989, as below).

——. 1988. "Baptism, Feminism, and Trinitarian Theology." *Ecumenical Trends* 17 (May): 65–68.

——. 1989. "The Baptismal Formula, Feminist Objections, and Trinitarian Theology." *Journal of Ecumenical Studies* 26 (Spring): 235–250.

Lerner, Gerda. 1986. *The Creation of Patriarchy.* New York: Oxford University Press.

Lohse, Bernhard. 1966. *A Short History of Christian Doctrine.* Philadelphia: Fortress Press.

Lott, Bernice. 1987. *Women's Lives: Themes and Variations in Gender Learning.* Monterey, Calif.: Brooks/Cole.

McClimans, Heather. 1982. "Learning About Myself." *Womanspirit* 9 (Winter Solstice): 27.

McFague, Sallie. 1982. *Metaphorical Theology*. Philadelphia: Fortress Press.

———. 1987. *Models of God: Theology for an Ecological, Nuclear Age*. Philadelphia: Fortress Press.

MacKinnon, Catharine A. 1987. *Feminism Unmodified: Discourses on Life and Law*. Cambridge: Harvard University Press.

May, Melanie. 1985. "Conversations on Language and the Imagery of God." *Union Seminary Quarterly Review* 40 (3): 11–20.

Meier, John P., and Raymond E. Brown. 1983. *Antioch and Rome*. New York: Paulist Press.

Miller, Casey, and Kate Swift. 1976. *Words and Women*. Garden City, N.Y.: Anchor Press/Doubleday.

———. 1980. *The Handbook of Nonsexist Writing*. New York: Lippincott & Crowell.

Mitchard, Jacquelin. February 1980. "The Abuser." *Capitol Times*, Madison, Wis. One of a series of articles on incest. (On file in the Anna Howard Shaw Center, Boston University School of Theology.)

Mollenkott, Virginia Ramey. 1982. "Evangelicalism, Patriarchy, and the Abuse of Children." *Radix* 14 (January/February): 15–18.

———. 1983. *The Divine Feminine: The Biblical Imagery of God as Female*. New York: Crossroad.

Moltmann, Jurgen. 1980. *The Trinity and the Kingdom*. San Francisco: Harper & Row.

Morley, Janet, and Hannah Ward. 1987/1988. *Celebrating Women*. Wilton, Conn.: Morehouse-Barlow (North American distributor; originally published in London by Women in Theology and Movement for the Ordination of Women, 1986).

Morton, Nelle. 1985. *The Journey Is Home*. Boston: Beacon Press.

National Center on Child Abuse Prevention Research. 1990. "Current Trends in Child Abuse Reporting and Fatalities: The Results of the 1989 Annual Fifty State Survey." Working Paper 808. Chicago: National Committee for Prevention of Child Abuse.

National Council of the Churches of Christ in the U.S.A, Division of Education and Ministry, Inclusive Language Lectionary Committee. 1986. *An Inclusive-Language Lectionary: Readings for Year A*. Rev. ed. Atlanta: John Knox Press; New York: Pilgrim Press; Philadelphia: Westminster Press.

Neufer Emswiler, Sharon, and Thomas Neufer Emswiler. 1974. *Women and Worship*. New York: Harper & Row.

———. 1980. *Wholeness in Worship*. San Francisco: Harper & Row.

———. 1984. *Women and Worship*. Rev. ed. New York: Harper & Row.

Newman, Barbara. 1987. *Sister of Wisdom: St. Hildegard's Theology of the Feminine*. Berkeley: University of California Press.

Nida, Eugene A. 1964. *Toward a Science of Translating*. Leiden, Neth.: E. J. Brill.

Nida, Eugene A., and Charles R. Taber. 1969. *The Theory and Practice of Translation*. Leiden, Neth.: E. J. Brill.

Nikkal, Carolyn. 1988. "Incest, Psychology, and Power." Unpublished class paper, Boston University School of Theology. For "Power and Powerless" course, taught by Elizabeth Bettenhausen.

Nilsen, Alleen Pace, Haig Bosmajian, H. Lee Gershuny, and Julia P. Stanley, eds. 1977. *Sexism and Language*. Urbana, Ill.: National Council of Teachers of English.

Oakley, Ann. 1972. *Sex, Gender and Society*. Gower, England: Maurice Temple Smith.

Oliver, Harold H. 1987. "Myth and Metaphysics: Perils of the Metaphysical Translation of Mythical Images." In *Weltoffenheit des Christlichen Glaubens. Fritz Buri zu ehren*, edited by Imelda Abbt and Alfred Jager, 43–49. Bern: Verlag Paul Haupt.

Osborne, Grant R. 1976. "Redaction Criticism and the Great Commission: A Case Study Toward a Biblical Understanding of Inerrancy." *Journal of the Evangelical Theological Society* 19 (Spring): 73–85.

Oxford-Carpenter, Rebecca. 1984. "Gender and the Trinity." *Theology Today* 41 (April): 4–25.

Pagels, Elaine H. 1976. "What Became of God the Mother? Conflicting Images of God in Early Christianity." *Signs* 2 (2): 293–303.

———. 1979. *The Gnostic Gospels*. New York: Random House, Vintage Books.

Patte, Daniel. 1987. *The Gospel According to Matthew*. Philadelphia: Fortress Press.

Pellauer, Mary D., Barbara Chester, and Jane A. Boyajian, eds. 1987. *Sexual Assault and Abuse: A Handbook for Clergy and Religious Professionals*. San Francisco: Harper & Row.

Perrin, Norman. 1967. *Rediscovering the Teaching of Jesus*. New York: Harper & Row.

Plaskow, Judith. 1990. *Standing Again at Sinai*. San Francisco: Harper & Row.

Presbyterian Church (U.S.A.) and Cumberland Presbyterian Church. 1985. *Holy Baptism and Services for the Renewal of Baptism*. Philadelphia: Westminster Press.

Procter-Smith, Marjorie. 1987. "Liturgical Anamnesis and Women's Memory: Something Missing." *Worship* 61 (September): 405–424.

———. 1990. *In Her Own Rite*. Nashville: Abingdon Press.

Rahner, Karl. 1970. *The Trinity*. New York: Herder & Herder.

Ramshaw, Gail. 1983. "The Language of Eucharistic Praying." *Worship* 57 (September): 419–437.

———. 1984. "An Inclusive-Language Lectionary." *Worship* 58 (January): 29–36.

———. 1986a. *Christ in Sacred Speech*. Philadelphia: Fortress Press.

———. 1986b. "Naming the Trinity: Orthodoxy and Inclusivity." *Worship 60* (November): 491–498.

Ramshaw, Gail, and Gordon Lathrop, eds. 1987. *Lectionary for the Christian People: Cycle B of the Roman, Episcopal, Lutheran Lectionaries*. New York: Pueblo; Philadelphia: Fortress Press.

Richardson, Alan. 1957. *A Theological Wordbook of the Bible*. New York: Macmillan. (Original edition, London: SCM Press, 1951.)

Richardson, Cyril C., Eugene R. Fairweather, Edward R. Hardy, and Massie H. Shepherd. 1970. *Early Christian Fathers*. Library of Christian Classics, vol. 1. Philadelphia: Westminster Press; New York: Macmillan.

Ricoeur, Paul. 1976. *Interpretation Theory: Discourse and the Surplus of Meaning*. Fort Worth: Texas Christian University Press.

Riggs, John. 1988. "Traditions, Tradition, and Liturgical Norms: The United Church of Christ Book of Worship." *Worship* 62 (January): 58–72.

Rimbach, James A. 1986. "God Talk or Baby Talk: More on 'Abba.'" *Currents in Mission and Theology* (August): 232–235.

Rogers, Elizabeth Frances. 1976. *Peter Lombard and the Sacramental System*. Merrick, N.Y.: Richwood.

Roland, Billy, Paul Zelhart, and Richard Dubes. 1989. "MMPI Correlates of College Women Who Reported Experiencing Child/Adult Sexual Contact with Father, Stepfather, or with Other Persons." *Psychological Reports* 64, 1159–1162.

Routley, Erik. 1982a. "The Gender of God: A Contribution to the Conversation." *Worship* 56 (May): 231–239.

———. 1982b. "Scriptural Resonances in Hymnody." *Reformed Liturgy and Music* 16 (Summer): 120–125.

———, ed. 1985. *Rejoice in the Lord*. Grand Rapids: Wm. B. Eerdmans.

Royer, Harry G. 1986. "Baptism in the Evangelical and Reformed Tradition." *Prism* 1 (Spring): 40–49.

Ruether, Rosemary Radford. 1983. *Sexism and God-Talk: Toward a Feminist Theology*. Boston: Beacon Press.

———. 1985. *Women-Church: Theology and Practice in Feminist Liturgical Communities*. San Francisco: Harper & Row.

———. 1986. "Review of *Bread Not Stone* by Elisabeth Schüssler Fiorenza." *Journal of the American Academy of Religion* 54 (Spring): 141–143.

Russell, Diana E. H. 1986. *The Secret Trauma*. New York: Basic Books.

Russell, Letty M. 1979. *The Future of Partnership*. Philadelphia: Westminster Press.

——, ed. 1985. *Feminist Interpretation of the Bible*. Philadelphia: Westminster Press.

——. 1987. *Household of Freedom*. Philadelphia: Westminster Press.

Schaberg, Jane. 1982. *The Father, the Son, and the Holy Spirit: The Triadic Phrase in Matthew 28:19b*. Chico, Calif.: Scholars Press.

Schaffran, Janet, and Pat Kozak. 1988. *More than Words: Prayer and Ritual for Inclusive Communities*. Oak Park, Ill.: Meyer-Stone Books.

Schillebeeckx, Edward. 1979. *Jesus*. New York: Crossroad.

——. 1984. *The Schillebeeckx Reader*. Edited by Robert J. Schreiter. New York: Crossroad.

Schilling, S. Paul. 1983. *The Faith We Sing*. Philadelphia: Westminster Press.

Schmémann, Alexander. 1974. *Of Water and the Spirit*. Crestwood, N.Y.: St. Vladimir's Seminary Press.

Schneiders, Sandra M. 1986. *Women and the Word: The Gender of God in the New Testament and the Spirituality of Women*. New York: Paulist Press.

Schüssler Fiorenza, Elisabeth. 1983. *In Memory of Her: A Feminist Reconstruction of Early Christian Origins*. New York: Crossroad.

——. 1984. *Bread Not Stone: The Challenge of Feminist Biblical Interpretation*. Boston: Beacon Press.

——. 1985. "The Will to Choose or Reject: Continuing Our Critical Work." In *Feminist Interpretation of the Bible*, edited by Letty Russell, 125–136. Philadelphia: Westminster Press.

Schweizer, Eduard. 1975. *The Good News According to Matthew*. Richmond: John Knox Press.

Searle, Mark. 1980. *Christening: The Making of Christians*. Collegeville, Minn.: Liturgical Press.

——. 1981. "Liturgy as Metaphor." *Worship* 55 (March): 99–120.

Segundo, Juan Luis. 1976. *Liberation of Theology*. Maryknoll, N.Y.: Orbis Books.

Spender, Dale. 1980. *Man Made Language*. London: Routledge & Kegan Paul.

Stanley, Julia P. 1977. "Gender Marking in American English." In *Sexism and Language*, edited by Alleen Pace Nilsen et al., 43–76. Urbana, Ill.: National Council of Teachers of English.

Stein, Jess, ed. *The Random House College Dictionary. Revised edition*, s.v. "father." New York, N.Y.: Random House, 1988. (Original edition edited by Laurence Urdang.)

Stevick, Daniel. 1970. *Language in Worship.* New York: Seabury Press.

Stookey, Laurence H. 1982. *Baptism: Christ's Act in the Church.* Nashville: Abingdon Press.

———. 1983. "The Language of the Trinity. " *Reformed Liturgy and Music* 17 (Fall): 166–168.

Summit, Ronald. 1987. "Beyond Belief: The Reluctant Discovery of Incest." In *Sexual Assault and Abuse: A Handbook for Clergy and Religious Professionals,* edited by Mary Pellauer et al., 172–197. San Francisco: Harper & Row.

Swidler, Leonard. 1979. *Biblical Affirmations of Women.* Philadelphia: Westminster Press.

Tamar [pseud.]. 1987. "Tamar and Amnon Revisited." *Daughters of Sarah* 13 (September/October) 11–13.

Tamez, Elsa. 1987. *Against Machismo.* Oak Park, Ill.: Meyer-Stone Books.

Tennis, Diane. 1985. *Is God the Only Reliable Father?* Philadelphia: Westminster Press.

Thiselton, A. C. 1975. *Language, Liturgy, and Meaning.* Bramcote, Nottinghamshire, England: Grove Liturgical Study No. 2.

Thistlethwaite, Susan Brooks. 1989. *Sex, Race, and God.* New York: Crossroad.

Throckmorton, Burton. 1984. "Why the Inclusive Language Lectionary?" *The Christian Century* 101 (August 1–8): 742–744.

Thurian, Max. Refer to World Council of Churches. Faith and Order Commission.

Tillich, Paul. 1951. *Systematic Theology,* vol. 1. Chicago: University of Chicago Press.

Tracy, David. 1979. "Metaphor and Religion: The Test Case of Christian Texts." In *On Metaphor,* edited by Sheldon Sacks, 89–104. Chicago: University of Chicago Press.

Tracy, David, and Robert M. Grant. 1984. "Part 2." In *A Short History of the Interpretation of the Bible.* Philadelphia: Fortress Press.

Trible, Phyllis. 1978. *God and the Rhetoric of Sexuality.* Philadelphia: Fortress Press.

———. 1984. *Texts of Terror.* Philadelphia: Fortress Press.

Troeger, Thomas H. 1987. "Personal, Cultural and Theological Influences on the Language and Hymns of Worship." *Hymn* 38 (October): 7–15.

United Church of Christ Office for Church Life and Leadership. 1986. *Book of Worship: United Church of Christ.* New York: United Church of Christ Office for Church Life and Leadership.

United Methodist Church. 1988. Advance edition D-2. *Daily Christian Advocate* 7 (February 25).

————. 1989. *United Methodist Hymnal.* Nashville: United Methodist Publishing House.

Visser 't Hooft, W. A. 1982. *The Fatherhood of God in an Age of Emancipation.* Geneva: World Council of Churches.

Viviano, Benedict T. 1984. Review of *The Father, the Son, and the Holy Spirit,* by Jane Schaberg. *Catholic Biblical Quarterly* 46 (January): 177–179.

Wade, David L. 1987. "Specific Prayers." *The Christian Century* 194 (December 2): 1099–1100. (Letter to the editor in response to Barr's article cited above.)

Wainwright, Geoffrey. 1969. *Christian Initiation.* Richmond: John Knox Press.

————. 1980. *Doxology.* New York: Oxford University Press.

Walker, Alice. 1982. *The Color Purple.* New York: Pocket Books.

Watkins, Keith. 1981. *Faithful and Fair.* Nashville: Abingdon Press.

Wheelwright, Philip. 1962. *Metaphor and Reality.* Bloomington, Ind.: Indiana University Press.

Whitaker, E. C. 1965a. *The Baptismal Liturgy.* London: SPCK.

————. 1965b. "The History of the Baptismal Formula." *Journal of Ecclesiastical History* 16 (April) 1–12.

White, James F. 1983. *Sacraments as God's Self Giving.* Nashville: Abingdon Press.

Widom, Catherine Spatz. 1988. "Sampling Biases and Child Abuse Research." *American Journal of Orthopsychiatry* 58 (April): 260–270.

Williams, Delores S. 1986. "What Was Missed: The Color Purple." *Christianity and Crisis* (July 14): 230–232.

Williams, Michael A. 1986. "Uses of Gender Imagery in Ancient Gnostic Texts." In *Gender and Religion: On the Complexity of Symbols,* edited by Caroline Walker Bynum et al., 196–227. Boston: Beacon Press.

Wilson-Kastner, Patricia. 1983. *Faith, Feminism, and the Christ.* Philadelphia: Fortress Press.

————. 1987. "Theological Perspectives on Sexual Violence." *Sexual Assault and Abuse: A Handbook for Clergy and Religious Professionals,* edited by Mary Pellauer et al., 96–112. San Francisco: Harper & Row.

Winter, Miriam Therese. 1987. *WomanPrayer, WomanSong: Resources for Ritual.* Oak Park, Ill.: Meyer-Stone Books.

World Council of Churches. 1983. *Baptism and Eucharist: Ecumenical Convergence in Celebration,* edited by Max Thurian and Geoffrey Wainwright. Geneva: World Council of Churches; Grand Rapids: Wm. B. Eerdmans.

World Council of Churches Community of Women and Men in the Church. 1983. *The Community of Women and Men in the Church: The Sheffield Report*, edited by Constance Parvey. Geneva: World Council of Churches.

World Council of Churches Faith and Order Commission. 1982. *Baptism, Eucharist, and Ministry*. Faith and Order Paper 111. Geneva: World Council of Churches.

World Council of Churches Faith and Order Commission, edited by Max Thurian. 1986a. *Churches Respond to BEM*, vol. 1. Geneva: World Council of Churches.

————. 1986b. *Churches Respond to BEM*, vol. 2. Geneva: World Council of Churches.

————. 1987a. *Churches Respond to BEM*, vol. 3. Geneva: World Council of Churches.

————. 1987b. *Churches Respond to BEM*, vol. 4. Geneva: World Council of Churches.

————. 1988a. *Churches Respond to BEM*, vol. 5. Geneva: World Council of Churches.

————. 1988b. *Churches Respond to BEM*, vol. 6. Geneva: World Council of Churches.

Wren, Brian. 1989. *What Language Shall I Borrow?* New York: Crossroad.

Yarnold, Edward. 1971. *The Awe Inspiring Rites of Initiation*. Middlegreen, Slough, England: St. Paul Publications.

Zeller, Dieter. 1981. "God as Father in the Proclamation and in the Prayer of Jesus." Translated by Nora Quigley and the editors. In *Standing Before God*, edited by Asher Finkel and Lawrence Frizzell, 117–130. New York: Ktav.

Zikmund, Barbara Brown. 1987. "The Trinity and Women's Experience." *The Christian Century* 104 (April 15): 354–356.

NAME INDEX

SUBJECT INDEX